Cases in Financial Accounting
Intermediate and Advanced

Edited by Eldon J. Gardner
Accounting Education Resource Centre
University of Lethbridge

John Wiley & Sons
Toronto New York Chichester Brisbane Singapore

DEDICATION

This book is dedicated to Lynda and Keri whose efforts and encouragement made it possible.

Copyright © 1990 by John Wiley & Sons Canada Limited

All rights reserved. No part of this work covered by the copyrights hereon may be reproduced or used in any form or by any means—graphic, electronic or mechanical—without the prior written permission of the publisher.

Any request for photocopying, recording, taping or information storage and retrieval systems of any part of this book shall be directed in writing to the Canadian Reprography Collective, 379 Adelaide Street West, Suite M1, Toronto, Ontario M5V 1S5.

Care has been taken to trace the ownership of copyright material contained in this text. The publishers will gladly receive any information that will enable them to rectify any reference or credit line in subsequent editions.

Canadian Cataloguing in Publication Data

Main entry under title:

Cases in financial accounting: intermediate and advanced

Result of a competition sponsored by the Accounting Resource Centre at the University of Lethbridge in 1988.
ISBN 0-471-79515-1

1. Accounting — Case studies. 2. Accounting — Case studies — Competitions. I. Gardner, Eldon J. II. University of Lethbridge. Accounting Resource Centre.

HF5635.C38 1990   657'.044   C90-093790-4

Cover Design: Brant Cowie

Printed and bound in Canada by Gagne Press Ltd
10 9 8 7 6 5 4 3 2 1

PREFACE

This series of case books has been developed from the first Accounting Case Writing Competition sponsored by the Accounting Education Resource Centre of the University of Lethbridge. The cases in these books are based on real situations and have been developed by some of the finest case writers in the world. The editor and the authors are confident that these cases, and future books planned in this series, will prove to be a valuable addition to the pedagogy of accounting.

THE UNIVERSITY OF LETHBRIDGE

Sometimes called Canada's Centennial University, the University of Lethbridge is a small liberal arts university located in southern Alberta. Lethbridge, Alberta's third largest city, is 200 kilometres (120 miles) south of Calgary.

The University has gained a reputation as an institution with a 12.5 to 1 student to faculty ratio that allows for small classes and an intimate learning environment. Its faculty has a reputation for good teaching and increasingly ambitious research.

THE FACULTY OF MANAGEMENT

The Faculty came into existence on July 1, 1989 after operating for eight years as the School of Management. Its first Director, now Dean, Dr. George Lermer has administered its growth and development. Today the faculty number forty. Its curriculum is a blend of case teaching, skills training and academic rigour that meets the needs of under-graduate students.

THE ACCOUNTING EDUCATION RESOURCE CENTRE

The Centre was founded on July 1, 1987 and Dr. Eldon Gardner was appointed its first Co-ordinator. The bi-annual Accounting Case Writing Competition, from which a selection of cases is being published in this book, is its major undertaking. The mandate of the Centre is to develop educational materials for use in academic and professional accounting programs.

BACKGROUND TO THE CASE BOOK

The cases in this book are the best of those submitted in the Accounting Case Writing Competition of 1988. The cases have been thoroughly reviewed and edited for publication. The following individuals contributed to the reviewing process:

- Dr. Daniel McDonald Simon Fraser University
- Dr. Henry Kennedy   University of Alberta
- Dr. George Baxter   University of Saskatchewan
- Dr. Peter Tiessen   University of Alberta
- Lorne Baxter   University of Calgary
  (retired from Touche Ross)
- Ronald Baines   University of Lethbridge
  (retired from Arthur Anderson)
- Professor Allan Hunter   University of Lethbridge.

Eldon Gardner edited the cases with the capable assistance of Katherine (Kate) Beaty Chiste.

FINANCIAL SUPPORT

The financial resources needed to support the Centre and this case writing and publishing venture were provided by several sources:

(1) The Accounting Education Foundation of the Institute of Chartered Accountants of Alberta provided initial funding for three years.
(2) The Government of Alberta provided matching funds for this initial three years.
(3) Supplementary funding was provided by the Burns Foods Endowment of the Faculty of Management.

ACCOUNTING CASE WRITING COMPETITION

The first Accounting Case Writing Competition selected five finalists who presented their cases to a student audience in a simulated class room environment at the Kananaskis Inn in Kananaskis, Alberta in May 1988. The following prizes were awarded:

(1) The first prize of $5,000 (U.S.) was awarded to Professor David Bateman of St. Mary's University, Halifax, Nova Scotia for his case entitled *City Autoparts Distributors Limited*.

(2) The second prize of $1,500 (U.S.) was awarded jointly to Professor Cynthia Heagy of the University of Georgia, Athens, Georgia and Mr. Richard Heagy, then of Clemson University, Clemson, South Carolina for their case entitled *Dane Manufacturing Company*.

(3) Three other prizes of $500 (U.S.) each were awarded to each of the following:

Jointly to Professors Ralph Drtina and Charles Brandon of Rollins College, Winter Park, Florida for their case entitled *Winter Park Brewery Company*.

Jointly to Professors Hugh Grove and Patsy Lee of University of Denver, Denver, Colorado for their case entitled *Snafu Sports Shop*.

Jointly to Professors Jeffrey Kantor and Teviah Estrin of University of Windsor, Windsor Ontario and Professor Murray Bryant of University of Toronto for their case entitled *Flawless Tool and Manufacturing Limited*.

The judges for the final competition were:

William Stephen, Chairman of the Board of the Accounting Education Foundation of Alberta,

Dr. Ross Archibald of the University of Western Ontario, and

Dr. Michael Gibbins of the University of Alberta.

USES OF THE CASE BOOK

This case book has been designed to be used as a supplement to widely used accounting texts. The Teaching Notes contain a list of texts and cases that are linked to the various specific chapters in those textbooks.

The Teaching Note for each case is provided to assist the instructor in the use of the case and to outline the recommended solution. In some cases the actual events are known and are described. In others, no specific solution or outcome is available.

Each case has been assigned a level of difficulty as follows — simple, moderate or complex. Generally those with a narrower focus (and with less detail) are classified as simple or moderate. Complex cases usually have a broad focus and sufficient detail to provide students a rich learning opportunity.

ACKNOWLEDGEMENTS

This book has been made possible by the support and encouragement of many people, some of whose names appear in what follows.

The authors of the cases deserve praise for the quality of their initial work. All of them have described interesting and timely situations with realism and relevance for accounting education. Their imagination and creativity have provided some challenging opportunities for readers.

Dr. George Lermer, Dean of the Faculty of Management, had the initial vision of the case writing competition. His unswerving support and dedication to the program assisted, in no small measure, in its success.

The Advisory Committee to the Centre provided support and guidance and put a large amount of effort in ensuring its success. Its members were:

Dr. George Lermer, Chair

Professor Allan Hunter

Professor Lawrence Merkley

Ian Kinnell of Peat Marwick Thorne, Lethbridge and member of the Board of the Accounting Education Foundation of Alberta

Dr. Eldon Gardner, Co-ordinator.

Kate Chiste's editorial work has made these cases eminently readable without losing the flavour and direction intended by the authors.

A number of people provided secretarial and administrative assistance, including Marilyn Hawryluk, who organized the case reviewing and judging processes.

Rosemarie Gattiker assisted Kate Chiste in the editorial process. Barbara Driscoll, Carrie Kanashiro, Marlene Lapointe and Stella Kedoin typed the manuscripts.

The editor wishes to thank in particular his wife, Lynda Gardner. She painstakingly worked to develop the appropriate format and style for the cases. Her patience and persistence when faced with so many varied and different authors' styles and formats was vital to the success of these case books.

The publishers of these volumes, John Wiley & Sons Canada Ltd., and their senior publisher, Hilda Gowans, deserve credit for taking the risk of publishing these books. It is Dr. Gardner's hope, as editor, and theirs that these volumes will be a valuable addition for accounting educators and practitioners around the world. Users should find that these cases provide many opportunities for developing judgmental, analytical, decision-making and evaluative skills (JADE skills) in the context of studying accounting.

Finally Dr. Gardner wishes to thank the many academic colleagues who have offered their encouragement for this case writing endeavour.

TABLE OF CONTENTS

Case 1	**City Autoparts Distributors Limited** D. Bateman	1
Case 2	**Commercial Design Inc.** B. Larochelle	19
Case 3	**Automik Limited** L.-P. Lauzon	47
Case 4	**Principal Group Limited** J. Lawson	73
Case 5	**Merrion Products** P. Clarke	79
Case 6	**Omega Group Limited** L.-P. Lauzon	87
Case 7	**Oxford Communications** A. Bhimani	103
Case 8	**Murphy Oil Company Limited** B. Boze	117
Case 9	**The Nabu Network Corporation** F. Simyar and K. Argheyd	123
Case 10	**The University and the Faculty Association** J. Amernic	155
Case 11	**Mark Gooden Explorations** E. Gardner	179
Case 12	**Rolls-Royce Privatization** A. Steele	185
	Interest Tables	215
	Glossary	227

CASE 1

CITY AUTOPARTS DISTRIBUTORS LIMITED

D. Bateman
Saint Mary's University
Halifax
Nova Scotia

INTRODUCTION AND BACKGROUND

The time was 9:45 a.m. on Monday, September 18, 1989 when Peter Bean's private deskphone startled him with its electrifying ring.

Peter: Bean, Wax & Associates, Chartered Accountants, Peter Bean speaking.

Caller: Good morning Peter. It's Everet Wantz of City Autoparts. I can't really talk over the phone right now because I have a 10:00 meeting with our lawyer, but we have some serious problems with our accounting systems and I was wondering if we could get together tomorrow to discuss them. I know we didn't exactly see eye to eye the last time we talked, but the events of the past few months have proven that I should have heeded your advice a little more closely. I hope that the incident is water under the bridge and that you will at least hear me out tomorrow.

Peter: (Hesitantly) Ah yes, I believe that we can meet. There is, however, the matter of last year's unpaid audit fee. How about 10:00 a.m. tomorrow at your office?

Everet: That sounds good. I'll dig out your bill and I'm sure that we can work something out. I can't talk any more just now, see you there tomorrow. Bye.

Peter: Bye. (To himself.) A fountain of information as usual.

As Peter placed the phone back down he began to wonder what kind of a mess he was facing. Things must be bad if Everet was willing to swallow his pride. News travelled fast and Everet had made some serious misjudgements since graduating from university the year before and taking over his father's business after the death of Max Wantz, the original founder of City Autoparts. At least Peter wasn't going into tomorrow's meeting completely cold; he had a good idea of the real problems (besides Everet) at City Autoparts. As auditor of the company over the past seven years, he felt he had a good understanding of the problems that Everet was alluding to in their brief conversation. At their last meeting, Everet had convinced the ailing Wantz that auditors were just a bunch of expensive score keepers. Following a heated discussion over the year's audit bill and a disagreement over how to proceed with a possible computerization plan, Everet made it clear to Peter that he would call if Peter's services were required further. Peter's informal discussions with Brad Mitchell, an ex-City Autoparts' employee and softball teammate, had revealed the fiasco that took place when Everet became the new President.

In Brad's words, it was "unbelievable". Everet considered himself the new whiz kid and a computer was going to be his first toy. Before anyone on the staff knew what was happening, an office was vacated and the new computer was brought in. Jim Locke, the only one on staff with any previous computer experience, had suggested that perhaps they should seek the outside help of their accountants or a business consultant. But Everet snubbed Jim's idea, exclaiming that he knew what he was doing and that "experts" would charge too much.

The ultimate computer and software choice had been made in a big huff over dinner one night when the IPM salesman told Everet that the lower priced NPR machine and software package couldn't do what City Autoparts wanted. That was all Everet needed—the next day he signed an NPR contract and as time went on, the IPM salesman's warning came true. After four months of start-up problems which forced the company to keep using their old manual system, Everet got fed up. He called NPR to come and pick up their machine before he threw it out in the street. Pretty soon, each was suing the other for lack of performance and damages.

"Oh well, things are never as bad as they first seem," Peter thought. "And besides, I owe it to Max Wantz to at least hear Everet out. After all, Everet must respect my skills or he wouldn't have called. It would be nice to get our largest client back on side again. I'll just play it by ear tomorrow and make my decision then whether to accept or reject this assignment."

The 10:00 a.m. meeting at Everet's office proved to be quite a surprise. In spite of the Continental parked in the company lot and the expensive furniture in the office, Everet had been humbled by his first year in the "real world". He had summed it up quite nicely when he said, "You don't fake your way through out here. If you don't know what you're doing you'll get a set of very expensive lessons in a hurry."

Everet addressed the matter of the outstanding audit bill of $10,000, and his solution caught Peter a bit off guard. Because of the firm's current tight cash position, Everet proposed to offer office facilities in a new complex owned by an associated holding and investment company, ABC Properties Limited, located in the Burnside Industrial Park, in lieu of a cash payment. He mentioned that he had thought of this solution when he saw Bean, Wax & Associates' announcement of a new partner and their expansion into computer services. He wondered how the firm's current facilities were handling this extra burden and whether they were looking for new office accommodations.

Peter told him that they were considering a move in the near future, but he would have to discuss the issue with his partners. Everet assured him that the lease would be with ABC Properties and that the rates would be the same as for other tenants, but that they could have first choice of the suites that were available.

Before leaving the audit fee issue, Everet asked Peter for a relatively "tight" figure for the expected fee for this year's audit and the systems work. His banker had suggested that he consider getting bids from other CA firms. He was quite sure that he didn't want to do that at this time, but he did want a good idea of the total expected costs.

The meeting concluded with the following comments:

Everet: Pete, I know I haven't got much of a reputation and what little there is probably isn't good, but I've learned a lot out here and one thing I've learned is that if you don't know what you're doing, hire somebody who does. Things got so bad a few months ago that I almost took up one of our competitor's offers to buy us out. I still might, but right now I want to prove to Dad that his company can still make it in the modern market place.

Peter: Well, thanks for the vote of confidence. I'm sure we can get things back on track. However, the key to success or failure of whatever system we come up with is going to be top management involvement and support of the system.

Everet: I guess that means me. I found out the hard way that the computer doesn't solve problems by just flicking the **ON** switch. I know that we're going to have to do a lot more planning if this thing is to be done right, and I'm willing to put the time into it since I know it's an important step for the company's future.

Peter: That's the type of attitude I wish more managers had. I think we'll be able to work well together. I'll need a few days to try to get a feel for where we are with our old system and whether a computer application is the right move. After all, we have to consider all alternatives. Maybe we don't need our own computerized system.

Everet: You know, I hadn't really given much thought to that possibility. I guess we've got to know where we're coming from in order to make the right decision. We might have some problems with respect to the old accounting system, as we had difficulties in generating our interim financial statements for the bank and our gross profit seems to be down about five points. I guess with the new system coming on the old system didn't get the attention it should have. I hope that doesn't cause too many problems. If there is anything I can do to provide additional information, feel free to call me. We have a spare office you can use. As well, I'll talk to our staff right away so they know what's going on and are available to assist in providing any necessary information.

Peter: That sounds like a good start. I'll give you a damage report as soon as I can. I think that maybe it would be advisable if you and your upper management team could get together and specify the goals and objectives of the company and what information each functional area requires. We'll have to prioritize this list because we will not be able to do everything at once, and I want to make sure that any system we implement does what was intended. This means that you will have to plan with foresight. We can't just plan for the status quo; look at least at a three-to five-year time horizon.

Everet: That seems like a logical starting point. We'll put our heads together and get something out to you as soon as possible. I agree with you that communication is the key if we're going to get the system we really want.

Peter: That's exactly right, and as an outsider I have to be sure that our plans for any systems design or development are in phase. Just a small reminder that this won't be a quick fix, and we are looking at 1988 before we'll be able to get anything going.

Everet: Sounds good to me, Pete. A little feedback from all of us certainly can't hurt things. One last thing Pete, I really want it done right this time. I don't want to get stuck with something that can't do the job, so be sure to ask if you need anything. By the way, I've heard that you like to stroke the golf ball, and since Dad's spot is open maybe we can get together for golf this Saturday. I have a standing tee-off booking for Saturday at 10:00 a.m. maybe we can pencil you in as a regular?

Peter: That sounds fine, I'm willing to give it a try for this week.

As a first step Peter informally gathered a management skills profile of all of City Autoparts' key staff (Exhibit 1). A preliminary review and confirmation of the accounting systems as documented by their control flowcharts (Exhibits 2 through 4) indicated that things were pretty much back on track utilizing the manual system used before the attempted computerization. However, most of the staff felt that the information in the accounting system might be suspect, due to less attention being paid to controls in the first six months of 1989 during the attempted conversion and implementation of the NPR system.

After renewing a few old acquaintances at City Autoparts, Peter went back to his office. He realized that the 1989 audit and the system review engagement were going to pose some interesting challenges, and he began to make mental notes of the information he would need for each project.

On September 27, 1989 Everet presented Peter with a written statement of the company's objectives and user requirements, which had been determined by a meeting of top management and potential users (Exhibit 5). After receiving the memo Peter was pleased to see that Everet and City Autoparts Distributors seemed to be moving in the right direction and that they realized some changes from the top down were going to be necessary. "I guess the ball's in my court now," thought Peter. "With a little bit more direction on my part, it shouldn't be too difficult to get some real priorities and evaluation criteria" (Exhibit 6).

BACKGROUND DATA

Auditor Profile

Wax, Bean & Associates, Chartered Accountants, had been in business since 1980, when Peter Bean and David Wax formed a partnership. Business had grown well (over 150 clients); their youthful energy and aggressive style were attractive to many small developing businesses. Their firm motto of "Meet the Clients' Needs With Personal Service" was typified by the private phone line and automatic call forwarding to the partners' personal residences (off-hours calls). Clients appreciated being able to reach the partners quickly on urgent matters. In most cases this additional service posed little inconvenience to the partners as usage was minimal; however, it was proving to be a great marketing device that differentiated their firm from all the others.

The client mix within the office was diverse, with a fairly even split between audit and non-audit engagements. City Autoparts had been the firm's first client. Max Wantz, who respected Peter Bean's work as a staff auditor with a large firm, decided to switch to the new firm when Bean went out on his own. City Autoparts had always been the firm's largest client, with annual fees ranging from $6,000 to $12,000 depending on the extent of special work performed.

The partners recognized the growing impact of information technology on the majority of their clients (small to medium sized businesses), and they felt that there was a real void in the marketplace with regards to the quality of computer consultative services provided to small businesses. Bean, Wax & Associates felt that they had the expertise to fill this niche.

Peter Bean, having a strong background in computerized accounting information systems and auditing, was placed as the partner in charge of this area, with 50% of his time budgeted in systems and the remainder in the audit area. The firm had purchased hardware and software facilities which allowed them to provide off-site computing facilities to their clients (batch processing). Negotiations and reviews of several hardware and accounting software vendors and their products were conducted. The firm standardized its hardware to one line of popular microcomputers (DOS-IBM Compatible) and two accounting packages, one a small business package (stand-alone) and the other for larger businesses (network capable). Long-term arrangements were made with these vendors so that volume discount prices could be obtained and the client's purchases would be done through the firm. One full-time computer specialist was hired to handle the more technical issues and provide customized programming if necessary, along with a full-time data entry operator.

The partners were not in complete agreement about the firm's decision to become involved in computer sales. There was considerable discussion that the CA designation would be tarnished by the accompanying role of computer salesmen. However, in line with the firm's motto of complete customer service and the actions undertaken by competing firms, it was decided this had to be the direction of the firm. It was hoped that in addition to servicing existing clients' computing needs, the development of a reputation in this area would attract external computing services clients who might also become auditing clients at some future date.

Initial response by the marketplace had been slow, as it was difficult to get the word out about the quality and type of services which could be provided. However, as each year end for the company's clients occurred the auditor in charge would introduce the new line of computing services available, and more interest seemed to be coming their way.

The regular audit stream practice was growing rapidly since the addition of another partner who brought in a significant number of new clients. At the last partners' meeting, the question of advertising as a means of improving their profile in the community was explored. It was agreed that with the firm's move towards specialized services (Peter in MIS and David in tax) that a more aggressive strategy aimed at achieving further exposure was warranted. Growth opportunities would mean increased profits for the partnership, and the possibility of additional expansion was already being explored.

Everet had been right in assessing the firm's need for new office space. Since last year, the addition of a new audit partner (bringing the total to four) had allowed Peter Bean to move more extensively into the management advisory and the computer consulting side of their practice. The addition of new staff and equipment and the expansion of the firm's audit business had put a significant burden on their old office space. The Burnside Industrial Park location would be ideal for the company, as it tied in well with their strategy of trying to show their clients that they were readily available. The firm wanted to portray a different image from the big national firms who were located in high-rise waterfront downtown offices. Approximately 40% of their clients were in this industrial park, and ABC's property was one of the few locations which had been designed to provide office space.

COMPANY PROFILE

Background Information

City Autoparts Distributors Limited is a wholesale distributor of automotive parts. It was incorporated in 1949 by Max Wantz. From its initial start in the stockroom of a truck garage in Halifax, Nova Scotia, the Company had grown to be one of the more successful independent auto parts distributors in the Maritimes. Growth had been steady and controlled by Max Wantz, who had an uncanny ability to sense and seize opportunity when it arose. His careful scrutiny of the day-to-day operations prevented any major disasters.

It was only in the last two to three years that problems had begun to arise. Due to his poor health, Max was not able to give the business the increasing attention that it needed. As a result of the company's operational structure, (one man centralized decision-making), decisions were beginning to bottleneck; the biggest complaint was a lack of information needed to make decisions. As a result of the increased size of the business, Max could not digest all the information necessary to make timely decisions. The accounting, marketing and logistics systems simply had not kept pace with increased growth. Just before his death, Max and top management had come to the conclusion that some revamping of the present system was necessary. It was hoped that Everet, who would soon be graduating from business school, would organize the needed change. On February 15, 1989 Max died suddenly and Everet, as the sole beneficiary, became President.

Company Details

Detailed information on City Autoparts' financial condition and company operation for 1987 and 1988 are contained in Exhibits 7 and 8. Additional company information is as follows:

> The company serves as a distributor of automotive parts with one warehouse location in Halifax, Nova Scotia. The number of parts carried in stock reaches approximately 6,000. Customers are predominantly auto repair shops, partsretailers and garages distributed throughout the region. The company has had an excellent reputation for quality brand name parts and reliable distribu-

tion to customers, but this reputation was beginning to tarnish due to head office problems.

Sales are made by a sales force of 15 agents distributed throughout all the major centres in the Maritimes. These salesmen are paid on a commission basis (5% of gross sales). They are expected to follow the firm's standard price lists, but do have the authority to initiate special discounts with approval of the sales manager. Standard discounts are allowed on sales according to trade classification of the customer, 30% for jobbers and 15% for retailers.

Goods are delivered by truck, bus or air; the method of transport is determined by the size of the shipment and requested delivery date. Freight charges, if any, are included on all invoices.

The company has a client listing of approximately 1200 customers. The average number of accounts which move each month is approximately 800. The average number of sales invoices produced each day is 300, with an average of 10 items per invoice. Sales invoice volume tends to be high relative to the number of customers because many of City Autoparts' customers use the Halifax warehouse as their stockroom, thus increasing their frequency of ordering.

With a product line of some 6,000 various auto parts and pieces of repair equipment ranging from a 10 cent washer to a $10,000 hydraulic car lift, inventory control and ordering has always been problematic for the company. As can be seen from a review of the company's flow charts (Exhibits 2, 3 and 4), inventory is controlled by means of a Kardex system, updated by a pool of inventory clerks. All purchasing is done by the Purchasing Agent, Joe Eddy, who reviews the inventory Kardex periodically and makes a decision as to whether to order, how much, and from whom. Joe prepares a purchase order and enters it into the accounting system. Based on time constraints and the volume of various parts, this inventory review and ordering cycle is usually conducted four or five times a year. Provisions are made for items which have stocked out to be ordered immediately. Experience in the past has found actual stock-out occurrence to be low, as Joe has usually lessened that possibility by ordering a large amount of safety stock. However, in the past year direct promotional activities initiated by several of their suppliers have caused more frequent stockouts in certain products, leading to increased customer dissatisfaction.

The warehouse is organized in a systematic layout by bin and part number and has been laid out to facilitate efficient picking. The sales order serves both as the picking order and the packing slip. Warehouse activities are controlled by Bill Bailey, an ex-naval officer, and a crew of five or six men, with the work flow remaining relatively smooth except for periods when a sales promotion is on to move certain products, as this usually increases the number of orders handled.

Purchasing, as discussed earlier, is conducted and controlled by Joe Eddy. The company buys from a list of approximately 200 possible vendors with the majority of purchasing and payments going to about 75 of them. Cash and volume discounts are available from most vendors. The existence of these special terms and discounts as well as bulk (container) deals has made discount monitoring difficult within the existing manual system. Recent federal sales tax amendments have placed the collection and monitoring of federal sales tax at the wholesale level, and this has caused significant tracking and adherence problems.

CASE REQUIREMENT

Your task is to assume the role of Peter Bean, C.A., as auditor of City Autoparts Distributors Limited and prepare feasible solutions to their audit and MIS problems. In those situations where additional material is required please make reasonable assumptions, and continue with your analysis and recommendations. Such would be the case in the imperfect environment of the "real world".

EXHIBIT 1
CITY AUTOPARTS DISTRIBUTORS LIMITED
TOP MANAGEMENT PROFILE

President

Everet Wantz
Age 28

Recent graduate of MBA program. Limited knowledge of business and of EDP systems.

Sales Manager

Larry O'Brien
Age 61

Had been Max's first salesman and had been with the company since 1950. His forte was sales and due to the dominating position of Max he had played only a small role in any general management activities. (No contact with EDP of any kind.)

Controller

Henry Dobbs
Age 50

A CGA with about 20 years of accounting. Had been with the company the last 15 years and set up the present accounting systems. EDP knowledge was very limited and was relieved when the NPR machine went.

Purchasing Manager

Joe Eddy
Age 43

Had come to the company from one of City Autoparts' major suppliers. Had an irreplaceable knowledge of the automotive parts industry. Had been with the company 10 years and since that time inventory controls had seemed strong (very few unexplained inventory shortages). No EDP experience.

Chief Accountant

Jim Locke
Age 29

Recent CMA graduate (1985). Had been with the company since 1984. Has had some EDP experience through previous jobs and part-time studies in computer applications at a local university. Had worked hard at the NPR installation and was frustrated that it never became operational.

Shipper Receiver

Bill Bailey
Age 46

Ex-naval officer. Very sharp and proficient in his job. (No EDP experience).

Credit Manager

Joan Sloan
Age 35

Former loans officer local bank. Only recent employee of firm (1 year). Has had minor exposure as a user to EDP systems in the bank.

EXHIBIT 2
CITY AUTOPARTS DISTRIBUTORS LIMITED
SALES — RECEIVABLES — RECEIPTS — BILLINGS

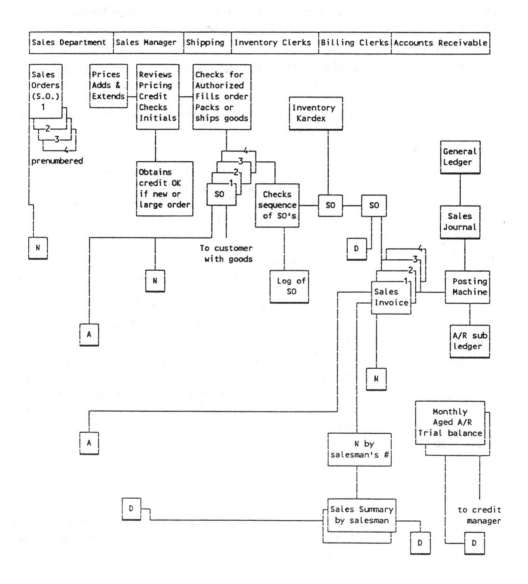

EXHIBIT 3
CITY AUTOPARTS DISTRIBUTORS LIMITED
COLLECTIONS AND CASH RECEIPTS

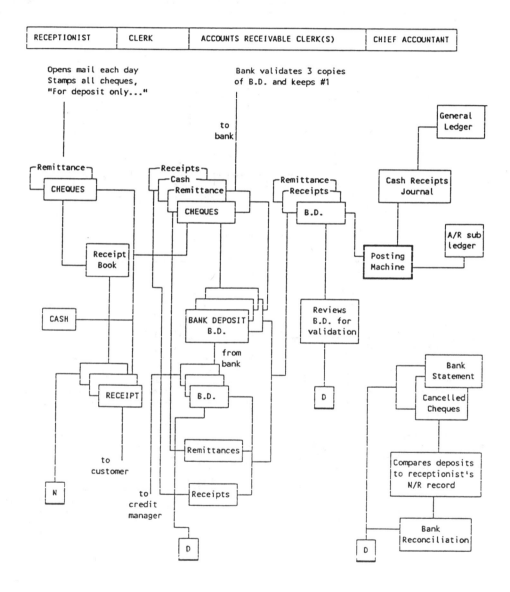

EXHIBIT 4
CITY AUTOPARTS DISTRIBUTORS LIMITED
PURCHASES — RECEIVING — PAYMENTS

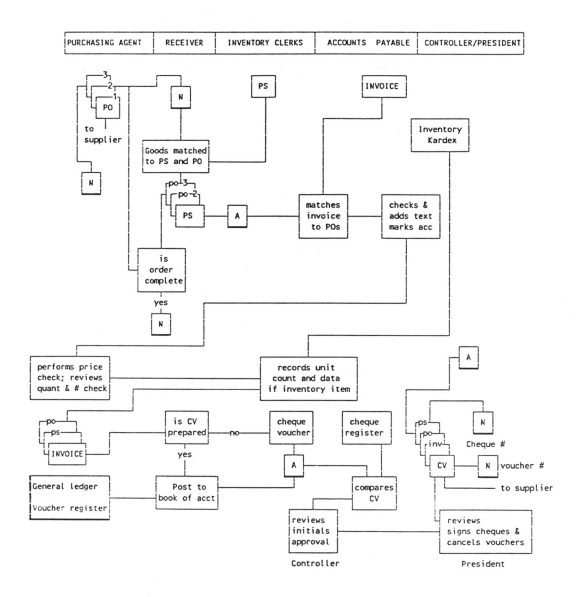

EXHIBIT 5
CITY AUTOPARTS DISTRIBUTORS LIMITED
EXTRACTS FROM MINUTES OF COMPANY STRATEGY MEETING OF SEPTEMBER 22 AND 26, 1989

The President called the meeting on September 20 to give all key staff an opportunity to contribute to the development of corporate goals and objectives and to identify information necessary to accomplish those objectives.

Present at the meeting were: Everet Wantz, Larry O'Brien, Henry Dobbs, Joe Eddy, Jim Locke, Bill Bailey and Joan Sloan.

September 22, 1989

Company objectives were summarized as follows:

The primary objective of City Autoparts Distributors is to improve on its past growth rate of 13% to 18% in sales and to improve profitability without exposing the company to any excessive financial risk. Management feels that this is definitely possible by:

(1) selective expansion of its product lines to carry complementary products (several American suppliers had made queries as to City Autoparts Distributors becoming their exclusive agents in Atlantic Canada), and

(2) critical examination of present sales and intensifying activities on those products which offer the greatest probability of success.

Management estimates that present facilities could withstand a doubling of current sales levels without any significant increase in capital expenditures. Such growth would of course require additional investment in working capital.

City Autoparts Distributors will continue to be a family owned and managed business; however, past growth has necessitated some expansion or sharing of top management functions and reorganization in this area will be likely, pending the preliminary results of our systems evaluation. Our tentative restructuring will be as follows: Henry Dobbs will become Vice-President of Finance and Operations and Jim Locke will become Controller, with a new staff member to be hired to fill Jim's position. This proposed reorganization in conjunction with a revised information system will hopefully minimize the bottlenecks presently occurring in the company. As one of Jim's new responsibilities we will place him in charge of systems development, and he will work closely with our external consultant.

September 26, 1989

Jim Locke had solicited from each potential computer user the areas where information improvements were necessary. The following list summarizes the major areas and concerns briefly.

Inventory

Sales and purchasing, both need more information on inventory levels and activity to plan appropriately.

Invoicing

At present the manually prepared invoices are taking too many hours to produce and very little other useful management information is coming from the system. Such desired information would be sales and profits per geographic area, sales representative, product, etc.

General Ledger Package

Interim financial statements are difficult to obtain on a timely basis. Information is needed faster if good decisions are to be made.

The meeting ended with all members optimistic about the opportunities available to the company.

EXHIBIT 6
CITY AUTOPARTS DISTRIBUTORS LIMITED
MEMO

TO: Peter Bean
FROM: Everet Wantz
SUBJECT: Systems Priorities
DATE: September 28, 1989

We have specified our earlier systems requirements and evaluation criteria as you requested. As a group, we unanimously feel that the inventory and billing systems must be our first priorities for system implementation.

Our goals for the new system are as follows:
(1) Reduced investment in inventory levels without impairing customer service.
(2) An improved (more scientific) method of ordering.
(3) Information relative to inventory age and turnover, gross profit and commissions.
(4) Retention of sales data so as to allow analysis for buying and marketing decisions.
(5) Flexibility within the system.
(6) Improved response time to satisfy customer ordering queries.
(7) Improved invoice preparation and billings.
(8) Reliability — system must be prone to few errors and breakdowns.
(9) Timely implementation — to have the system operational as soon as possible.

Our criteria for evaluation will be as follows:
    (1) Tangible savings   30%
    (2) Percentage of goals met   20%
    (3) Intangible benefits   20%
    (4) Time to implement   15%
    (5) Total cost   15%

I trust this will be satisfactory.

EXHIBIT 7
CITY AUTOPARTS DISTRIBUTORS BALANCE SHEET
as at December 31, 1988
(in dollars)

ASSETS	1988	1987
Current Assets		
Cash	63,000	82,000
Time Deposits	42,000	113,000
Receivables Less Allowance of 110,000 in 1986 and 80,000 in 1985	1,650,000	1,480,000
Inventories	1,510,000	1,206,000
Prepaid Insurance, Taxes, etc.	85,000	76,000
Total Current Assets	3,350,000	2,957,000
Property, Plant and Equipment	1,561,000	1,333,000
Less Accumulated Depreciation	743,000	690,000
Total Assets	4,168,000	3,600,000
LIABILITIES AND OWNERS' EQUITY		
Current Liabilities		
Short Term Note Payable	330,000	24,000
Current Portion of Long Term Debts	90,000	86,000
Accounts Payable	755,000	580,000
Accrued Liabilities	474,000	444,000
Taxes Payable	75,000	110,000
Total Current Liabilities	1,724,000	1,244,000
Long Term Debt (Net of Current Portion)	385,000	475,000
Deferred Income Taxes & Other Credits	210,000	204,000
Shareholders' Equity		
Common Shares Par Value $1.00 authorized 1,000,000 issued 40,000 1988, 39,000 1987	40,000	39,000
Paid in Capital	50,000	49,000
Retained Earnings	1,759,000	1,589,000
	1,849,000	1,677,000
Total Liabilities and Shareholders' Equity	4,168,000	3,600,000

EXHIBIT 8
CITY AUTOPARTS DISTRIBUTORS LIMITED
STATEMENT OF INCOME
For the Year Ended December 31, 1988
(in dollars)

	1988	1987
Net Sales	10,134,000	8,900,000
Cost of Goods Sold	8,208,000	7,116,000
Gross Income	1,926,000	1,784,000
Selling, General & Administrative Expenses	1,401,000	1,126,000
Operating Income	525,000	658,000
Less Interest Expense	95,000	60,000
Income Before Taxes	430,000	598,000
Less Provision for Income Taxes	150,000	210,000
Net Income	280,000	388,000

STATEMENT OF RETAINED EARNINGS
(in dollars)

Balance January 1, 1988	1,589,000
Plus Net Income	280,000
Less Dividends Paid	110,000
Balance December 31, 1988	1,759,000

CASE 2

COMMERCIAL DESIGN INC.

B. Larochelle
Concordia
University
Montreal, Quebec

INTRODUCTION

James Smith was the youngest child in a Winnipeg family of nine children. Having left high school at the end of Grade 11, James, now 42, began working as a laboratory assistant for a local photographer where he stayed for ten years. Deciding to strike out on his own, James quickly developed a successful commercial photography business which he operated as a proprietor. James' success was such that he could have expanded operations to include several employees. However, James was uncomfortable with the prospect of managing others, and so restricted his operations by referring surplus work to other commercial photographers.

In 1975, three of James' brothers, Joe, Sam and Fred, approached James with a proposition that they join him in the photography business. The brothers had observed the extent of business that James turned away and felt that there was a significant opportunity for them all to make money. The brothers wished to form an equal partnership with James. James, who rarely disagreed with his brothers, reluctantly agreed to their proposal.

During the first years of its existence, the partnership business expanded to include commercial film processing and advertising design. Advertising design included developing and mounting photographs taken by other photographers, as well as direct design, layout and photography. James developed a particular expertise in the commercial photography and marketing segments of the business. The industry was subject to much technological innovation, but James appeared to find it easy to keep abreast of technological developments. James' technical abilities enabled him to price jobs so that the partnership was quite price-competitive even though its profit margins were large. James' weakness was that he was socially uncomfortable although clients were

© John Wiley & Sons Canada Ltd. All rights reserved.

attracted to his trustworthiness.

None of James' brothers possessed his technical expertise. Joe, the eldest, and Sam, the second eldest, had backgrounds in office equipment sales. The third brother, Fred, had some accounting training but had had a checkered work history prior to going into business with his brothers. Like James, none of the brothers had completed high school.

In 1981, the partnership had purchased a building and invested in state-of-the-art equipment. The purchase of the building was a particular source of pride to the Smith brothers, since other companies in the industry did not have the cash flow or creditworthiness to purchase a building. The profitable state of the partnership caused the brothers to establish Commercial Design Inc. in 1982 and to transfer the partnership assets to the corporation. All four brothers had an equal number of shares in the new corporation.

Annual net income fluctuated greatly since it was dependent on how much the brothers left in the business, as opposed to taking out of it in salaries. All brothers were paid the same salary, irrespective of effort. Decisions as to salary and other business expenses were to be made with the consent of all brothers. However, it developed that Joe, Sam and Fred would "get together" and determine what would be a "fair" compensation arrangement. James would be presented with the plan and, as he had done most of his life, would defer to the wishes of his older brothers.

TROUBLED DEVELOPMENTS AND THE BUYOUT

Notwithstanding the profitability of Commercial Design Inc., James Smith was becoming increasingly dissatisfied. For example, the salary arrangements of the brothers had resulted in a small loss in Commercial Design's first year of operations. None of his brothers was devoting as much time to the business as James was. Joe and Sam occupied themselves with sales, though only with respect to clients which James had developed. Fred had appointed himself the accountant for Commercial Design. However, he only devoted about half his working day to his accounting activities; the balance of Fred's day was spent out of the office "developing new business", which never appeared to develop. In addition, Fred's accounting knowledge appeared to be quite rudimentary. Fred's accounting "work" consisted primarily of preparing cheques and presenting cheques to one of his brothers for countersignature. All of his brothers worked no more than thirty-five hours per week; James, on the other hand, often worked nights and weekends and took work and business worries home.

James' dissatisfaction was reinforced by the sentiments of his wife, Jane. James and Jane had been high school sweethearts who married two years after James left high school. Jane had completed high school and worked as a department store clerk until one year after the marriage, when the first of their three children was born.

James normally discussed business matters with Jane when he was unhappy about the way matters were going, and Jane knew very little about Commercial Design Inc. other than what her husband told her. Jane rarely socialized with her brothers-in-law or their families. She became convinced that James was being exploited by his three brothers and encouraged him to "take them out – for once in your life, you have to stand up to them!"

James gradually came to agree with his wife's sentiments, but didn't know how to confront his brothers. His financial position and creditworthiness were such that he could pay his brothers handsome premiums for their interests. However, as the youngest child in the family, his role in relation to his brothers had always been to defer to what he perceived to be their better judgement. James could not remember any occasion when he had challenged his brothers – how could he now persuade them to sell him their interests?

STRUCTURE OF COMMERCIAL DESIGN INC. AT THE TIME OF THE BUYOUT DECISION

At the time of James' deliberations with respect to buying out his brothers, Commercial Design Inc. was organized as follows:

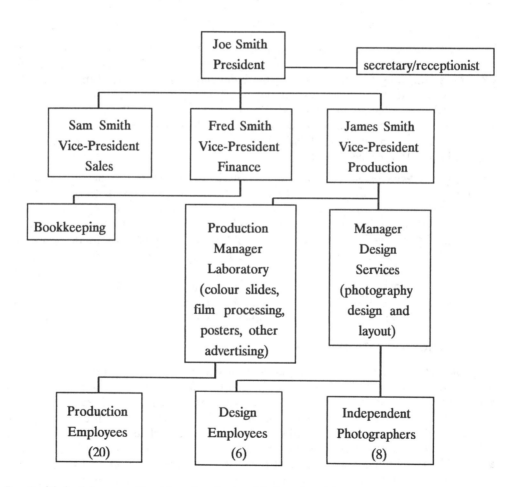

Joe Smith had become President by virtue of being the eldest brother. Meetings among the brothers were ad hoc, primarily in the context of signing cheques. A typical day for

James would involve meetings with customers and discussions with the production and design departments to ensure that customers' specifications were met. Sam would meet with James if a customer called with a repeat order and Sam had taken the call. The receptionist referred all new customer calls to James and, through James, had learned which customers should place repeat orders through Sam.

James was intimately familiar with the production and design functions, having worked in both capacities for many years. His talents as a photographer and designer were well-known locally. However, as business grew, James became less directly involved with both departments. The main business activities were split into the Design and Laboratory Departments. The Departments ran themselves; the demand for Commercial Design's services was so strong that employees worked overtime most weekends, though overtime was not compulsory. Local community college students studying design and photography would be hired as temporary workers to meet the demand.

All jobs were priced by James, who also supervised all billings and collections. It seemed to James that more and more of his time was devoted to administrative tasks. He would often walk through the production department "to get a fresh perspective on things," as he would say. All new employees were hired by James. Turnover was slight, with employees appearing to be attracted to the independent atmosphere. While employees were paid hourly, their hours varied depending on job demands. Often employees would work two fifteen-hour days and then take the next day off. All employees had keys to the premises, to facilitate weekend work. Since most of the production and design work could be performed independently, the flexibility of an employee's hours did not impede the processing of jobs.

Review of the work prior to delivery was primarily the responsibility of the production and design managers. Most larger jobs were reviewed by James prior to billing. James also reviewed all jobs where unique specifications had been agreed to between James and the client. In the event that James was dissatisfied, he would express his dissatisfaction to the production manager who would relate the problems to the employee responsible. An employee was rarely chastised for an unsatisfactory job unless there had been several instances of deficient work. In the history of Commercial Design and the predecessor partnership, very few employees had ever been fired. On those rare occasions, the firing was done after James had expressed his dissatisfaction to the department supervisor. The supervisor, rather than James, would fire the employee.

THE NATURE OF THE INDUSTRY

The commercial design industry was an industry composed of a few large "players" and many small ones. It was highly competitive due to the fact that entry into the industry was relatively easy, if one possessed the requisite expertise in one of several fields — such as photography, film processing, mounting, design and layout. The industry was distinguished from retail photography in that its primary clientele was composed of advertising and communications agencies, rather than the general public. Persons with artistic talent and temperament were attracted to the industry based on its offering an opportunity for creative expression and independence. While entry into the photography and film processing segments of the industry involved significant equipment investments, most equipment could be leased.

Demand was unpredictable, depending on contacts won by particular advertising or communications agencies. Such work was distributed based on the reputation of the particular design firm and relationships among principals developed over time. Given the number of industry "players", the fortunes of which were often tied to certain industry relationships, the industry was plagued by frequent failures of participants and accounts receivable collection problems.

A LAWYER TO THE RESCUE: EFFECTING THE BUYOUT

James Smith's childhood friend, Pete Sneet, had continued his education while James had dropped out of high school. Eventually, Pete had qualified as a lawyer. For nearly twenty years, Pete had practised law, becoming a senior partner in a mid-sized downtown law firm. It was a source of pride to James that he knew a lawyer of such stature. The corporate lawyer for Commercial Design was a lawyer chosen by James' brothers; James, however, used Pete Sneet exclusively for any legal work which James required.

James enjoyed his time with Pete Sneet. On occasion, James was able to convince Pete to go out to lunch with him. One day in early 1983, James described to Pete the frustration he was having with the business arrangement with his brothers. Pete devised a plan to buy out the brothers, to be financed in part through the sale of the building which was now owned by Commercial Design Inc. The strategy was to be very blunt with the brothers, indicating James' intention to contribute no greater time to the business than that contributed by the brothers, if they wouldn't let him buy them out. The brothers would be advised in no uncertain terms that James' decreased activities would cause the brothers' interests to quickly diminish in value.

The plan was proposed to the brothers at a meeting called by Pete but not attended by James. The brothers reluctantly agreed to the buyout. James was contacted by Joe Smith, the eldest brother, and berated for "betraying the family interests". All of the brothers, notwithstanding being compensated for their interests, vowed to have nothing further to do with James.

THE "NEW" COMMERCIAL DESIGN INC.

Exhibit A contains the financial statements of Commercial Design Inc. from the time of its foundation to its most recent (1987) year end. The buyout arrangement was proposed at the beginning of the 1983-84 fiscal year of the company. James ultimately found himself owning all of the shares of Commercial Design, but was compelled to move the business premises due to the sale of the building as part of financing the buyout.

While James' wife was quite happy that he now owned the business, James was at a loss as to what to do next. He wanted to get more advice from Pete Sneet. However, the demands of Pete's practice were such that this was not possible. The business was moved to the newer premises and James found himself conducting business much as he had previously, whereby he was involved in both production and marketing. The functions previously performed by his brothers were assumed by Commercial Design's bookkeeper. Since the work could be performed autonomously and the staff was accustomed to working independently, production continued much as it had previously.

However, moving the business premises of Commercial Design had its costs. James suddenly found himself committed to a long-term lease (negotiated by Pete Sneet), plus significant leasehold improvements. This expenditure lowered the amount which James could take out of the business, which displeased his wife. "After all," she said, "you are your own boss. Surely you can manage our money better than that."

MANAGEMENT SEMINARS AND THE FIRST GENERAL MANAGER

James was concerned that, while he now owned Commercial Design, he didn't know how to manage or expand it. He decided to attend a series of strategic management seminars offered by a local university as part of its executive development program. James enjoyed attending the program, since he felt that he was mixing with attendees who were members of the local business elite. While James was uncomfortable contributing to the sessions, he was quite proud of his response to the seminar leader's question, "Describe your current business interests." James had said, "I am the President and Owner of Commercial Design Inc."

During the breaks in the sessions, James discussed general business issues with the seminar leader. After a session on "Delegation of Authority," James mentioned to the seminar leader that the session had convinced James that he needed a general manager. James wondered if the seminar leader knew of anyone he could recommend. The seminar leader suggested a recent M.B.A. graduate whom he had taught in several classes. Based on this recommendation, in June of 1984 James hired Angela White as the general manager of Commercial Design Inc. Her duties were undefined, since the idea of hiring a general manager had first occurred to James at the management seminar.

Angela had been recommended by the seminar leader because she was a top student academically and had previous management experience. She had spent two years as the district manager of an electronics retailer prior to entering the M.B.A. program. In her work, Angela adopted a "take charge" attitude, which she brought with her to her new employment. After quickly learning the nature of James Smith's business, Angela effectively took it over. She assumed that she was in charge of production as well as general business matters, including marketing. Her attitude caused some consternation for James. At the same time, he wasn't certain why he was concerned, and also was unsure how to express his reservations to Angela.

James Smith was, at least as it appeared externally, a fairly easygoing person. Employees liked him because he didn't interfere with their work. The employees regarded James as "a fair boss to work for — weak, but fair." Angela was viewed quite differently.

One of the most objectionable aspects of Commercial Design, in her view, was the fact that employees did not work regular shifts and that recording of time worked was based on the honour system. Angela thought Commercial Design should be "more like a regular factory", as she put it. Accordingly, without consulting James, she implemented production schedules, establishing target quotas and proposed that the employees work regular shifts. When some of the employees complained, Angela's response was, "Look, I'm in charge here. My objective is to increase the profitability of Commercial Design. You can't operate without a boss."

Subsequent to the buyout and the hiring of Angela, the structure of Commercial Design looked like this:

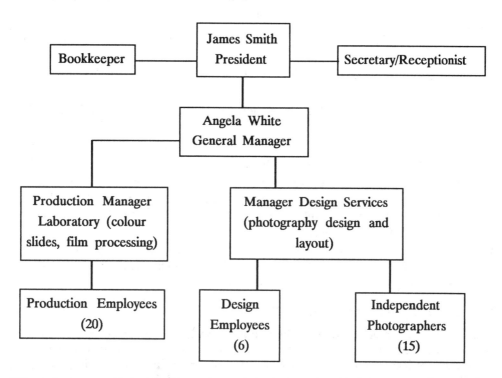

Other changes which Angela proposed included the alteration of accountability relationships, whereby both the production and design managers would be under her direct control rather than that of James, as well as the curtailment of overtime. Angela's belief was that the employees should become more productive during their regular working hours. She also proposed the termination of the relationship with the independent photographers. Angela felt that there was inefficient control over their work and that hiring one or two photographers as employees would make more sense, from a control perspective.

The production and design managers immediately complained to James Smith. James readily agreed with their complaints, telling them, "If she thinks she's in charge here, I have a few things to tell her. Leave it with me." However, when James spoke to Angela, the conversation focused on how Angela was enjoying the new job. James' only comment as to her performance was, "Don't go so fast with the changes. I guess that they're needed, but it takes time to get people used to them." The changes proposed by Angela were subsequently implemented. In addition, Angela proposed that all marketing functions be assumed by her, and that James spend his time with older, established accounts.

"After all," said Angela, "The chief executive officer delegates authority and does not become involved with the day-to-day operations of the organization."

"I guess you're right," replied James, with some hesitation.

Soon afterwards, James found himself with nothing to do. The work seemed to be getting out, though James noticed that when employees passed him in the hall, they appeared to be unhappy and looked at James in a questioning fashion. He had a feeling that the changes implemented by Angela weren't working. This was confirmed by July of 1985 when both the production and design managers threatened to quit unless Angela was removed. At the same time, customers were expressing dissatisfaction over the fact that, in most cases, they were no longer dealing directly with James. James decided to call Pete Sneet.

"I need a new manager, but I don't know how to get rid of the old one," he said. "Can you help me get rid of her? She thinks that she owns the company."

"This is outside of my normal legal practice," said Pete. "However, I'll help you out, since I know that this must be giving you a fair amount of pressure."

"Pressure like you wouldn't believe," replied James. "I'm all alone in this. My wife pushed me into this and now, when I have difficulties, she doesn't want to talk about them. This move has cost me many thousands of dollars and I'm getting calls from the bank. My employees are quitting. I have to talk strategy with someone."

The next day, James didn't go to the office. Pete Sneet appeared with a letter signed by James which dismissed Angela, effective immediately. A generous cash settlement was offered and accepted. The day after, James returned.

THE SECOND GENERAL MANAGER

After interviewing several people who responded to a newspaper advertisement for a general manager, James settled on Dave Sophistico. Dave had attended two years of community college, after having dropped out of university. His previous work experience was two years as an assistant manager for a local design firm. Dave appeared to be extremely enthusiastic about the new position. While like Angela he adopted a "take charge" attitude, he did listen to James, who wanted the organization to function as it had prior to Angela.

Dave became James' "right-hand person." While his job was nominally that of general manager, he basically performed whatever task James gave him on any given day. Since James was not consistent with respect to the activities which he reserved to himself, soon Dave had been exposed to all major aspects of Commercial Design. Dave found that he was well-liked by most employees. Soon, like Angela, he considered that he effectively controlled the business.

Dave made sure that James was satisfied with matters by informing him selectively with respect to the day-to-day operations of the business. Dave also eased James out of certain functions without James being aware of it. For example, Dave would offer to "take care" of a certain client, if James was busy. Soon the client would only be dealing with Dave rather than James. Whereas before, James was involved in the hiring process, Dave would suggest that he could do the "prescreening" to make things easier. As a result, Dave was able to ensure that anyone who might be a potential threat to himself was not hired.

Once again, James often found himself with nothing to do. He became depressed since he thought he should be busy, yet he wasn't. Dave appeared to be doing an excellent job; in fact, the business seemed to run quite well without James. However, it was quite apparent that Dave was running the business in his own way.

PROFITABILITY PROBLEMS

James had ordered the installation of a computerized accounting system at Commercial Design. Every month, he received extensive financial information, including itemized income statements and balance sheet accounts, showing every transaction affecting a particular account. James reviewed these transactions but was at a loss to understand what they meant. He relied on a representative of the external accountant for Commercial Design who prepared the year-end financial statements and would generally spend an hour or so with James discussing their significance.

By the end of the 1984-85 fiscal year, James had decided to change accounting firms, in the hope of obtaining a greater degree of personal service. The change had come about as a result of a business trip which James had taken to Saskatoon, Saskatchewan. While working out at the hotel's athletic club, he had encountered Frank Shades, a partner with Bright, Green and Shades, a Saskatoon firm of Chartered Accountants. Frank had listened with great interest to James' discussion of his concerns. James was greatly impressed with Frank and asked that he immediately take over the account. Frank's firm assumed the account as of the beginning of Commercial Design Inc.'s 1986 Fiscal year.

During the 1986-87 fiscal year, the bank manager began to call James more frequently, pointing out to James that the account of Commercial Design was in serious overdraft. James was quite upset since he had guaranteed the indebtedness of Commercial Design Inc. by pledging the family home as security and had no idea that the cash position of Commercial Design was that perilous.

Most of the pricing had been taken over by Dave. In addition, while receivables had previously been collected by James and the bookkeeper, Dave had volunteered to assume the collection function. Having volunteered to collect the funds, Dave had soon lost interest. When James called Dave into his office to discuss the financial difficulties of Commercial Design, Dave said that the problems were due to increased costs and general collection difficulties; he expressed the opinion that both conditions were temporary.

While the explanation satisfied James at the time, he remained depressed. During a one-week period he thought about several courses of action as his moods changed: (1) sell the business and do something else; (2) merge with a design firm of a comparable size; (3) take over another design firm; (4) expand the business by purchasing or leasing new equipment. In fact, James had very little to do at Commercial Design other than contemplate what to do in the future.

One course of action contemplated by James was a merger or association with Faible Inc. Exhibit B contains the financial statements of Faible Inc. which were presented to James for consideration. Faible's primary business was photographic enlargements and commercial displays, such as displays for trade shows and advertising campaigns. The principals of Faible wanted to merge with Commercial Design, an action which James considered to involve a fusion of the two companies. However, James was uncertain whether this was a preferred course of action. After all, at this time Commercial Design Inc. was not cash rich; in addition, James did not know the management of Faible very well. James estimated that equipment of Commercial Design with a market value of approximately $70,000 could be adopted to Faible's line of business.

James' reluctance was due in part to remembering a previous investment in Clickum Inc. which he had made with his brothers. Together they had acquired 40% of the outstanding common shares of Clickum, a private company which marketed specialized photography equipment. That investment had been sold shortly after the incorporation of Commercial Design Inc., as a result of acrimonious difficulties with the majority owners of Clickum Inc.

THE BANKRUPTCY FRAUD

In May 1987, ABC Inc., a major supplier of Commercial Design, suddenly made an assignment in bankruptcy. At the time, James had taken a short vacation with his family and had left Dave in charge. Dave received a call from an assistant to the controller of ABC. The assistant was reviewing the accounts receivable of ABC and noted that Commercial Design owed ABC Inc. $20,000. For a cash payment of $400, the assistant offered to eliminate the receivable prior to the bankruptcy proceedings, which were imminent.

James had given Dave signing authority on the corporate bank account. Accordingly, Dave went to the bank with a cheque made payable to "cash", cashed the cheque and presented the $400 to the assistant to the controller of ABC Inc. The receivable was eliminated thereafter. When ABC Inc. went bankrupt, as far as the bankruptcy trustee could tell, it was not owed any money by Commercial Design Inc.

In early June 1987, when James returned from his vacation, Dave proudly told him what he had done. "For $400, I saved the company $20,000," he said.

James was initially pleased but he soon began to have some doubts. He had never been involved with something like this in all his years he had been in business with his brothers. What if someone were to find out? What would his wife say? He immediately called Pete Sneet.

"Dave was a bit aggressive while I was away," James told Pete, and then related what Dave had done. Pete expressed serious concerns about the actions.

"What was done amounts to a fraud," Pete said, "a fraud for which you could be held responsible. I think that you should fire Dave immediately for being involved in bribery. You should also call the trustee in bankruptcy and acknowledge the debt."

"You talk to Dave. You talk to the trustee," replied James. Pete appreciated that the issues relating to Commercial Design Inc. were becoming quite complex and that the advice of a multi-skilled professional was perhaps in order. Accordingly, Pete has contacted the management consulting firm of Pensum Inc., with which you are associated. You have been asked to provide a report to Pete addressing several issues. The report will be shown to James Smith and will be used by James and Pete in any further actions that they take.

CASE REQUIREMENTS

1. With respect to James Smith's buyout of his brothers, discuss fully the accounting, tax, managerial and audit/review concerns that should have arisen at the time of the buyout. Your answer should include suggested provisions to be included in the buyout agreement, as well as a suggested purchase price, from the perspective of James Smith, making any assumptions considered necessary under the circumstances.

2. Discuss fully the accounting, tax, managerial and audit/review issues relating to the current position of Commercial Design Inc. and the development of the company subsequent to the buyout by James Smith, making any assumptions considered necessary under the circumstances.

3. Assuming that James Smith wishes to involve Commercial Design Inc. in some form of business arrangement with Faible Inc., discuss fully the options available to Commercial Design Inc. Your answer should include a discussion of the accounting, tax, managerial and audit/review issues of each option, from the perspective of Commercial Design Inc. and the needs of James Smith. Include in your answer a recommendation, with reasons, as to which option should be chosen, making any assumptions considered necessary under the circumstances.

4. Critically evaluate James' management and control practices.

EXHIBIT A — COMMERCIAL DESIGN INC.
BALANCE SHEET — Year Ended May 31 (in dollars)

ASSETS	1983	1984	1985	1986	1987
Current Assets					
Cash on Hand	-0-	-0-	13,665	300	300
Term Deposit	-0-	-0-	-0-	50,000	-0-
Accounts Receivable (Note 3)	186,944	169,230	239,222	108,641	204,180
Inventory	15,966	10,824	13,063	13,277	11,226
Prepaid Expenses	2,919	3,033	6,998	14,592	8,828
Corporate Taxes Receivable	-0-	-0-	-0-	12,264	-0-
Total Current Assets	205,829	183,087	272,948	199,074	224,534
Advance to Shareholder	-0-	2,411	1,230	-0-	-0-
Investment, at Cost Shares — Clickum Inc.	5,008	-0-	-0-	-0-	-0-
Fixed Assets (Note 4)					
Cost	270,965	279,455	283,327	451,074	408,832
Less Acc. Depreciation	23,720	46,977	68,839	82,029	115,765
	247,245	232,478	214,488	369,045	293,067
Other Assets					
Goodwill, at Amortized Cost	65,700	62,242	58,784	55,326	51,868
Total Assets	523,782	480,218	547,450	623,445	569,469

EXHIBIT A
COMMERCIAL DESIGN INC.
BALANCE SHEET
Year Ended May 31 (in dollars)

LIABILITIES	1983	1984	1985	1986	1987
Current Liabilities					
Bank Overdraft	3,707	18,938	-0-	8,698	15,680
Bank Loan (Note 5)	112,000	77,000	50,000	65,000	65,000
Renovation Loan	-0-	-0-	-0-	82,780	-0-
Accounts Payable and Accrued Expenses	39,967	36,015	98,246	90,502	110,701
Bonuses Payable to Employees	-0-	-0-	24,673	-0-	-0-
Shareholder Loan	-0-	-0-	-0-	-0-	12,937
Income Taxes Payable	-0-	-0-	17,400	-0-	24,215
Instalments on Long-Term Debt	19,894	8,554	13,508	66,349	10,950
	175,568	140,507	203,827	313,329	239,483
Due to Shareholders					
W/O Repayment Terms	8,451	-0-	-0-	-0-	-0-
Long-Term Debt (Note 6)	80,802	72,191	57,113	71,747	69,956
Total Liabilities	264,821	212,698	260,940	385,076	309,439

SHAREHOLDERS' EQUITY

Capital Stock Authorized
Unlimited number of class A shares, voting and participating
Unlimited number of class B shares, voting and non participating
Unlimited number of class C shares, voting and non participating with the exception of a dissolution
Unlimited number of class D shares, non cumulative, non participating, non voting, redeemable at amount paid plus any declared unpaid dividend
Unlimited number of class E shares, cumulative, non participating, non voting, redeemable at the amount paid plus any declared unpaid dividend

Issued and Fully Paid

	1983	1984	1985	1986	1987
Class D Shares	260,000	257,142	222,846	188,550	140,000
Class A Shares	100	100	100	100	100
	260,100	257,242	222,946	188,650	140,100
Retained Earnings (Deficit)	(1,139)	10,278	63,564	49,719	119,930
	258,961	267,520	286,510	238,369	260,030
Total Liabilities & Shareholders' Equity	523,782	480,218	547,450	623,445	569,469

EXHIBIT A
COMMERCIAL DESIGN INC.
EARNINGS AND DEFICIT
Year Ended May 31 (in dollars)

	1983	1984	1985	1986	1987
Sales	731,107	801,962	948,093	706,554	783,389
Cost of Sales	383,801	351,834	432,692	351,496	406,279
Gross Earnings	347,306	450,128	515,401	355,058	377,110
Operating Expenses					
Salaries and Benefits	97,711	179,513	205,219	174,248	173,010
Promotion	32,637	18,777	35,691	27,054	26,549
Advertising Expense	2,461	14,859	-0-	-0-	-0-
Training and Travelling	11,622	3,802	1,466	2,226	112
Office Expenses	21,267	16,921	28,518	17,080	18,498
Equipment Rental	13,003	16,175	6,274	7,712	3,873
Property Expense	21,396	23,820	23,931	-0-	-0-
Maintenance and Repair					
Equipment	6,019	10,112	2,103	1,740	1,028
Vehicles	4,051	9,472	6,796	-0-	-0-
Building	-0-	-0-	-0-	6,402	11,615
Telephone	9,704	14,057	15,348	7,367	5,523
Insurance	9,846	8,928	9,580	10,352	6,883
Rent	3,010	8,638	9,236	17,621	49,200
Interest and Bank Charges	18,271	15,285	15,549	9,998	11,331
Vehicle Rentals	18,398	22,170	5,021	-0-	-0-
Gas and Oil	12,733	20,151	10,046	-0-	-0-
Bad Debts	8,413	3,555	7,550	571	2,920
Professional Fees	24,978	20,243	28,950	12,330	8,562
Interest on Long-Term Debt	10,538	12,100	10,972	8,951	9,936
Depreciation of Fixed Assets	23,720	24,221	21,862	16,054	50,151
Amortization of Goodwill	3,458	3,458	3,458	3,458	3,458
Loss on Disposal of Equipment	-0-	815	-0-	-0-	-0-
Moving	-0-	-0-	-0-	3,475	7,708
Heat, Water and Hydro	-0-	-0-	-0-	8,397	12,646
Automobiles	-0-	-0-	-0-	23,296	12,664
Municipal Taxes	-0-	-0-	-0-	5,992	6,874
	353,236	447,072	447,570	364,324	422,541
Other Revenue	4,791	8,361	2,855	-0-	-0-
	348,445	438,711	444,715	364,324	422,541
Net Earnings	(1,139)	11,417	70,686	(9,266)	(45,431)

EXHIBIT A
COMMERCIAL DESIGN INC.
RETAINED EARNINGS (in dollars)

	1983	1984	1985	1986	1987
NET EARNINGS					
Before Taxes and Extraordinary Items	(1,139)	11,417	70,686	(9,266)	(45,431)
Income Taxes					
Current	-0-	-0-	17,400	-0-	-0-
Extraordinary Items					
Recovery of Income Taxes Due to Losses Carried Back	-0-	-0-	-0-	750	2,357
Gain on Sale of Fixed Assets	-0-	-0-	-0-	9,466	125,345
Total Extraordinary Items	-0-	-0-	-0-	10,216	127,702
Earnings at Year End	(1,139)	11,417	53,286	950	82,271
RETAINED EARNINGS					
Beginning of the Year	-0-	(1,139)	10,278	63,564	49,719
Add:					
Earnings for Year End	(1,139)	11,417	53,286	950	82,271
	(1,139)	10,278	63,564	64,514	131,990
Deduct					
Dividends	-0-	-0-	-0-	14,195	12,060
Interest on Tax Arrears	-0-	-0-	-0-	600	-0-
				14,795	12,060
End of the Year	(1,139)	10,278	63,564	49,719	119,930

EXHIBIT A
COMMERCIAL DESIGN INC.
CHANGES IN FINANCIAL POSITION
Year Ended May 31 (in dollars)

Source of Funds	1983	1984	1985	1986	1987*
Earnings (Net Loss/ Net Income)	(1,139)	11,417	53,286	(9,266)	
Items not Affecting Funds					
Amortization of Goodwill	3,458	3,458	3,458	3,458	
Depreciation of Fixed Assets	23,720	24,221	21,862	16,054	
Profit/Loss on Sale of Fixed Assets	(1,270)	815	-0-	-0-	
Funds Provided from Operations	24,769	39,911	78,606	10,246	
Realization of Investments	-0-	5,008	-0-	-0-	
Long-Term Loan	90,188	-0-	-0-	81,501	
Proceeds from Sale of Fixed Assets	8,550	900	385	9,466	
Decrease in Advance to Shareholder	-0-	-0-	1,181	1,230	
Income Tax Refund	-0-	-0-	-0-	750	
	123,507	45,819	80,172	103,193	
Application of Funds					
Dividends	-0-	-0-	-0-	14,195	
Additions of Fixed Assets	15,139	11,170	4,257	170,611	
Investments in Shares	5,008	-0-	-0-	-0-	
Decrease in Loans Due to Shareholders	86,556	10,861	-0-	-0-	
Interest on Tax Arrears	-0-	-0-	-0-	600	
Installments on Long-Term Debt	19,061	8,611	15,078	66,867	
Redemption of Shares	-0-	2,858	34,296	34,296	
	125,764	33,500	53,631	286,569	
Increase/Decrease in Funds	(2,257)	12,319	26,541	(183,376)	
Working Capital Beginning of Year	32,518	30,261	42,580	69,121	
End of Year	30,261	42,580	69,121	(114,255)	

* 1987 was computed on a cash basis, and is entered separately on the following page.

EXHIBIT A
COMMERCIAL DESIGN INC.
CHANGES IN FINANCIAL POSITION
(Based on a Cash Basis)

Year ended May 31, 1987

(in dollars)

Operating Activities	
Net Loss Before Extraordinary Item	(45,431)
Items Not Involving Cash	
Amortization of Goodwill	3,458
Depreciation of Fixed Assets	50,151
	8,178
Variation in Non-Cash Working Capital Components	(73,508)
Funds Provided (utilized) from Operations	(65,330)
Financing Activities	
Proceeds (payment) of Long-Term Debt	(1,791)
Income Tax Refund	2,357
Gain on Sale of Fixed Assets (after tax)	125,345
Redemption of Shares	(48,550)
Funds Provided from Financing Activities	77,361
Investment Activities	
Dividends	(12,060)
Net Addition to Fixed Assets	25,827
Funds Provided (utilized) by Investment	13,767
Increase in Funds	25,798
Funds at the Beginning of the Year	(106,178)
Funds at the End of the Year	(80,380)
Items Constituting Funds	
Cash	300
Term Deposit	-0-
Bank Overdraft	(15,680)
Bank Loan	(65,000)
	(80,380)

EXHIBIT A
COMMERCIAL DESIGN INC.
NOTES TO FINANCIAL STATEMENTS

1. Governing Statute and Nature of Operations

The Company, incorporated under the Canada Business Corporations Act, has operated a photographic business since June 1, 1982.

2. Significant Accounting Policies

Inventory

Inventory is valued at the lower of cost and replacement cost. Cost is determined by the first in, first out method.

Fixed Assets

Fixed assets are recorded at cost and depreciated over their estimated useful lives under the diminishing balance method at the following annual rates:

Cameras	20%
Equipment	10%
Furniture	20%
Building	10%

Goodwill

Goodwill is amortized on a straight-line basis over 20 years, until 2002.

3. Accounts Receivable

	1983	1984	1985	1986	1987
Trade Accounts	200,281	164,164	241,051	108,725	206,222
Allowance for Doubtful Accounts	14,670	929	1,863	600	2,042
	185,611	163,235	239,188	108,125	204,180
Other Receivables Clickum Inc.	1,333	5,995	34	516	-0-
Total	186,944	169,230	239,222	108,641	204,180

4. Fixed Assets

Cost	1983	1984	1985	1986
Leasehold Improvements				85,431
Land	37,030	37,030	37,030	37,030
Cameras	8,570	8,570	8,570	8,570
Equipment	154,032	156,801	159,263	240,488
Furniture	10,796	16,517	17,927	19,018
Building	60,537	60,537	60,537	60,537
Total	270,965	279,455	283,327	451,074

36 COMMERCIAL DESIGN INC.

Net Book Value	1983	1984	1985	1986
Leasehold Improvements				85,431
Land	37,030	37,030	37,030	37,030
Cameras	6,856	5,488	4,390	3,512
Equipment	140,047	128,526	117,890	188,820
Furniture	8,829	12,411	11,057	10,131
Building	54,483	49,023	44,121	44,121
	247,245	232,478	214,488	369,045

For the year 1987, fixed assets are recorded at historical cost and depreciated over their estimated useful lives under the following rates:

	Method	Rate	Cost	Accumulated Depreciation	Net Book Value
Leasehold Improvements	Straight line basis	20%	116,874	24,947	91,927
Cameras	Declining balance	20%	8,570	5,761	2,809
Equipment	Declining balance	10%	252,453	71,700	180,753
Furniture	Declining balance	20%	30,935	13,357	17,578
			408,832	115,765	293,067

5. Bank Loan

The bank loan is secured by a general security agreement covering all assets and a collateral third mortgage on the building owned by the company.

6. Long-Term Debt

	Current Portion	1983	1984	1985	1986
8 3/4% loan[A]	5,833	5,833			
9 1/2% Mortgage[B]		4,675	4,675		
Loan Payable at Prime Rate Plus 1 3/4%[C]	9,386	90,188	80,745	70,621	57,643
	19,894	100,696			
Installments Due Within One Year		19,894	8,554	13,508	
Total Long-Term Debt		80,802	72,191	57,113	

Notes

[A] Payable in monthly installments of $833, maturing October 18, 1983.

[B] Payable in monthly installments of $425, maturing April 23, 1984 (lien on Fixed Assets which have a Net Book Value of $155,732 in 1983).

[C] In monthly installments of $1,758, principal and interest, maturing in September.

7. Capital Stock

Under an agreement between the shareholders and the Company, the Company has a commitment to redeem 120,000 Class D shares for a total consideration of $120,000 over a forty-two month period expiring in October 1987.

The Company has redeemed Class D shares for the year ended May 31, for total considerations as below:

	# of Shares	Amount
1984	2,858	2,858
1985	34,296	34,296
1986	34,296	34,296
1987	48,550	48,550

Authorized

Unlimited number of class A shares, voting and participating

Unlimited number of class B shares, voting and non participating

Unlimited number of class C shares, voting and non participating with the exception of a dissolution

Unlimited number of class D shares, non cumulative, non participating, non-voting, redeemable at amount paid plus any declared unpaid dividend

Unlimited number of class E shares, cumulative non participating, non voting, redeemable at the amount paid plus any declared unpaid dividend

8. Cost of Sales

	1983	1984	1985	1986
Salaries, Commissions and Benefits	270,279	226,856	218,163	188,662
Material and Supplies	104,449	118,102	134,374	78,880
Shipping	9,073	6,876	80,155	83,954
	383,801	351,834	432,692	351,496

9. Long-Term Leases

Under long-term leases expiring at different dates until April 1986 for the rental of vehicles and in October 1987 and September 1988 for the equipment rental, the Company has a commitment to pay a total amount of:

1983	1984	1985
84,076	44,575	36,112

The equipment leases include a purchase option at 10% of cost. The Company could exercise these options at the end of the first 60 month period for each of the leases. (January 1987 and December 1987)

The rental expense for vehicles for the year ended May 31, 1983 aggregates $18,398 and $7,300 for the equipment. The annual rentals for the next five years are as follows:

Years	Long-Term Lease Committments				
	1983	1984	1985	1986	1987
1984	30,385				
1985	23,890	17,711			
1986	20,468	16,498	18,744		
1987	7,601	8,133	12,123	73,707	
1988	1,732	1,853	3,956	67,751	64,136
1989		380	1,289	65,084	61,469
1990				63,280	59,665
1991				53,115	49,500

10. Directors' Salaries

A total amount of $107,200 was paid to the four directors during the year for salaries.

11. Income Taxes

The disparity between the earnings before income taxes and the income tax expense is principally a result of the fact that the Company is entitled to a business investment tax purposes.

12. Comparative Figures

Certain comparative figures have been reclassified to conform with the presentation adopted in the current year.

13. Subsequent Events

On June 16, 1986, the Company sold the building located in the city of Winnipeg for a total consideration of $245,000. Net proceeds from the sale of the building were utilized to discharge amounts owing to the Royal Bank of Canada for renovations and leasehold improvements made at the new location situated in the city of Winnipeg and to pay part of the long term debt owing to the bank.

EXHIBIT B
FAIBLE INC.
BALANCE SHEET
As at January 31 (in dollars)

ASSETS	1984	1985	1986	1987	July 1987
Current					
Deposit Certificate	26,000	26,000	26,000	-0-	
Accounts Receivable	179,375	212,321	514,821	378,270	629,588
Inventory (Notes 1, 2)	147,414	172,870	455,300	445,700	385,500
Prepaid Expenses	8,589	7,300	13,000	13,700	34,385
Income Taxes Recoverable	264	-0-	46,252	65,749	52,343
Total Current Assets	361,642	418,491	1,055,373	903,419	1,101,816
Deferred Development					
Costs (Note 1)	-0-	-0-	104,257	100,813	70,813
Fixed (Notes 1 & 3)	77,841	90,177	242,230	191,954	224,594
Total Assets	439,483	508,668	1,401,860	1,196,186	1,397,262
LIABILITIES					
Current					
Bank Overdraft	11,705	33,957	49,426	-0-	
Bank Loan (Note 4)	117,000	140,000	262,000	379,605	520,207
Accounts Payable	166,581	130,054	592,432	224,392	275,489
Income Taxes Payable	-0-	8,127	-0-	-0-	
Current Portion of Long-Term Debt	3,804	3,029	18,360	51,720	56,980
Deferred Revenue	-0-	-0-	-0-	32,675	-0-
Total Current Liabilities	299,090	315,167	922,218	688,392	852,676
Long-Term Debt	3,122	200	24,400	44,880	36,660
Deferred Income Taxes	-0-	-0-	15,382	15,578	15,578
Total Liabilities	302,212	315,367	962,000	748,850	904,914
SHAREHOLDERS' EQUITY					
Capital Stock					
Authorized					
5,000 Common Shares of No Par Value, Aggregate Consideration not to Exceed $50,000					
Issued					
100 Common Shares	100	100	100	100	100
Excess of Appraisal Value of Equipment Over Cost	30,000	30,000	30,000	30,000	30,000
Retained Earnings	107,171	163,201	409,760	417,236	462,248
Total Shareholders' Equity	137,271	193,301	439,860	447,336	492,348
Total Liabilities & Shareholers' Equity	439,483	508,668	1,401,860	1,196,186	1,397,262

© John Wiley & Sons Canada Ltd. All rights reserved.

EXHIBIT B
FAIBLE INC.
STATEMENT OF RETAINED EARNINGS (in dollars)

	1984	1985	1986	1987	July 1987
BALANCE					
Beginning of the Year	106,132	107,171	163,201	409,760	417,236
Net Income for the Year	1,039	56,030	246,559	7,476	45,012
BALANCE					
End of Year	107,171	163,201	409,760	417,236	462,248

STATEMENT OF INCOME (in Dollars)

	1984	1985	1986	1987	July 1987
REVENUE					
Manufacturing	1,421,019	2,182,313	3,399,849	2,751,130	1,586,991
Rentals	38,747	32,474	34,709	49,100	17,960
Other					24,815
Total Revenue	1,459,766	2,214,787	3,434,558	2,800,230	1,629,766
Cost of Goods					
Manufactured	1,071,483	1,651,219	2,305,331	2,093,857	1,213,593
GROSS PROFIT	388,283	563,568	1,129,227	706,373	416,173
EXPENSES					
Administrative Salaries	64,233	74,725	154,173	128,790	65,508
Advertising	6,968	22,037	32,023	26,858	11,652
Bad Debts	23,239	13,556	9,390	9,299	14,000
Delivery	64,091	78,552	86,857	76,561	41,528
Depreciation	8,214	9,829	22,357	28,897	14,953
Freight	38,149	63,831	95,113	57,161	24,104
Insurance and Licenses	2,563	3,369	15,512	9,223	6,420
Interest, Bank Charges	20,313	20,031	29,408	62,790	27,907
Office	40,901	56,396	61,605	43,597	22,955
Professional Fees	7,752	6,778	13,200	11,959	7,987
Sales Commissions & Salaries	49,968	78,220	214,961	170,422	87,563
Selling	10,045	10,718	15,411	15,426	7,793
Telephone	15,266	15,589	19,694	29,006	11,192
Trailer	14,800	-0-	-0-	-0-	-0-
Travel	20,314	45,790	74,132	24,784	14,799
Total Expenses	386,816	499,421	843,836	694,773	358,361
INCOME FROM OPERATIONS			285,391	11,600	57,812
Gain on Sale of Equipment			-0-	1,090	-0-
Net Income Before Income Taxes	1,467	64,147	285,391	12,690	57,812
Provision for Income Taxes	428	8,117	38,832	5,214	12,800
NET INCOME	1,039	56,030	246,559	7,476	45,012

EXHIBIT B
FAIBLE INC.
STATEMENT OF CHANGES IN FINANCIAL POSITION (in dollars)

	1984	1985	1986	1987*
SOURCE OF FUNDS				
Operations				
Net Income for the Year	1,039	56,030	246,559	
Items Not Requiring Working Capital				
Depreciation	14,428	16,504	40,426	
Deferred Income Taxes	-0-	-0-	15,382	
	15,467	72,534	302,367	
Increase in Long-Term Debt	-0-	-0-	24,200	
	15,467	72,534	326,567	
APPLICATION OF FUNDS				
Purchase of Fixed Assets	19,960	28,840	192,479	
Reduction in Long-Term Debt	3,804	2,922	-0-	
Increase in Deferred Development Costs	-0-	-0-	104,257	
	23,764	31,762	296,736	
INCREASE (DECREASE) IN WORKING CAPITAL	(8,297)	40,772	29,831	
WORKING CAPITAL				
Beginning of Year	70,849	62,552	103,324	
End of Year	62,552	103,324	133,155	

* Computed on a cash basis. Entered separately on the following page.

EXHIBIT 2
FAIBLE INC.
STATEMENT OF CHANGES IN FINANCIAL POSITION
(in dollars)

	Jan. 1987	July 1987
CASH PROVIDED BY (USED FOR)		
Cash from Operations		
Net Income for the Year	7,476	45,012
Items Not Involving Cash		
Depreciation	55,436	28,081
Deferred Income Taxes	196	-0-
Amortization of Development Costs	133,625	49,836
	196,733	122,929
Net Change in Non-Cash Working Capital		
Balances Related to Operations	(209,411)	(179,975)
	(12,678)	(57,046)
FINANCING ACTIVITIES		
Long-Term Debt Proceeds	100,000	25,000
Long-Term Debt Payments	(46,160)	(27,960)
	53,840	(2,960)
INVESTING ACTIVITIES		
Purchase of Fixed Assets	(5,160)	(60,721)
Development Costs	(130,181)	(19,875)
	(135,341)	(80,596)
INCREASE (DECREASE) IN CASH POSITON DURING THE YEAR	(94,179)	(140,602)
Cash Position (Bank Indebtedness)		
Beginning of Year	(285,426)	(379,605)
END OF YEAR	(379,605)	(520,207)

Non-cash working capital includes accounts receivable, inventory, prepaid expenses, income taxes recoverable, accounts payable and income taxes payable.

EXHIBIT B
FAIBLE INC.
NOTES TO FINANCIAL STATEMENTS

1. SIGNIFICANT ACCOUNTING POLICIES

(a) Inventory

Inventory is stated at the lower of cost and replacement cost, which is not in excess of net realizable value. Cost is determined on the first-in, first-out basis.

(b) Depreciation

Depreciation is provided as follows:

Furniture and office equipment	20% — reducing balance basis
Production machinery and equipment	20% — reducing balance basis
Equipment carried at appraised value	straight line basis over 15 years (1987 — the life of the lease)
Leasehold improvements	straight line basis over 7 years
Automobile	30% — reducing balance basis
Computer equipment	20% — reducing balance basis

2. INVENTORY

	1984	1985	1986	1987	July 1987
Materials	73,832	150,121	386,826	413,872	358,799
Work in Progress	73,582	22,749	68,474	31,828	26,701
	147,414	172,870	455,300	455,700	385,500

3. FIXED ASSETS

	1985 Cost	Depreciation	Net	1984 Net
Furniture and Office Equipment	12,791	7,282	5,509	6,365
Production Machinery and Equip.	63,904	24,933	38,971	6,854
Equip. Carried at Appraised Value	30,000	12,000	18,000	20,000
Leasehold Improvements	45,545	17,848	27,697	34,622
	152,240	62,063	90,177	77,841

	1986 Cost	Depreciation	Net	1985 Net
Furniture and Office Equipment	23,093	9,414	13,679	5,509
Production Machinery and Equip.	168,817	43,218	125,599	38,971
Equip. Carried at Appraised Value	30,000	14,000	16,000	18,000
Leasehold Improvements	65,717	27,293	38,424	27,697
Automobile	13,982	2,098	11,884	-0-
Computer Equipment	43,110	6,446	36,644	-0-
	344,719	102,469	242,230	90,177

44 COMMERCIAL DESIGN INC.

	1987 Cost	Depreciation	Net	1986 Net
Furniture and Office Equipment	27,393	12,600	14,793	13,679
Production Machinery and Equip.	166,853	64,368	102,485	125,599
Equip. Carried at Appraised Value	30,000	16,000	14,000	16,000
Leasehold Improvements	65,717	39,261	26,456	38,424
Automobile	13,981	5,662	8,319	11,884
Computer Equipment	43,404	17,503	25,901	36,644
	347,348	155,394	191,954	242,230

	July 31, 1987 Cost	Depreciation	Net	Jan/87 Net
Furniture and Office Equipment	28,482	14,134	14,348	14,793
Production Machinery and Equip	225,784	78,746	147,038	102,485
Equip. Carried at Appraised Value	30,000	17,000	13,000	14,000
Leasehold Improvements	65,717	45,245	20,472	26,456
Automobile	14,682	6,962	7,720	8,319
Computer Equipment	43,404	21,388	22,016	25,901
	408,069	183,475	224,594	191,954

4. BANK LOAN

The bank loan is secured by a deposit held by the Bank and a general assignment of accounts with interest at bank prime rate plus 1.25%.

5. LONG-TERM DEBT

	1984	1985	1986	1987
Bank Loan	6,926	3,239	42,760	
Repayable in Principal Payments of $1,530 monthly, maturing May, 1988				24,000
Repayable in Principal Payments of $2,780 Monthly, Maturing March, 1989				72,000
Current Portion	3,804	3,039	18,360	51,720
	3,122	200	24,000	44,280

As at July 31, 1987

Bank Loan, Repayable in Principal Payments of $700 Monthly, Maturing April, 1990	22,000
Bank Loan Repayable in Principal Payments of $1530 Monthly, Maturing May, 1988	15,220
Bank Loan Repayable in Principal Payments of $2,780 Monthly, Maturing March, 1989	55,520
	93,640
Current Portion	56,980
	36,660

The bank loan is secured by a first charge against certain production equipment and an assignment of inventories, and is guaranteed by personal term deposits of two directors.

6. RELATED PARTY TRANSACTIONS

The Company has leased premises from a related party expiry July 31, 1989 at a yearly rental of:

1985	59,000	
1986	63,700	(The Company paid $61,250.)
1987	66,144	

The Company rents equipment from related companies with annual rental payments of:

1985	10,000	
1986	14,000	
1987	25,000	each.

EXHIBIT B
FAIBLE INC.
SCHEDULE OF COST OF GOODS MANUFACTURED (in dollars)

	1984	1985	1986	1987	July 1987
MATERIALS					
Inventory Beginning of Year	86,189	147,414	172,870	455,300	445,700
Purchases	589,784	821,144	1,439,623	765,839	446,759
Freight	19,277	35,661	50,661	78,388	20,934
	695,250	1,004,219	1,663,154	1,299,527	913,393
Inventory End of Year	147,414	172,870	455,300	445,700	385,500
	547,836	831,349	1,207,854	853,827	527,893
EXPENSES					
Casual Labour and Sub-Contractors	30,413	28,018	17,400	40,898	18,748
Depreciation Machinery & Equipment	6,214	6,675	18,069	26,539	13,128
Design	-0-	88,481	205,244	114,509	49,028
Direct Labour	329,220	458,738	573,970	524,001	342,847
Equipment Rentals	15,518	22,139	14,504	32,317	12,906
Erection	-0-	42,653	38,891	97,956	49,251
Heat, Light and Power	18,033	20,099	22,696	20,697	9,944
Insurance	4,040	3,488	4,880	10,502	10,012
Payroll Benefits	54,363	57,269	86,144	83,024	50,760
Research & Development	-0-	-0-	-0-	133,625	49,836
Rent	47,339	54,120	69,595	125,712	60,507
Small Tools & Supplies	9,771	19,192	25,552	14,309	8,461
Taxes	8,736	18,998	20,532	15,941	10,272
	523,647	819,870	1,097,477	1,240,030	685,700
Total Cost of Goods Manufactured	1,071,483	1,651,219	2,305,331	2,093,857	1,213,593

CASE 3

AUTOMIK LIMITED

L.-P. Lauzon
Université du Quebec
Montreal, Quebec

BACKGROUND

Automik Ltd., an automotive parts and service company, was founded in 1964 by its current majority shareholder, Thierry Planchet. Planchet was born in Bordeaux, France, and emigrated to Canada in 1960. He became a Canadian citizen in 1970, and is now 59 years old.

Since 1980, Automik has been regulated by the Canada Business Corporations Act. It became a public corporation in 1982, when class A shares with one vote each and class B shares with 100 votes each were issued. The company's head office is in Drummondville, Quebec. The corporation's class A and class B common shares are traded on the Toronto and Montreal Stock Exchanges. In the coming year, Planchet plans to register his corporation's common shares on the Vancouver Stock Exchange, Canada's third largest stock market. This way Automik will become better known in Western Canada, a region which, according to Planchet, is destined for great expansion. (See Appendix I – III for Automik's financial statements.)

By means of his Canadian subsidiary Pradex Ltd., which owns all of his French company's (Pradex S.A.) outstanding shares, Planchet has his mind set on expanding his operations to his native country in the very near future, and also to the French-speaking countries of Morocco and Tunisia where he has many friends and relatives. According to Planchet, the Canadian market has almost reached its saturation point, and future expansion should take place in Europe and North Africa. As a native Frenchman and former Foreign Legion soldier in North Africa, he thinks he has far more knowledge and experience than his competitors to expand his operations to the European and African markets. As is the case with his French company, Pradex S.A., the future foreign subsidiaries would be directly managed by the parent company.

Since its establishment, Automik has been serving the motor vehicle market for parts and service. Needless to say, Automik operated in a highly competitive sector of the economy, along with hundreds of other companies. Except for a few large organizations, the spare parts industry is fragmented, with virtually no structure. Competitiors are many, and the individual distributors' impact on the whole market is not significant. Although Automik may not be considered one of Canada's largest public corporations, it is in fact one of the ten largest in its commercial sector.

It has become more and more difficult for an entrepreneur or a company to gain access to the spare parts distribution market. The start up and maintenance costs of a distribution network have been skyrocketing. Similarly, changes in automobile technology have resulted in more numerous, more sophisticated and more expensive automobile parts and components; inventories thus require larger investments and more elaborate control methods.

Although competition is fierce in this sector, Automik has experienced a regular and continued growth since its foundation in 1964. If in 1984 it had not lost money due to the shutdown of two warehouses (one in Western Canada, and one in the Maritime provinces), and on foreign currency conversion, and if it had not incurred considerable charges for setting up a new pension plan and equipping the company with a data processing system, 1984 would have been Automik's best year ever.

The corporation converted its foreign currency accounts according to the current rate method. With this method, all asset and liability items in foreign currencies, including the foreign subsidiary's, are converted at a foreign exchange rate in effect at the end of the fiscal year. During the fiscal year, profits and expenses are converted at the average monthly foreign exchange rate.

The total exchange gains and losses resulting from the foreign subsidiary's financial statements' conversion are recorded in the foreign currency conversion cumulated adjustment account as common shareholders' equity. If the foreign subsidiary is sold, or if the net investment in the foreign subsidiary is considerably reduced, an appropriate portion of the foreign currency conversion cumulated adjustment account is entered in the results for the current year.

Canadian legal entities' foreign exchange gains and losses are entered in the income statement, except for those pertaining to long-term foreign currency debt items. As for debt items considered as the foreign subsidiary's net investment margin, foreign exchange gains and losses are entered in the foreign currency conversion cumulated adjustment account. As for the remaining long-term foreign currency debt item protion, foreign exchange gains and losses are deferred and amortized over the remaining periods of the various obligations. Foreign currency gains and losses on long-term debt items subject to a margin by means of a foreign exchange term contract are offset by losses and gains resulting from these foreign exchange term contracts.

Needless to say, Thierry Planchet keeps a very close watch on the French economy. The steady fall of the French franc is for Planchet a highly welcome opportunity to purchase French companies now, and at a good price.

CORPORATE STRUCTURE

Automik's organization chart is outlined in Appendix IV. The company now comprises four divisions:

Autogros wholesale divisions,
Autopak retail division,
Econoprix specialized auto repair division,
Pradex truck mechanics division, and its French subsidiary, Pradex S.A.

These divisions are individual companies whose shares are owned 100% by the parent company, Automik Ltd. (See Appendix V.) Formal weekly meetings have been planned between head office's executive officers and the subsidiaries' managers; however, this policy is seldom enforced due to the very heavy workload of everyone involved.

Autogros Division

The wholesale division now accounts for 300 stores, usually occupying about the same floor area and displaying the same Autogros banner. Fifty of these stores belong to Autogros: 40 are located in Quebec, and the remaining 10 are in Ontario. Automik has just received a purchase offer from a wealthy Ontario entrepreneur for the 10 stores located in Ontario. Planchet is interested in this offer and wonders how much he should be asking. (Additional information pertaining to this offer can be found in Appendix XIII.) The other 250 stores, which are affiliated-wholesalers, are spread across Canada. The latter take part in the "Autogros Associates" program which allows them to take advantage of Autogros' managerial advice and technical assistance, besides offering their customers well-known products and fast and efficient service. The majority of Autogros stores are profit-making and achieve an identical output rate.

The wholesale network stores get their supplies from 15 distribution centres spread across Canada and owned by Autogros. Each of these centres consists of a huge automobile and truck part warehouse.

Autopak Division

The Autopak retail division was set up in 1980 when Autopak Limited was acquired, thereby securing a place for Automik in the retail market. This division operated four separate warehouses which serve affiliated retailers in Quebec, Ontario and the Maritime provinces. These retailers operate small and average floor space stores which sell automobile parts directly to the consumer, sometimes offering mechanical assistance and other services. This subsidiary now includes 100 retailers: 85 are associated stores, and 15 are directly owned by Autopak. The latter are all located in Quebec, except for one in New Brunswichk.

Econoprix Division

The Econoprix specialized auto repair division was established in 1982, in order to monopolize a high-growth economic sector. It consists of mechanics' shops specializing in a particular kind of automobile repair: mufflers, shock absorbers and brakes. The Econoprix division was set up to group together these mechanics who make such repairs into one common company by offering them a specific identity, advertising, training, as well as excellent pruchasing conditions. The Econoprix division now has 200 retailers: 100 in Quebec and 100 in Ontario. Only 10 of them belong directly to the

Econoprix company; the other 190 are affiliated stores. The 10 Econoprix-owned stores are all located in Quebec. This division has four ultramodern warehouses: two in Quebec and two in Ontario.

Pradex Division

The Pradex truck mechanics division serves the trucking industry. It consists of a distribution centre which, among other things, looks after ignition systems and the rebuilding of diesel engine injection pumps. It also specializes in heavy truck parts, the remanufacturing of crankshafts, engine blocks, and cylinder heads. The truck mechanics division is the only Automik subsidiary located outside Canada. The Pradex S.A. company operates its distribution centre in Bordeaux, France. Thierry Planchet, who bought this company from his cousin Herve Robic, currently Pradex S.A.'s chief executive manager, congratulates himself for acquiring it, as he plans launching the other three divisions on the French market, using Pradex S.A. as his turntable. Detailed information of sales and profits may be found in Appendix VI.

HUMAN RESOURCES

During the 1983 fiscal year, the total number of employees varied from 1,607 to 1,694. In 1982, it fluctuated between 1,805 and 1,686. The number was reduced to 1,482 employees by the 1984 fiscal year end, which resulted in a noticeable deterioration of relations with the unions. In the near future, Automik hopes to cut back at least 150 more employees. The unions hold the data processing system partly responsible for these cutbacks.

The following table shows the break-down as at December 31, 1984:

	Number of Employees
Head Office and Services	171
Autogros Wholesale Division	673
Autopak Retail Division	177
Econoprix Auto Repair Division	107
Pradex Truck Mechanics Division	265
French Pradex S.A.	89
	1,482

About 20% of Automik's employees are represented by various negotiating agents for 12 separate collective agreements. Unions represent from five to 120 members, for an average of 25 members per union. Most of the collective agreements expire in the final months of 1984. Two of them have been renewed, and four more are being negotiated. The last labour conflict dates back to 1980, when Autogros employees stopped working for more than five months, and the French Pradex S.A.'s employees went on a six month strike.

In order to ease employer-employee tensions after the job cutbacks and a company-imposed wage freeze, Automik's management has recently been more generous regarding job tenure for its regular employees, safer working conditions, training and upgrading, and statutory holidays. On the other hand, management is inflexible regarding a shorter work week. This currently constitutes the employees' main demand.

During the 1984 fiscal year, Automik officially adopted a new benefit-based pension plan. Appendix VII summarizes the plan's most important provisions. According to actuarial calculations, the updated value of benefits irrevocably awarded salaried employees for past service amounted to $8,500,000 as at December 31, 1984; current service cost would amount to $550,000 approximately for each calendar year from 1984 to 1989. Management intends to pay the whole cost of current service by depositing $550,000 annually in the pension fund for the years 1984 to 1989. Moreover, the $8,500,000 cost for past service will be amortized and capitalized (at a rate of 11 1/2 %) over 15 years. The plan will cover all current full time Automik and subsidiary employees, except those working for the French Pradex S.A.

THE INDUSTRY

The automobile parts sector has become extremely complex, due on the one hand to the increasing number of parts required for automobile maintenance and on the other hand to the number of automobile models currently available on the market. This is compounded by fast-changing automotive technology, which accounts for very large inventories of required parts.

Thanks to a distribution network strategically located throughout Canada, Automik believes that several factors have had a positive effect on its growth and performance. First of all, according to automobile industry statistics, vehicles now on the road are getting old; the average age of vehicles registered in Canada is now close to seven years, compared to 5.5 years in 1970. The reason is two-fold: cars last longer and they are more expensive to buy new, so they are not replaced as often as they used to be. Automik is in a position to take direct advantage of the increasing number of older cars on the road, because it is closely linked to a potentially widening spare parts market.

Automik subsidiaries' 23 specialized warehouses each have inventories varying from $800,000 to $8,000,000 in cash value, depending on their volume of business. The stocklist consists of 32,000 to 45,000 separate car and truck parts; it also includes a range of specialized tools required by those who perform mechanical maintenance, such as electronic tune-ups, wheel alignments, and hoists.

DATA PROCESSING

At Automik, 1984 was an important year as far as data processing was concerned. The first computer was installed in April at an Autopak associated retail store in Longueuil. By the end of 1984, 20 of the 100 Autopak corporate and associated retailers, as well as two of its four distribution retail centres had been equipped with a computer. By the end of 1985, 20 more retailers and the remaining two distribution centres will be added to the list, and by 1990 the majority of the Automik conglomerate will be using the computer.

A number of factors have contributed to the decentralization of data processing at Automik and the installation of computers in corporate and associated retail stores. Among them are the rapid changes in automotive technology which will necessitate a great many additions to a stocklist already numbered at nearly 45,000 items. In a sector where prompt service is crucial, effective computer systems guarantee progress with customers.

Data processing installation required substantial investments of about $3,000,000 for the 1984 fiscal year alone. The current and future equipment net cost, after deduction of investment credits which the corporation expects will be granted, is financed through leasing contracts. The corporation's next objective is to improve the operating system and to clarify the managing and forecasting systems.

FINANCIAL RECORDS

The corporation's bookkeeping is the responsibility of the Vice-President Finance and Treasurer, Philippe Planchet. Keeping records of cash and credit merchandise sales and customers' accounts receivable is the subsidiaries' responsibility. They also look after controlling all corporate store and warehouse bank accounts. The payment of some operating expenses, such as electrical power, minor repairs, telephone, etc., is also the subsidiaries' responsibility. On the other hand, wages, purchases, payments of suppliers' accounts, subsidiaries' managers' travel and entertainment expenses, capital expenditure, advertising, etc., are head-office controlled. Furthermore, the recording of sales made by affiliated or associated stores, i.e. Autogros, Autopak or Econoprix dealers, as well as the latter's monthly dues collection, come entirely under head office. This way, since subsidiaries' managers have little bookkeeping to do, they have more time to carry out their controlling, planning and coordinating tasks.

At head office, salary and purchase recording is carried out through data processing. With the installation of computers in the subsidiaries, corporate stores, and warehouses, head office hopes to speed up customers' credit sales and accounts receivable bookkeeping procedures considerably. During the last fiscal year, subsidiaries' managers asked that sales come under their responsibilities, but head office refused, advocating that by centralizing the system at head office subsidiaries can greatly benefit from bulk purchase rebates and better credit conditions. For the past few years, however, subsidiaries' managers have been responsible for setting, right from the start of the fiscal year, the minimum inventory level they wish to keep in stock, and very often head office's executive members have held discussions before adding or dropping a product or a line of products.

Next year, Automik wants to offer all its associated stores a new accounting service by which, in return for fees set ahead of time, the parent company will do most of their bookkeeping and will provide them with monthly financial statements.

Financial statements are prepared by head office for each subsidiary, each corporate store, and each warehouse on a monthly basis. Once compiled, they are examined by head office's executive members and the Board of Directors. After analyzing them, they are forwarded to subsidiaries' managers, who have to answer questions raised by head office and explain notable budget discrepancies.

Budget provisions constitute a priority item with Automik, and they are very carefully prepared. Head office personnel take more than a month to compile them in proper form, and two more weeks are required for discussion and approving them with subsidiaries' managers. As a matter of fact, the pay cheques of subsidiaries' managers are partly related to their monthly sales.

THE AUDITORS

The other day, after a good tennis match, Aubert Ricard, a wealthy industrialist and close friend of Philippe Planchet, mentioned something to him about price variance effects. Like Ricard, Philippe Planchet (son of Thierry and company accountant) does not want to show financial records based on current costs in the future. Instead he insists on generating public information based on original costs indexed at general price levels, in order to preserve operational capacity. However, he wants to leave out of the supplementary financial statements both deferred taxes and the financial structure adjustment. Philippe insists on his auditor helping him to compile and prepare such statements. He says that such financial reports will be useful when negotiating with the unions. According to him, these statements will show the firm's true operating results by eliminating elusive profits caused by inflation. As part of choosing the general price level index, he insists on using the implicit gross national expenditure deflation index, which he believes to be higher than the consumer price index; and he intends to use the price index in effect at the end of the fiscal year, and not the year average index. Philippe would appreciate being given an explanation of the nature of gains or losses due to general price level changes. He would also like some indications as to what these gains or losses will be for the 1984 fiscal year. Additional information on this effect can be found in Appendix XI.

Automik's current auditor, Remi Dupont, does not know how to do these supplementary statements, since he never had to do any such thing for other clients. However, he is willing to familiarize himself with this topic by reading the CICA Handbook's new chapter on price variance effects.

Last year, Automik drastically changed the format of its statement of changes in financial position. It is now done on a cash flow basis (cash in hand) instead of the more conventional working capital basis. Remi Dupont was at first opposed to such an interpretation of the expression "working capital," but, after much discussion, he was been won over and decided not to carry out his threat to put forward an audit report with reservation. However, Philippe Planchet and his long-time friend and auditor, Remi Dupont, had another disagreement regarding the recording of taxes on deferred profits. On this topic, Philippe is inflexible; he no longer wants to see a deferred tax heading in his financial statements, starting with the 1985 fiscal year.

Behind the scenes, Automik's bankers, legal advisors and financial analysts have for a long time been urging Thierry Planchet to change auditors. The accounting firm Dupont, Dupont & Associates currently audits Automik's and its subsidiaries' books, except for the French company Pradex S.A., whose financial statements are audited by a large U.S. based international firm. This latter firm has also recently increased its efforts to have Dupont, Dupont & Associates removed. As the senior Mr. Dupont is French and a long-time friend of Thierry Planchet, both of them having fought side by side in Morocco and Tunisia, the latter has strong hesitations about replacing him. Moreover, Dupont's son has just married the daughter of Planchet's brother Didier, who is Automik's current chief executive officer and president. Didier Planchet's daughter is employed by Automik's marketing department.

Thierry Planchet, however, took it upon himself to tell his current auditor that, as early as 1985, he planned to entrust the Canadian national accounting firm Rachel, Duclos with the task of auditing his most important subsidiary, Autogros Inc. Feeling sorry for his friend Remi Dupont, who stands to lose his most important client, Planchet introduced Dupont to Mr. Duclos, with a view of instigating negotiations for a future merger between these two accounting firms. Duclos believes that, whether there is a merger or not within the next three years, he will be given the mandate to audit Automik and all its subsidiaries. Except for auditing Automik's accounts, Dupont, Dupont & Associates remains a marginal accounting firm whose usual customers have little in common with those dealing with Rachel, Duclos.

EXPANSION OPPORTUNITIES

At the end of the 1984 fiscal year, Mr. Planchet received two very appealing offers. The first one was an opportunity to purchase the corporation Rano Inc., one of Autopak's competitors. Rano's financial statements can be found in Appendix VIII. Rano's current majority shareholders want $4,000,000 cash for their 80% interest. As for the minority shareholder who has 20% of the voting shares, Adelin Lathier, a resident of Lausanne, Switzerland, he wants $1,200,000 for his block of shares. The majority shareholders' interest may be acquired regardless of Mr. Lathier's shares.

Although Rano has suffered operating losses during the 1982 and 1983 fiscal years, Planchet is very interested in acquiring this corporation, especially because of his distribution network. Rano relies on a chain of 90 affiliated or associated retailers established in the Maritime provinces, Ontario and Quebec, and five corporate stores located in the Montreal area. According to Planchet, this acquisition will prove profitable in the long run. Rano is a corporation that reached its peak ten years ago. It then enjoyed a very enviable reputation with consumers, and practised a very aggressive advertising and marketing policy. It had a network of 12 associated retailers and 12 corporate stores. However, five years ago it completely withdrew from western Canada in order to consolidate its activities in the provinces east of Ontario. After three executive managers had resigned Rano began to collapse and was no longer in a position to face up to competitors like Autopak, Automik's subsidiary.

If the purchase takes place, Thierry Planchet intends to dissolve Rano Inc. in order to integrate it into Autopak. That way, Autopak would almost double its sales outlets, and the former Rano stores would bear the Autopak banner. After consolidation, Planchet plans to close two of the five Rano-affiliated stores located in the same neighbourhood as existing Autopak stores. In the short run, Automik will have to invest approximately $4,000,000 in the Rano stores, to make them profitable again. Close to 60% of this additional capital outlay will be devoted to capital expenditure.

The other project Planchet is considering consists of merging common interests with the corporation Bamax Inc., which has more than 300 corporate or affiliated garages spread throughout Canada and in the north-eastern U.S. Bamax operates garages specializing in automobile maintenance and repair, and it competes directly with Econoprix. Bamax's latest financial statements may be found in Appendix IX.

Although negotiations are just beginning, the Bamax family proposes that Planchet merges the two corporations. After the merger, Automik's current shareholders would have about one quarter of Bamax's voting shares and would be entitled to a fair representation on the Board of Directors. Bamax's current shareholders would end up with 45% of the common shares, and the balance of 30% of the shares would be held by the public at large. Bamax Inc. is a public corporation whose common shares are traded on the Toronto and Vancouver Stock Exchanges.

Should this initial offer be turned down, however, the Bamax family has already suggested a second alternative. A new managing corporation would be set up under the corporate name of Pico Inc., and Bamax's common shares, held by the Bamax family, as well as 100% of Autopak's, Econoprix's and Autogros' shares would be transferred to Pico Inc. The Planchet family would then have 20% of the voting shares, and the Bamax family would have the rest. Afterwards, the managing corporation, Pico Inc., would become a corporation open to the public, with its common shares registered on the Toronto, Montreal and Vancouver Stock Exchanges. After this public offer, the Bamax family would own about 40% of the common shares, the Planchet family approximately 10%, and the public at large 50% of the remaining shares. Furthermore, the Bamax family would offer the Planchet family, at market price less a 5% rebate, 10% of the shares it would have in Pico Inc.

If a provision in the merger offer did not prevent the Planchet family from owning more than 30% of Pico's shares, Mr. Planchet would have at once accepted this second offer and would have bought, without the Bamax family's knowledge, enough common shares to gain Pico's legal control. These shares would have been bought on the open market. But if he could convince an important silent shareholder, such as Caisse de depot et d'investissement (a provincial crown corporation), a bank, a trust company or an insurance company to provide financing, Mr. Planchet would counter-offer to the Bamax family and propose to buy all of Bamax's common shares. Obviously, if the latter scenario ever came about, Mr. Planchet would shelve his projects to expand in France and North Africa for a few years. He could then concentrate on the American market for the immediate future. Bamax's approach to Automik is an attempt to counteract the competition of such giants as Canadian Tire, Goodyear and Firestone. Bamax believes that, in the long run, neither it alone nor Econoprix alone could compete against such large companies.

THE FUTURE

On this day, May 18, 1985, overtaken by all these recent developments, Thierry Planchet has decided to ask Renaud Duclos of the firm Rachel, Duclos to advise him regarding all his projects and his company's smooth operation. He would like to be given precise recommendations to improve his corporation's short and long term operations and financial situation.

CASE REQUIREMENT

Assume the role of Renaud Duclos, and prepare a report for Thierry Planchet on his company's financial situation, short and long term operations, and two prospects for expansion and merger.

TABLE OF APPENDICES
AUTOMIK LTD.

I	Audited consolidated income statement for the fiscal year ended December 31, 1984 – Automik Limited
II	Audited consolidated balance sheet at December 31, 1984 – Automik Limited
III	Notes to financial statements – Automik Limited
IV	Automik Limited's organization chart
V	Automik Limited's distribution network
VI	Divisional/regional sales, and divisional net profits
VII	Automik's and subsidiaries' pension plan provisions
VIII	Rano purchase project: Rano Inc.'s audited financial statements
IX	Bamax merger project: Bamax Inc.'s audited financial statements
X	Automik's and Bamax's common stock market value
XI	Information regarding price variance effects
XII	Subsequent events
XIII	Offer to purchase the 10 Ontario Autogros stores

APPENDIX I
AUTOMIK LTD.
CONSOLIDATED INCOME STATEMENT
For the Fiscal Year Ended on December 31
(in thousands of dollars)

Income	1984	1983
Sales	198,264	177,584
Cost of Sales	119,159	105,731
Margin	79,105	71,853
Operating Expenses		
Amortization	1,980	1,630
Bad Debts	32	18
Heating and Lighting	2,190	2,151
Interest	1,590	950
Wages	44,111	45,123
Advertising	3,300	3,100
Social Security Benefits	8,410	6,591
Taxes	3,196	1,443
Maintenance and Repairs	2,112	1,047
Others, Free of Certain Products	7,300	6,866
	74,221	68,919
Profits Before Exceptional Items	4,884	2,934
Exceptional Losses (Note 6)	(5,027)	
Profits (Losses) for the Fiscal Year	(143)	2,934

APPENDIX II
AUTOMIK LTD.
CONSOLIDATED BALANCE SHEET
as at December 31
(in thousands of dollars)

	1984	1983
SHORT TERM ASSETS		
Cash in Hand	132	500
Short Term Investments	2,000	2,000
Debit Accounts and Other Debits	20,134	15,006
Inventories	46,343	40,118
Services Receivable	1,436	1,029
	70,045	58,653
LONG TERM ASSETS		
Fixed Assets (Note 2)	12,661	11,317
Deferred Expenses (Note 3)	357	140
Goodwill	2,779	2,779
	15,797	14,236
Total Assets	85,842	72,889
SHORT TERM LIABILITIES		
Bank Loans and Outstanding Cheques	5,692	5,247
Suppliers and Accrued Liabilities	23,280	16,113
Taxes	2,058	406
Long Term Debt Fraction Within the Year	2,128	1,761
	33,158	23,527
LONG TERM LIABILITIES		
Bonds and Debentures (Note 4)	12,420	13,397
Deferred Taxes	851	917
	46,429	37,841
EQUITY CAPITAL		
Capital Stock (Note 5)	15,034	10,403
Contributed Surplus	492	615
Retained Earnings	23,887	24,030
	39,413	35,048
Total Liabilities & Capital	85,842	72,889

© John Wiley & Sons Limited. All rights reserved.

APPENDIX III
AUTOMIK LTD.
NOTES TO FINANCIAL STATEMENTS

1. SUMMARY OF BOOKKEEPING PROCEDURES

Consolidation

The corporation's subsidiaries have been consolidated, and all the intercompany accounts and transactions have been eliminated.

Inventories

Inventories are evaluated at the lesser of the net realization cost and value.

Amortization and fixed assets

Bookkeeping and amortization is calculated according to the maximum rates allowed by taxation authorities, except for buildings and equipment which are amortized according to the linear amortization method at the rates of 2 1/2% and 10% respectively. Fixed assets are recorded at cost.

2. FIXED ASSETS

(in Thousands of Dollars)

	Cost	Accumulated Depreciation
Land and Improvements	1,510	61
Buildings	7,240	2,253
Equipment	12,800	9,197
Others	3,750	1,128
	25,300	12,639

3. DEFERRED COSTS

Long Term Debt Issue Cost and Rebate	210
Feasibility Study — Data Processing	
Installation and Staff Training	112
Actuarial Study — Pension Plan	35
	357

4. BONDS AND DEBENTURES

Secured Debenture, Series A, 9 3/4%, Falling Due in 1986	2,850
Secured Debenture, at Prime Rate until 1985, Raised 1/4% thereafter, Payable in U.S. Dollars and Falling Due in 1987	6,000
Purchase Price Balance, 14 1/2%, Due in 1990	850
Purchase Price Balance, 13%, Due in 1988, and Payable in French Francs	3,110
Other Loans Secured through First Mortgages at Interest Rates Between 11 3/4% and 15 1/2%	1,063
Interest Free Shareholder's Advances with No Due Date and No Specific Mode of Repayment	675
	14,548
Minus: Current Portion	2,128
	12,420

5. CAPITAL STOCK

Authorized, Unlimited
Class A Shares, with Cumulative Dividend of $0.50, and One Vote Each
Class B Shares, with Non Cumulative Dividend of $0.25, with 100 Votes Each

Issued and Paid

892,470 Class A Shares	12,028
122,610 Class B Shares	3,006
	15,034

During the 1984 fiscal year, in accordance with a share purchase plan offered certain high managers, the Corporation issued 25,000 Class A shares and 11,600 Class B shares. This issue is subject to shareholders' ratification. 120,000 Class A share purchase rights, and 26,500 Class B share purchase rights are in circulation as at December 31, 1984. They make it possible for the bearers to purchase the Corporation's shares at market price less 25%.

6. EXCEPTIONAL LOSSES

Shut Down of 2 Warehouses	3,830
Foreign Currency Conversion — Long Term Debt, and French Subsidiary	228
Pension Plan — Cost of Past Service	1,750
Data Processing Installation, and Exceptional expenses (Breakings, Breaking-in)	328
	6,136
Minus: Due and Deferred Taxes	1,129
	5,007

APPENDIX IV
AUTOMIK LIMITED'S ORGANIZATION CHART

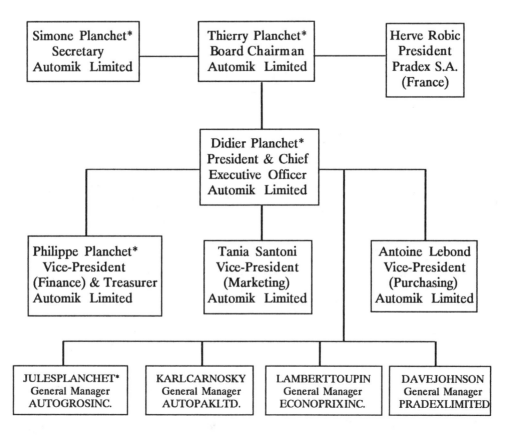

NOTES

The majority of Class B shares are held by the Planchet family members. Thierry Planchet owns 61% of them, and the other family members own 29%. The balance is owned by the public at large. Only 18% of the Class A shares are owned by the Planchet family, and the rest by the public at large, of which a 17% block is owned by an investment company partly controlled by the Canadian Government.

The Ontario Securities Commission is currently carrying out an investigation into the legality of Class B shares. These shares are believed to be discriminatory in comparison with Class A shares.

Herve Robic wants Automik to give him 20% of Pradex S.A.'s common shares, otherwise he will be resigning in 1985.

* Members constituting Automik Limited's board of directors.

© John Wiley & Sons Limited. All rights reserved.

APPENDIX V
AUTOMIK LIMITED'S DISTRIBUTION NETWORK

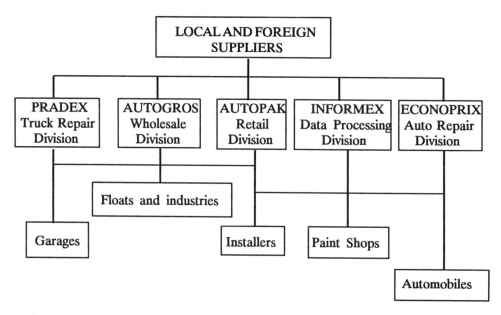

NOTE

After Automik has acquired a certain degree of competence in data processing, it plans to set up a consulting subsidiary in this field of activity. This way it hopes to make its data processing department profitable. The plans are to add a new sector to the corporation's organization in 1985, a data processing department with its own vice-president (finance) and treasurer, Mr. Philippe Planchet. It is quite probable that Guy Jutras, 27 years old, who has a computer science diploma from Control Data Institute, will be appointed to the position of vice-president (information). Mr. Jutras is now employed by a competitor of Automik Limited, and negotiations are on the verge of success. It seems quite probable that Mr. Jutras will soon be joining Automik's ranks.

APPENDIX VI
AUTOMIK LTD.
DIVISIONAL/REGIONAL SALES AND DIVISIONAL NET PROFITS
For the Fiscal Year Ended on December 31, 1984
(in thousands of dollars)

	Corporate	Associated	Total
Divisional Sales			
Autogros	13,900	85,673	99,573
Autopak	4,215	26,952	31,167
Econoprix	2,010	44,533	46,543
Pradex — Canada	34,111		34,111
Pradex — France	12,600		12,600
Intersector Sale Write-Off			(25,730)
			198,264
Regional Sales			
Western Provinces			21,007
Ontario			55,231
Quebec			88,155
Maritime Provinces			21,271
France			12,600
			198,264
Divisional Net Profits			
Autogros	324	2,589	2,913
Autopak	118	885	1,003
Econoprix	31	765	796
Pradex	172	-0-	172
	645	4,239	4,884

APPENDIX VII
AUTOMIK LTD.
AUTOMIK'S AND CANADIAN SUBSIDIARIES' PENSION PLAN PROVISIONS

1. Benefits

All participating employees who have reached the age of sixty (60) will be entitled to a retirement pension until their death. Those who, by retirement time, have accumulated twenty (20) consecutive years of service for the company, will receive an annual pension equal to 70% of their last three (3) years' average wages. Retiring employees with fewer than twenty (20) years of service will be awarded prorated pensions.

2. Award of Benefits

Entitlement to future benefits will be granted participating employees after a period of five (5) uninterrupted years of service, or on their forty-fifth (45th) birthday, whichever occurs first.

3. Transferability

The pension plan will be entirely transferable. Acquired benefits by a participating employee who leaves the company can be transferred to any other registered pension plan of his/her choice when leaving.

4. Contributions

No contributions will be required from salaried employees, and the plan will be entirely financed through employer's contributions.

5. Actuarial Appraisals and Plan Changes

Every three years, the plan will be re-appraised, and revised if need be. However, no amendment shall in any way affect the benefits hitherto attributed participating employees.

6. Past Service

When the plan comes into effect, all the years of past service will be recognized for all eligible employees.

7. Effective Date

When approved, the plan will be retroactive to December 31, 1983.

APPENDIX VIII
AUTOMIK LTD.
RANO PURCHASE PROJECT
RANO INC.'S AUDITED FINANCIAL STATEMENTS
(in thousands of dollars)
STATEMENT OF CONSOLIDATED RESULTS
For the Year Ended December 31, 1983

	1983	1982
Sales	17,900	18,416
Cost of Sales, Operating Expenses and Financial Charges	<u>19,077</u>	<u>19,060</u>
Before-Tax Loss	1,177	644
Collectible Taxes		<u>140</u>
Fiscal Year Loss	1,177	504
Net Loss Per Share	3.09	1.30

RANO INC.
STATEMENT OF CONSOLIDATED DEFICIT
For the Fiscal Year Ended on December 31, 1983

	1983	1982
Fiscal Year Opening Balance	5,550	4,836
Plus:		
Fiscal Year Loss	1,177	504
Declared Dividends	<u>135</u>	<u>210</u>
Fiscal Year Closing Balance	<u>6,862</u>	<u>5,550</u>

RANO INC.
BALANCE SHEET
at December 31, 1983
(in thousands of dollars)

	1983	1982
SHORT TERM ASSETS		
Cash in Hand	40	125
Debit Accounts and Other Debits	1,610	1,920
Inventories	3,717	4,815
Services Receivable	172	190
Taxes	86	180
	5,625	7,230
LONG TERM ASSETS		
Land	178	178
Buildings	121	143
Accumulated Depreciation	(86)	(76)
Equipment	3,412	3,785
Accumulated Depreciation	(850)	(810)
	2,775	3,320
Total Assets	8,400	10,450
SHORT TERM LIABILITIES		
Bank Loans	1,300	610
Suppliers and Accrued Liabilities	2,060	2,950
	3,360	3,560
EQUITY CAPITAL		
Common Stock Capital		
480,610 Issued Shares	7,002	7,325
Contributed Surplus	4,900	5,115
Deficit	(6,862)	(5,550)
	5,040	6,890
Total Liabilities and Equity Capital	8,400	10,450

APPENDIX IX
BAMAX MERGER PROJECT
BAMAX INC.'S AUDITED FINANCIAL STATEMENTS
STATEMENT OF CONSOLIDATED RESULTS (in thousands of dollars)
For the Fiscal Year Ended on August 31, 1984

	1984	1983
Sales	197,957	195,661
Cost of Goods Sold	108,155	104,150
Margin	89,802	91,511
Cost of Sales and Administration	77,275	78,120
Interest	3,119	4,318
	80,394	82,438
Before Tax Profits	9,408	9,073
Taxes	3,478	3,269
Fiscal Year Profits	5,930	5,804

CONSOLIDATED BALANCE SHEET

	1984	1983
Short Term Assets		
Customers and Notes Receivable	38,085	29,859
Inventories	79,291	74,072
Services Receivable	462	267
Deferred Taxes	401	139
	118,239	104,337
Fixed Assets (Note 3)		
Fixed Assets	30,763	26,568
Minus Accumulated Depreciation	10,659	9,350
	20,104	17,218
Other Asset Items		
Investment	662	
Undepreciated Cost Related to Debenture Issues	262	282
Goodwill	1,945	1,965
	2,869	2,247
Total Assets	141,212	123,802
Short Term Liabilities		
Bank Loan	18,328	8,893
Suppliers and Accrued Liabilities	34,150	27,299
Income Taxes and Other Taxes Payable	2,467	1,705
	54,945	37,897
Long Term Debt (Note 4)	18,525	19,850
Equity Capital		
Common Stock Capital 2,000,000 Shares Issued	27,843	27,421
Retained Earnings	39,899	38,634
	67,742	66,055
Total Liabilities and Equities	141,212	123,802

© John Wiley & Sons Limited. All rights reserved.

BAMAX INC.
ADDITIONAL NOTES
August 31, 1984

1. BOOKKEEPING PROCEDURES

Consolidation

The consolidated financial statements include Bamax Inc. and subsidiaries' books.

Conversion of Foreign Currency Entries

The assets and liabilities items in foreign currency are converted in $CDN according to foreign exchange rates, in effect at balance sheet time, and complete operations' exchange gains and losses are charged against the results of the fiscal year when they occurred.

Inventories

Inventories, including used material and rented units, are evaluated at cost or at net realization value, whichever is the lesser of the two.

Fixed Assets and Amortization

Fixed assets are recorded at cost. Amortization is calculated according to the degressive amortization method, except for rental improvements, at the following rates:

Buildings	either 5% or 10%
Material	20%
Rolling Stock and Computers	30%
Rental Improvements	Linear Amortization Over Set Lease Term

Other Assets

Investment is recorded at cost, and profit is entered as soon as dividends has been received.

Debenture issue related costs are amortized over the issue period.

The Corporation is of the opinion that goodwill constitutes a permanent value. Goodwill resulting from acquisitions made before the end of 1973 has therefore been entered as an undepreciated asset; goodwill resulting from acquisitions made after 1973 has been amortized over future profit forecast period, which must not exceed forty years.

Activity Sector

In accordance with Article 47 of the Canada Business Corporations Act regulations, the board of directors has determined that the Corporation's activities can be classified in a single sector, i.e. the operation of garages specializing in automobile maintenance and repairs.

2. DIVIDENDS

During the fiscal year, the corporation has declared the following dividends (in thousands of dollars):

	1984	1983
Common Shares	4,665	4,640

3. **FIXED ASSETS**

Land and Buildings	14,108	12,475
Minus Accumulated Depreciation	1,618	1,224
	12,490	11,251
Material and Rental Improvements	16,655	14,093
Minus Accumulated Depreciation	9,041	8,126
	7,614	5,967
	20,104	17,218

4. **LONG TERM DEBT**

Sinking Fund Debentures, 8 3/4%, Series A, Due on March 1, 1993	3,250	3,500
Sinking Fund Debentures, 11 3/4%, Series B, Due on October 15, 1995	2,600	2,800
Sinking Fund Debentures, 11 1/4%, Series C, Due on October 1, 1999	14,000	14,000
	19,850	20,300
Minus Short Term Portion Included in Suppliers and Accrued Liabilities	1,325	450
Total Long Term Debt	18,525	19,850

The debentures are secured by a floating charge on the Corporations's possessions. Sinking fund annual payments amount to $1,325,000.

The long term debt interest has amounted to $2,187,000 ($2,233,000 in 1983).

5. **COMMITMENTS**

Commitments in accordance with long term leases amount to $9,409,000.

Payments due for the next five fiscal years are as follows:

1985	1,613,000
1986	1,271,000
1987	1,015,000
1988	948,000
1989	826,000

6. **EMPLOYEES' PENSION PLAN**

The last employees' pension plan actuarial examination as at August 31, 1983, has shown that the fund had a surplus. The plan was amended in 1984 to improve it by making use of a fraction of the surplus.

APPENDIX X
AUTOMIK'S AND BAMAX'S COMMON STOCK MARKET VALUE

AUTOMIK	COMMON SHARES	
	Class A	Class B
	$	$
December 31, 1980	19 1/4	22 5/8
June 30, 1981	22 3/4	26 1/4
December 31, 1981	23 5/8	28 1/4
June 30, 1982	21 7/8	25 3/8
December 31, 1982	20 1/8	24 7/8
June 30, 1983	20 1/2	25 1/8
December 31, 1983	23 3/4	29 3/4
June 30, 1984	25 3/8	33 1/8
December 31, 1984	28 1/2	36 1/4

Class B common shares are traded at a market value higher than Class A shares due to the fact that they carry one hundred votes each. On the other hand, as few Class B shares are issued to the public and there is little stock market activity with these shares, their market value has been negatively affected.

BAMAX	COMMON SHARES
December 31, 1980	40 1/8
December 31, 1981	42 3/4
December 31, 1982	42 5/8
December 31, 1983	43 1/2
December 31, 1984	44 1/4

APPENDIX XI

INFORMATION REGARDING PRICE VARIANCE EFFECTS

Here are the approximate dates of the net fixed asset acquisitions, accompanied by the mid-year consumer price index:

1974	100
1980	130
1982	150
1984	170

To make things more simple, fixed asset purchases are imagined to have been made towards the middle of the year and equally distributed over these four (4) dates.

Current operating proceeds and expenses have take place evenly over the course of the 1984 fiscal year.

The June 30, 1984 price index was 170, and the December 31, 1984 was 180. The June 30 index is believed to be identical to the year average index. The general price index was 160 on January 1, 1984.

Here are the dates at which the following assets were acquired, or accounted for:

1. **Inventories:** second half of 1984 fiscal year.
2. **Short Term Investments:** deposit certificates acquired on June 30, 1984.
3. **Customers and Suppliers:** date back approximately sixty (60) days.
4. **Goodwill:** mid-year 1980.

Here are certain items' market values on December 31, 1984:

Fixed assets	32,000,000
Inventories	68,000,000
Class A Shares	28 1/2
Class B Shares	36 1/4

Inventories' and fixed assets' market values are often required by lenders. For this reason, Mr. Planchet wonders whether it would be useful to report a balance sheet with three (3) columns: original cost, original cost indexed on general price level and net realized value.

APPENDIX XII

SUBSEQUENT EVENTS

On March 31, 1985, Mr. Thierry Planchet made an offer to buy back all the Class B shares in circulation at December 31, 1984 through his private management company, Planchet Investment Corporation. He offered a purchase price of $40 per share.

APPENDIX XIII
OFFER TO PURCHASE THE 10 ONTARIO AUTOGROS STORES

Mr. Sam Greenwich offered to purchase from Automik the ten (10) Autogros stores it owns provided the following terms are agreed upon:

$200,000 Paid Cash at Purchase Time.

$500,000 Payable Over Ten (10) Years at the Annual Interest Rate of 8%

Furthermore, an amount equivalent to 10% of the net profits realized by the ten (10) stores will be paid Automik annually for the ten (10) fiscal years following the purchase of the stores by Mr. Greenwich.

CASE 4

PRINCIPAL GROUP LIMITED

J. Lawson
St. Mary's University
Halifax,
Nova Scotia

INTRODUCTION

Recent years have witnessed tremendous change in the Canadian financial industry. Trust companies, which were once controlled by the same influential group which also ran the country's chartered banks, and whose business consisted primarily of the trusteeship of estates, have changed radically. Increased competition and an influx of new entrepreneurial owners have resulted in many upheavals. Aggressively managed investment companies frequently have sought rapid growth through investment in real estate and mortgages. Often these strategies resulted in success, although there have been many casualties as well. The succession of trust company failures that occurred in the late 1970s and early 1980s has illustrated an underlying problem; a common theme has been a lack of responsibility on the part of companies' management, overly aggressive investment strategies, and ineptitude on the part of the federal and provincial regulatory agencies.

Alberta, with its cyclic economy, has been the setting for several bank and trust company failures, including the Northland Bank, The Canadian Commercial Bank, and Peter Pocklington's Fidelity Trust.

The subject of this case is another trust company, one whose reputation as a pillar of the western Canadian financial community was firmly established, yet whose downfall was rooted in the same economic events that were responsible for putting several other financial institutions out of business. What is unique about Principal Group is that although the company fell into a precarious position as early as 1982, it was not until August 10, 1987 that the company finally declared bankruptcy.

© John Wiley & Sons Canada Ltd. All rights reserved.

COMPANY HISTORY

First Investors Corp. was incorporated in Edmonton in 1954 by Donald Cormie. A graduate of Harvard Law School with entrepreneurial ideas, Cormie became bored with his position as a partner in an Edmonton law firm. Inspired by the philosophy of thrift that he had learned from his father, he set out with the dream of establishing a western Canadian savings company. Cormie's partner in business was Kenneth Marlin, a railroad dispatcher and vacuum cleaner salesman. Marlin had been impressed with Cormie's background and accomplishments and, after listening to his plans for building a western based financial institution, he was convinced that his future lay with First Investors Ltd.

First Investors' primary vehicle was investment contracts. Individuals who purchased them as savings plans were promised a set rate of 4% interest plus, at the discretion of the company, "additional credits" which would reflect the profits realized on investments. The contract company's investments included mortgages, stocks and bonds. For several years, Cormie and Marlin concentrated their efforts on building up the business of First Investors. Under Marlin's direction, a network of sales people was established across Alberta, British Columbia and Saskatchewan. The investment company's profits grew, and in 1962 Cormie and Marlin were able to buy out a competitor, Associated Investors of Canada Ltd. By the early 1960s Cormie and Marlin had assembled a network of companies under the umbrella of Principal Group Ltd. as the management company that owned the two investment contract firms and other subsidiary companies. Principal Group, in turn, was owned by Collective Securities Ltd., a holding company in which Marlin had a 10% interest, the balance being owned by Cormie.

A major advancement for Principal Group occurred in 1965, with the incorporation of Principal Savings and Trust Co. By adding a trust company, Principal gained access to low-cost deposits from small savings and chequing accounts, as well as a branch network which facilitated the distribution of investment contracts. During the next few years Principal also established seven mutual funds which were marketed through the trust company branches. (Appendix 1 illustrates graphically the structure of Principal Group.)

Principal Group's operation was characterized by an aggressive strategy involving several actions. First was the promise of interest rates to investors which always equalled or exceeded those of the competition. Second was the acceptance of investments which were of higher risk than those accepted by the competition; this was particularly true in real estate and mortgages. Finally the company engaged in very aggressive marketing tactics with the public to obtain sales of investment contracts at a rate of growth far in excess of that of many of its competitors.

During the 1970s the Principal Group grew to the point where it was the largest western Canadian based financial institution. The company's impressive growth during this period could be attributed both to its aggressive strategy and to the boom in Alberta's economy which stimulated demand for real estate, (in which First Investors Ltd. and Associated Investors Ltd. invested a considerable amount of their capital). The crowning achievement occurred when the company moved into an impressive thirty story skyscraper in downtown Edmonton. Cormie's dream had finally been realized.

Principal Group Ltd. had also become a leader in the application of computer technology. Its sophisticated computer system was the only one in North America that permitted the redemption of mutual funds from an automatic teller. The company was also a participant in the revolutionary "Instinet" system which permitted the computerized trading of shares by its investment management team.

The company's good fortunes began to change, however, following the oil price declines of 1982. Real estate prices in Alberta dropped sharply, and as a result of hard times many Albertans stopped making their mortgage payments. The Principal companies, as well as many other competing lenders in the province, started to feel the pinch as they were left with millions of dollars worth of foreclosed real estate. At this point Principal's investment contract companies started to experience cash flow problems.

Principal Group made several attempts to expand into the lucrative market of southern Ontario. In 1983 the company applied to the Ontario government for permission to sell investment contracts in that province, but when the Superintendent of Insurance requested additional financial information about Associated Investors Ltd. the company abandoned the application. In 1984 Principal made an application through one of its subsidiaries to acquire a small Ontario chartered trust company; however, when Ontario investigators discovered that Principal Trust was financially extended (indebted) beyond what they considered acceptable, the application was refused.

In 1984 the Canada Deposit Insurance Corp., as a condition of continued deposit insurance, imposed a plan on Principal Savings & Trust under which the company was instructed to increase its capital base and write off some problem loans, as well as make other improvements. In response to these demands Principal Group Ltd. engineered a series of transactions in which cash was paid by investment contract companies to the trust company for mortgages and real estate which were transferred to the investment companies. The result of these procedures was that while the companies appeared to be worth more, all that stood behind this increase in value was real estate and mortgages of questionable value because many of them were the problem loans noted above.

In a further attempt to improve its financial position, First Investors filed a prospectus with the Alberta Securities Commission for a $50 million preferred share issue early in 1985. This prospectus provided the government with an indication of the full extent of the problems by its disclosure that, at the end of 1984, up to 63% of all mortgages held by First Investors had been in arrears for 90 days or more. As a result of this disclosure, the Alberta government refused to approve the prospectus and the preferred share issue was not allowed to proceed.

Apart from the dilemma caused by the slump in the real estate market, Principal's problems originated from its policy of being a leader in the effective rates offered on its investment certificates. During the 1950s and 1960s, when interest rates were low and did not change significantly from year to year, the investment contract concept had worked well for Principal Group. However, in the early 1980s when interest rates rose to over 18%, the investment contracts became liabilities. Although in theory the company was not forced to pay out "additional credits" on its uninsured investment contracts, in practice it was obliged to in order to compete with companies offering investment contracts backed by the Canadian Deposit Insurance Corporation; otherwise, no one could be persuaded to buy them. As a result of the increased cash outflows resulting from maturing certificates, First Investors and Associated Investors were losing money by 1982. This situation became so severe that by 1986 the companies were obliged to keep selling investment contracts in order to have enough cash to pay off the maturing certificates as they came due.

The province's Financial Institutions department was transferred to Treasury from Consumer and Corporate Affairs in the summer of 1986. As Treasury officials scrutinized the Principal financial reports, they developed some serious concerns about the book values of the Principal companies' real estate holdings; the regulators called in the accounting firm Price Waterhouse for an independent opinion. As it turned out, Price Waterhouse valued the real estate at market prices, while Principal had arrived at more generous figures based on the potential resale price. The two valuations were millions of dollars apart.

At this point (May 1987) it was determined by the Alberta Treasury Department that the investment companies should be shut down. The next issue to be addressed was how this would be accomplished. While Cormie and Marlin might have preferred to continue operating the companies and pay off the investment contracts only as they came due, to allow the companies to continue operation would have required the province to keep renewing their licenses. Provincial regulations stipulated that the licenses could only be renewed if the companies were solvent. But for the companies to take an immediate writedown on the foreclosed real estate, which was required in accordance with Generally Accepted Accounting Principles, would have resulted in immediate bankruptcy.

After refusing a series of bail-out proposals from Cormie and Marlin, the Alberta Treasury officials informed Principal Group Ltd. that it would have to make immediate arrangements to have a manager appointed for First Investors and Associated Investors Ltd. In accordance with these instructions Coopers & Lybrand was appointed Receiver of the companies on June 30, 1987, and funds committed to the two were frozen. With public attention focussed on Principal Group, Cormie and Marlin faced a "crisis of confidence", a crisis which led to their voluntarily putting Principal into bankruptcy on August 10, 1987.

CASE REQUIREMENTS

1. Was the management of Principal Group Ltd. at fault in the application of Generally Accepted Accounting Principles to companies' financial data? If so, identify instances in the case that relate to specific sections of the CICA handbook.

2. Inquiries have revealed that Principal Group's investment contract companies were in precarious financial condition as early as 1982; however, public accounting firms continued to issue unqualified statements up until 1985. In 1984 Principal Group's Annual Report contained the unqualified opinion of a public accounting firm. The Notes to the Financial Statements contain sections on Mortgage Loans and Owned Property in which it is noted that these assets have been written down to some extent by the auditors. It has subsequently been revealed that, in order to accurately reflect the true market value of the real

estate, the values could have been written down to an extent far greater than was actually performed.

What should have been done to more appropriately reflect the market values? Explain.

3. Because First Investors Ltd. and Associated Investors Ltd. were private companies, no financial information was required to be made available to the public. Even the Principal Group itself, as a privately held company, was not required to disclose any financial information to the public. Principal Group Ltd.'s Annual Reports were in fact published, but because the consolidated financial statements show no breakdown of the subsidiary companies, they revealed little about the financial condition of First Investors or Associated Investors.

    In consideration of the above, what, if any, recommendations would you make concerning the requirements for public disclosure for companies that sell investment contracts and promissory notes?

4. Recent history has raised questions about the regulation of trust companies, either from the point of view of Federal and Provincial legislation, or the enforcement of that legislation, or both. The Federal Trust Companies Act stipulates that no more than 10% of an investment company's assets are to be invested in real estate; yet in repeated cases, such as Fidelity Trust and Principal Group Ltd., it has been shown that management disregarded this requirement.

    If you were in a position to influence public policy, what amendments if any would you recommend be made to the Federal Trust Companies Act and the Provincial Securities Acts with specific reference to requirements for financial disclosure? How would you recommend that this new legislation be enforced?

REFERENCES

Best, Patricia and Ann Shortell. *A Matter of Trust, Greed, Government and Canada's $60 Billion Trust Industry*. Toronto: Penguin Books, 1986, pp. 1-28, 193-212.

"Burned", *Globe & Mail Magazine*, October 1987, pp. 41-47.

"Closings didn't worry Cormie: Witness", *Globe & Mail*, Nov. 27, 1987, pp. B1, B4.

"Letter reveals Principal Group's agents feuded", *Globe & Mail*, Dec. 2, 1987, pp. B1-B2.

"Lost Investments: A Matter of Principal", *Atlantic Business*, Halifax, November/December 1987, pp. 50-53.

"Principal bust bitter irony for man of thrift", *Globe & Mail*, Aug. 5, 1987, pp. B1-B4.

"Principal collapse blamed on government", *Globe & Mail*, Nov. 11, 1987, pp. B1, B13.

"Principal furor good and bad news for accountants", *The Bottom Line*, September, 1987, pp. 1-2.

"Principal owner no pauper despite collapse of empire", *Globe & Mail*, November 7, 1987, pp. B1-B2.

"Principal VP admits deception after dramatic record hearing", *Globe & Mail*, November 25, 1987, pp. B1-B2.

"Top Principal salesman admits lying to auditors", *Globe & Mail*, November 19, 1987, pp. B1-B2.

OTHER

The Alberta Business Corporations Act, Canadian Securities Law Reporter, Government of Canada.

The Alberta Investment Contracts Act, Canadian Securities Law Reporter, Government of Canada.

The Alberta Securities Act, Canadian Securities Law Reporter, Government of Canada.

Financial Standards (Loan Companies Regulations), Government of Canada.

Financial Standards (Trust Companies Regulations), Government of Canada.

Trust Companies Act, Government of Canada.

CICA Handbook, Section 3050, "Long Term Investments"

CICA Handbook, Section 5000, "General Accepted Auditing Standards"

The Regulation of Financial Institutions: Proposals for Discussion, Ottawa, 1985.

Robinson, Lyman, **Report to the Minister, in the Matter of The Trade Practices Act**, Province of British Columbia, October 14, 1987.

Principal Group Ltd., Financial Statements 1981 to 1985

CASE 5

MERRION PRODUCTS

P. Clarke
University College
Dublin, Ireland

It was not the type of assignment that Kevin Byrne would have volunteered for. However, he felt obliged to help out his old pal, John Davis, who was the owner and managing director of Merrion Products. Since leaving college some years ago the two friends had lost contact with each other. Now, several years later, they met by chance at a weekend party. In a smoky atmosphere they traded anecdotes about the "old days" before updating each other on their current careers.

Kevin had qualified as an accountant and was now a sole practitioner. John, after his engineering studies, had set up a small manufacturing corporation trading as Merrion Products. From humble beginnings the company had grown to a modest size with annual turnover of about $800,000. The company manufactured metal boxes or casings which hold the electronic circuitry in audio equipment mainly in stereos. Their orders come primarily from large corporations specializing in the manufacture of audio equipment, and earlier this year Merrion Products had entered into a number of contracts.

At first sight the agreed contract prices had appeared lucrative compared with estimated costings. However, the company did not employ an accountant. The end result, admitted John, was that the accounting records were in a "terrible mess". John didn't know how his actual costs matched up with his original estimates. After a little persuasion, Kevin agreed to help his old friend and promised to pay a visit to the factory the following Friday.

Kevin arrived early Friday morning and took up temporary residence in John's office, which was littered with files, account books and paper. He opened the window to let some fresh air in. John pointed to a large file on the desk and said, "I've got everything here for you. The best place for you to start is with our financial position at the end of last year." The top page of the file represented the company's opening trial balance, with supporting schedules (Exhibit 1). "This is helpful," said Kevin.

© John Wiley & Sons Canada Ltd. All rights reserved.

EXHIBIT 1
(in dollars)

Trial Balance at June 30, 1987	Debit	Credit
Factory fixed assets (net)	40,000	
Raw materials control	50,000	
Work in progress*	30,960	
Capital and reserves		74,000
Bank overdraft		58,000
Debtors	45,040	
Creditors		36,000
Production overhead due		4,000
Administration expenses prepaid	6,000	
	172,000	172,000

* Analysis of work in progress.

Job No.	Materials	Labour	Production Overhead	Total
87 – 62	2,000	6,800	2,040	10,840
87 – 68	4,000	12,400	3,720	20,120
	6,000	19,200	5,760	30,960

John explained that a major problem was the general lack of production capacity. His production staff often had to work overtime in order to complete certain jobs on time. This was expensive since the basic labour rate was $20 per hour with overtime being paid at a premium of 50%. He continued, "Quality is of the utmost importance in our products. The metal casings must be engineered precisely to the manufacturers' specifications or else they will not take the electronic circuitry, dials and other components of the audio equipment."

Kevin asked, "How do the manufacturers let you know exactly what they want?"

John replied, "Let me run you through a typical scenario of a customer tender. That should answer some questions and highlight the type of problems we experience. It all starts with a marketing person in a customer company who wants to incorporate advanced technology in the audio equipment. This automatically changes the size of the metal boxes for the electronic circuitry. The modifications are passed on to their design office staff, who produce drawings and specifications for the metal boxes. These are sent out to companies like ours with a request for a quotation. Our estimator, Jack Kelly, with help from the Engineering Department, determines material and labour costs for the units under tender. Production overhead is added at the rate of 30% of direct labour expense and an additional 20% is added to total production cost to cover administration costs and leave a margin for profit. Jack eventually submits our estimate to the customer after liaising with our sales department. If our tender is successful, we receive a fixed price order with required delivery within a specified time.

"The estimating is crucial, as we must stick to our estimate once it is given and accepted. One of our problems is that different design specifications for each job can affect production time and material costs. As you will appreciate, one of the principal problems associated with estimating is identifying how long a job will take to pass through a work centre and the amount of materials required."

Kevin looked at the summary of labour hours worked and materials requisitioned for each job during the past six months (Exhibit 2). The direct materials figure had been obtained from the material requisitions dockets which were completed as material was issued for production. These dockets showed the amount and price of materials required for each job. The labour hours worked were summarized from detailed job cards. John confirmed that it was the responsibility of each production employee to manually enter the actual hours worked on each job on the appropriate card.

EXHIBIT 2
Usage of materials and labour for six months ended December 31, 1987

Quotation Price $	Job No.	Direct Materials $	Basic Labour Hours	Overtime Labour Hours
20,000	87 – 62		100	14
30,000	87 – 68		60	Nil
50,000	87 – 71	7,000	1,000	250
64,000	87 – 75	10,800	1,400	Nil
40,000	87 – 83	5,000	700	120
70,000	87 – 94	8,500	1,500	200
110,000	87 – 95	12,800	2,600	Nil
120,000	Various	14,000	2,700	200

Kevin asked to see any other information that John might have, especially in relation to cash movements, and goods purchased and sold. After some delay, John pointed to a summary page in the file (Exhibit 3).

EXHIBIT 3
Miscellaneous data for six months ended December 31, 1987
(in dollars)

Raw material purchase invoices	70,000
Invoices for production overhead expenses	56,000
Administration expenses incurred	62,000
Check payments for materials, production and administration overheads	170,000
Checks paid for wages	
— Basic (11,000 hours)	220,000
— Overtime (850 hours)	25,500
Receipts from debtors	400,000

John indicated that there were a few other pieces of information which might be useful in constructing a set of financial statements. All jobs worked on during the past six months had been completed with the exception of job No. 87 – 95, which was still in progress. All completed work had been delivered to customers and invoiced, although payments from some customers were still outstanding.

Kevin then queried depreciation policy in relation to factory fixed assets. "We depreciate these assets at the rate of $8,000 per annum," replied John. He added, "I hope you have enough information to build up some sort of financial picture of the company for the past six months. I'd also like your observations on what we're doing right or wrong in the company. I want to introduce you to the rest of our management team. I've asked each of them to spend some time with you discussing their own areas."

At this point the two left the office to meet the other members of the management team.

Terence Moore, the production manager, took Kevin for a tour of the shopfloor. They strolled along the central aisle as Terence described the various processes involved in the different manufacturing operations. Kevin couldn't help notice the cluttered conditions in some work areas such as welding and packing. When he enquired about this, Terence told him, "Stores are always short of parts or packing materials. Jobs are always having to be set aside until the required parts are delivered. Another problem is Tony Murray, our sales manager. He's forever charging down here and rushing through his priority orders. This leaves other work by the wayside."

Kevin wondered how this fitted into production scheduling as he knew it. His thoughts were interrupted by the arrival of Tony Murray.

Tony reached out a hand and said, "Welcome to the company, Kevin. Now, what can I tell you?"

"How about filling me in on the customer profile?" Kevin replied.

"Customers, yes, we supply to most of the big names in the business, but the market is fairly competitive. We must, therefore, keep our prices keen and our performance high."

"How are you doing in regard to sales?" Kevin asked.

"Up to six months ago I would have said fine," Tony answered. "Now, I'm not so sure. Our delivery record has been getting worse, and our customers are beginning to complain and refuse to accept delivery. What's more, Jack Kelly, he's the estimator, doesn't seem to realize how competitive the market is. He keeps producing prices that make it a bit harder than it used to be to get orders. I nearly always have to reduce his figures before making a final quotation. It's getting tougher to get orders."

Tony went on to draw a picture of potential disaster in the near future and complained about production being inefficient and disorganized and inventory nearly always being short of parts.

As Kevin left Tony's office, he wondered what he was letting himself in for. He consoled himself by putting the sales manager's pessimism down to paranoia, which he thought was common in sales people when dealing with other departments in their own company.

It was harder to get time with Bill Rodgers, the purchasing manager, who was making phone calls. After Kevin had been standing around for a few minutes Bill put the phone down. "Sorry to keep you waiting, Kevin," he said.

The phone rang again.

Bill sighed and suggested, "Let's go to the canteen for a cup of coffee and a chat. If we stay here we'll get no peace with people chasing me over parts."

In the relative safety of the no-smoking zone in the canteen Bill outlined the work of his department. "I'm responsible for purchasing and maintaining stores. In relation to the various raw materials we classify them as follows, with each group having its own coding system: sheet metal, packing materials including fasteners and cardboard boxes, and single piece parts for metal boxes.

"We keep the packaging material and a few other pieces in the store next to the welding area. There is a lot of heat in that area and as a result we don't have any dampness problems. Everything else is in the large, main store at the other end of the factory. Our stock records are kept on a cardex system. However, because of the nature of our business and occasional lack of communication, staff are constantly going into the inventory and taking parts for production."

Later in the day Jack Kelly, the estimator, and Pat Orr, the engineering manager, met with Kevin together. The two work closely together in drawing up labour and material estimates for quotes. The engineering department provides both a breakdown of the products components required for each job (bill of materials) and a description of the work to be performed (routing slip). Jack applies standard costs for material and labour to each job to give an estimate of direct cost. Direct labour costs are increased by 30% to cover production overheads and a 20% mark-up is added to cover administration costs and leave a profit margin. These figures are then discussed with Tony Murray, the sales manager, who has the option of reducing them before forwarding the estimate to the customer as a final tender price.

Before leaving Kevin paid a courtesy visit back to John. They agreed that there was much need and scope for improvement in the company's accounting and information system. John also indicated that the auditors had recently been unhappy about certain difficulties which they experienced during their annual audit.

After reviewing his notes Kevin confirmed that he had sufficient information, admittedly not verified by him, to construct a crude income statement for the six months ended December 31, 1987. The first thing he noticed was that the firm's bank overdraft had increased to $73,500. "Not a significant increase," thought Byrne, "but perhaps its trend was indicative of the general state of the company."

John added, "I think you should have a pretty good overview of what's happening here. I'd appreciate a memorandum, based on your initial observations, as to how things can and should change. I don't know a lot about accounting matters so be brief and succinct — a sort of mini action plan. I would also appreciate a separate memo on what current difficulties you think the auditors may be experiencing. Here are some documents which may be of some assistance to you: Standard Costing Procedure (Appendix 1), Invoicing Procedure (Appendix 2), and Organization Structure (Appendix 3).

© John Wiley & Sons Canada Ltd. All rights reserved.

CASE REQUIREMENTS

1. Prepare an income statement for the business for the six months ended December 31, 1987, showing the actual production cost of each job completed.
2. Indicate briefly what matters you would further investigate before finalizing your income statement.
3. Draft a memorandum for discussion with John Davis, indicating the main weaknesses and deficiencies of the company's operations which are apparent from your initial talks with the management team. Also, you should indicate the additional information and improved procedures that would be needed to correct the situation, bearing in mind the weaknesses and deficiencies which you have identified.
4. You should draft a note in relation to possible difficulties being experienced by the firm's auditors during the annual audit and how these will be corrected by your recommendation.

APPENDIX 1
STANDARD COSTING PROCEDURE

Materials

Bought in single pieces, parts are costed at the average price paid per unit over the last financial year plus 5%.

Sheet metal is a more complex issue. When the Engineering Department has decided what size sheet of metal is to be used and how it is to be cut, the cost of the sheet (calculated in the same way as for bought in single piece parts) is allocated to each piece cut in proportion to the area of metal used in it. This means the unused metal (wastage) is automatically costed into cut pieces to be used. However, metal recuts, if necessary, are ignored for costing purposes.

Packing materials are costed at the price charged by the suppliers.

Labour

Each work centre has a standard rate per hour allocated to it. This is established with reference to operative wage rates, based on a normal level of activity. Normal activity is based on a 35-hour working week for each operative.

Every job passing through a work centre takes a certain amount of time. This is composed of a set-up time and running time. The total time is divided by the number of units in each job and the results multiplied by the rate per hour, thus giving a work centre cost per unit produced.

APPENDIX 2
INVOICING AND ACCOUNTING PROCEDURE

Job comes into Stores from the shopfloor with a job card. The job number and actual labour hours recorded will have been hand written on the job card.

Stores prepares the job for shipment.

A 4-part document is raised by Stores regarding job:

Copy 1 — filed in Stores.

Copy 2 — advice note to customer is dispatched immediately.

Copy 3 — proof of delivery. Goes with delivery to customer where receiving officer signs it and it is then returned to be filed in the Stores.

Copy 4 — production control. Production files are updated to match jobs completed with job orders. Cost of materials issued is added to form by Stores personnel from their records. Form goes to accounts department where special charges such as transport are added and an invoice is raised based on the original quoted price for the job. This form is subsequently filed and referred to again only in the event of a customer query.

Problems

Several problems arise in relation to invoicing:

1. Wrong job numbers appear on documents raised by Stores so that wrong quotation prices are given on invoices.
2. Invoices include incorrect totals and extensions. Trade discounts are granted inappropriately.

Sources of Error

1. Incorrect job numbers and material codes appear on job cards. This is as a result of cards being lost on the shopfloor and operatives filling in new cards incorrectly since Stores will not accept jobs without completed cards. Operatives must identify material codes if Stores personnel are not present when goods are being withdrawn.
2. Recording of labour hours for each job is the sole responsibility of each operative. Some hours are not recorded due to negligence or genuine error.
3. Typing errors, since no cross checking takes place in accounts department before invoices go out.

APPENDIX 3
CURRENT ORGANIZATION STRUCTURE

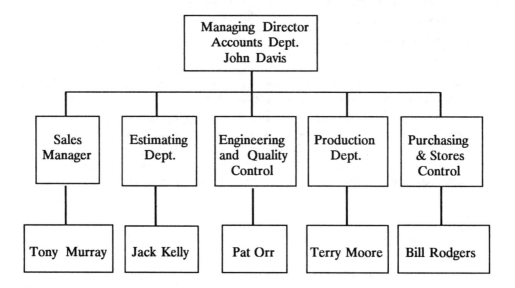

CASE 6

OMEGA GROUP LIMITED

L.-P. Lauzon
Universite du Quebec
Montreal, Quebec

Omega Group Ltd. of Montreal was incorporated under the Quebec Companies Act on February 12, 1978. It was set up as an umbrella corporation for the companies owned by the founding shareholders: Henri Pinard, Thomas Bathenay and Simone Latour. In the following years, besides operating these companies, the corporation established, alone or in conjunction with other corporations, and acquired new ones. Excerpts of Omega's financial statements and related notes may be found in Appendix I.

Omega Group operates in the field of communications, a highly competitive industry consisting of hundreds of companies, some large multinationals and some small proprietorships; Omega may be considered one of the 25 largest in this field. Among its main competitors are gigantic corporations like Thomson Newspapers Limited, with annual sales of $812 million in 1984; Southam Inc., with annual sales of $1,084 million in 1984; Quebecor Inc., with annual sales of $279 million in 1984; Tele-Direct (Canada) Inc. and its subsidiary Ronalds-Federee Limited with annual sales of $417 million in 1984 and Torstar Corporation, with annual sales of $619 million in 1984.

Omega Group deals mainly with three sectors: printing, publishing and distributing. Lately it has expanded its operations to the retail commercial sector by investing in Poly-Loisirs Inc. along with two other partners. Appendix II gives additional information about Poly-Loisirs, as well as an excerpt from its financial statements.

In the printing sector, Omega offers services which include advertising conceptualization and electronic composition, as well as printing per se. It has become one of the largest circular printers in Canada by constantly adapting to new technologies and adding new services. Omega operates three printing houses specializing in offset printing which, among other things, makes it possible to print a variety of products at high speed and with superior quality.

© John Wiley & Sons Canada Ltd. All rights reserved.

In the publishing sector, Omega (a French language publisher) publishes one weekly newspaper, three magazines, one monthly tabloid, encyclopedias, fascicles, and elementary, secondary, college and university educational textbooks. These specialized products are aimed at segmented, French-language markets. Omega also operates a mail-order company producing books and other printed material.

In the distributing sector, Omega operates a house-to-house printed material distribution firm, which also does the mailing of various products. This division looks after the distribution of the conglomerate's many products.

The organization chart below shows the trade names of the main subsidiaries and associated companies, along with their sectors as at October 31, 1985.

Ownership Holdings of Omega Group

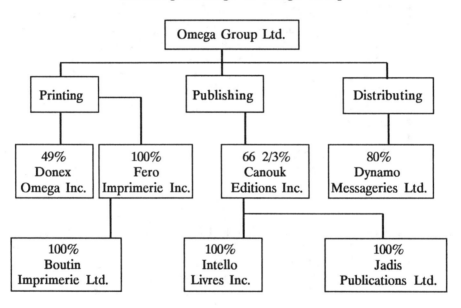

Omega is controlled by the corporation's three founding shareholders:

Henri Pinard	22%
Thomas Bathenay	16%
Simone Latour	16%

The remaining common shares are owned by twenty-eight (28) shareholders; the most important are: Assurances Canadou Ltd. with 8%, and the American pulp and paper company Donex Inc. with 5%. The Canadou Insurance Company also owns all of the 200,000 non-participating preferred shares with a $2 annual cumulative dividend, and it has two out of the twelve representatives on Omega's Board of Directors. Donex Inc. has one representative on the Board, and is the main supplier (about 85% of purchases) of the 50,000 metric tonnes of various types of paper products used by Omega. The paper purchases from Donex are covered by set price purchase contracts (in $ U.S.) which expire in 1988.

To improve its financial situation and to facilitate its expansion, on November 27, 1985, Omega issued 300,000 new preferred shares with a $1 annual dividend. These shares are to become voting shares if no cumulative dividend is paid during a consecutive two-year period. These shares have been bought by Gestion Primo Inc. which is effectively, but not legally, controlled by an external member of Omega's Board of Directors. These shares were issued for a $3,000,000 consideration.

Omega hopes to secure its development through new acquisitions in carefully chosen communication sectors. During the year 1985, it has committed approximately $150,000 to searching for such potential companies.

Lately it has become highly interested in purchasing the Canadian company Cosmos Publications Ltd., which is 100% controlled by the American company Cosmos Corporation. This purchase would make it possible for Omega to establish itself in Ontario and Western Canada, to increase its growth in the publishing sector, and to start marketing books written in English. Cosmos Publications specializes in elementary and secondary school textbooks.

The American Cosmos Corporation has decided to divest itself of its Canadian subsidiary. If Omega puts in a bid for Cosmos it will have to redeem the company's preferred shares, owned by a private investor now settled in Switzerland, then reimburse the American parent company and pay a fair price for all of the common shares it owns in its Canadian subsidiary.

A large Canadian trust company, Royal Trustco, could refinance the current loan of Cosmos Publications which is to be repaid to the American parent company through an $8,000,000 CDN loan at 12% annual interest with $250,000 repayable semi-annually.

An established Ontario publisher is interested in an equal partnership with Omega for the purpose of buying Cosmos Publications, but Omega's executive officers have shown little interest in this option.

Because it would like to be Cosmos Publications' sole owner, Omega Group has made an offer to Cosmos Corporation, along with a $50,000 deposit which is non-refundable if the parties cannot agree. The offer expires in 14 days. An excerpt of Cosmos Publications' main financial statements can be found in Appendix III along with relevant information pertaining to the eventual acquisition of this company by Omega Group. Omega also plans to purchase a firm in the Quebec publishing sector. Illico Editions Inc.'s financial statements, to be found in Appendix IV, have recently been received and are under examination.

Omega's activities are all distributed in profit centres. Currently, only Boutin Imprimerie and Intello Livres are in deficit, because of an obsolete plant and a bad location in the first case, and the publication of too sophisticated and too specialized a book selection in the second case. To make these two subsidiaries profitable, Omega's executive officers entrusted Pinard's two daughters, Berthe and Dina, 29 and 33 years old respectively, with the task of managing them; both women hold degrees in administration. The parent company, as the managing company of its subsidiaries, is responsible for planning and coordinating activities, and for their financial control. Furthermore, it offers consulting services in human resources management and provides data processing services to member companies. Omega encourages a decentralized form of management to ensure its subsidiaries' development. But because it is so intent on achieving its control and coordination objectives, the parent company defines the member companies' management policies, practices and procedures.

Each company in the group forwards a monthly financial statement to head office, with notes explaining unusual gaps and comparing the situation to previous corresponding periods, in order to appraise trends and take corrective action if applicable.

As noted, human resources management comes under the parent company. Thus hiring-related activities, employee relations, and training are coordinated by the human resources director, who draws up salary schedules for the conglomerate's internal positions in addition to managing the fringe benefit program. The preparation and negotiation of collective agreements also come under the parent company for the firms whose staff is unionized. On October 31, 1985, the group had 1,108 employees allocated as follow: head office, 26; data processing centre, 12; printing sector, 618; publishing sector, 248; distributing sector, 204.

During the 1985 fiscal year, negotiations took place for nine collective agreements. Seven of these, with 406 employees, were renewed; the remaining two, with 78 distributing sector employees, are still in dispute, even after a conciliator's involvement. In the coming fiscal year, four collective agreements for 301 printing and publishing sector employees will have to be negotiated. Head office and data processing centre employees are not unionized. Omega plans to set up a generous retirement pension plan for its non-unionized employees in the near future; it also plans to revise and restructure existing retirement pension plans for its unionized employees. However, the subsidiaries' retirement pension plans differ widely and Omega plans to consolidate them during the coming fiscal year. The controller would like to be given more details about the main pension plans in existence.

The parent company is also responsible for expansion or acquisition projects. It negotiates important contracts with suppliers and customers, manages the insurance portfolio, authorizes capital expenditures, and negotiates short and long term financing.

The books for Omega Group and its subsidiaries are audited by local accounting offices:

—Omega Group Ltd., Fero Imprimerie Inc., and Boutin Imprimerie Ltd. are audited by Pique, Avril and Associates;

—Canouk Editions Inc. and its two subsidiaries are audited by Beaudoin, Themes & Co.;

—Dynamo Messagerie Ltd. is audited by Lucien Poisson, C.A.

As for the associated corporation Donex-Omega Inc., its financial statements are audited by the prestigious accounting firm of Donut, Dunkin, Savard, C.A., which operates on a national scale. On the international level, this firm is associated with the firm Ritz, Pendleton, Markawitz & Co. Cosmos Publications' current auditor is the Toronto accounting firm Polash, Dixie & Co.

In 1986, Omega plans to change its recording method concerning its investment in Donex-Omega Inc. and to record the proportional interest consolidation instead of the investment value. In view of Omega's present size, its bankers, Canadou Assurance

Ltd., and Donex Inc. have lately put pressure on the company to replace the parent company's and subsidiaries' current auditors with a national accounting firm.

At first, the three founding shareholders would not hear of such a change, since Omega's and its subsidiaries's current auditors had been long-time personal friends of the three principal shareholders; Mr. Avril of Pique, Avril and Associates even does Mr. Pinard's personal income tax returns. However, after much consulting, advising, and even some arguing with one another, they agreed to meet with the chief partner of the firm as suggested by the bankers, Canadou and Donex, namely Homer Savard of the firm Donut, Dunkin, Savard, C.A. The chairman of Omega's Board of Directors, Henri Pinard, the chief executive officer and president, Simone Latour, and the senior executive vice-president, Thomas Bathenay, were very impressed with Savard's professionalism and decided to give him the task of auditing Omega's and all its subsidiaries' books, provided he presented a reasonable estimate of future audit charges. Savard's firm would also be called upon to audit Cosmos Publications' (incorporated under Ontario laws), and Illico Editions Inc., if Omega ever decided to proceed with the purchase of these companies. Moreover, the firm Donut, Dunkin, Savard, C.A. would be given a large consulting project regarding the accounting and auditing problems found in Omega.

As time is of the essence it is already March 1986 Homer Savard has decided to give this important consulting task to a young, ambitious and dynamic chartered accountant and team leader, Corina Avalino. Savard thinks it is essential to make a strong impression on Omega Group right from the start. Although the task to audit all the companies associated with Omega is not to begin until December, 1986, Savard has asked Avalino to give him a report regarding peculiarities and problems encountered when auditing the financial statements of Omega, all its subsidiaries, Cosmos Publications and Illico Editions. The 1985 financial statements of Omega, all its subsidiaries, and Cosmos Publications have been audited and the auditors' reports are positive.

At a meeting with Avalino and Savard, head office made certain things very clear: they want the accounting firm Donut, Dunkin, Savard, C.A. to provide them with judicious advice regarding their companies' management and financing, whether acquiring Cosmos Publications and Illico Editions is the right thing to do, what the purchase price should be for these companies, the relevance of their accounting standards, and any other points of importance. Moreover, as they do not know much about the type of accounting standards a company like Poly-Loisirs should adopt, they want Avalino to give them the broad lines of the main accounting standards to be adopted by this company to record its assets, liabilities, profits and expenses.

CASE REQUIREMENT

Play Corina Avalino's part, and write one report to Omega Group's executive and a separate report to Homer Savard, chief associate in the accounting firm Donut, Dunkin, Savard, C.A. This report should detail all of the accounting and auditing issues that are present in Omega Group Ltd.

TABLE OF APPENDICES
OMEGA GROUP LTD.

I **Omega Group Ltd.** – Excerpts of main financial statements, and summary of most important notes.

II **Poly-Loisirs Inc.** – Excerpts of main financial statements, and some additional relevant information.

III **Cosmos Publications Limited** – Excerpts of main financial statements, summary of most important notes and various additional information.

IV **Illico Editions Inc.** – Excerpts of main financial statements.

APPENDIX I
OMEGA GROUP LTD.
STATEMENT OF CONSOLIDATED RETAINED EARNINGS AND RESULTS
For the Fiscal Year Ending October 31 (in thousands of dollars)

	1985	1984
Revenue	124,115	95,831
Cost of Sales	99,456	79,700
Margin	24,659	16,131
Charges		
Commercial and Administrative	7,305	6,345
Financial	1,566	1,686
Amortization	2,921	2,501
	11,792	10,532
Operating Profits	12,867	5,599
Associated Company Profit (Loss) Share Held at 49% (Note 9)	361	(181)
Before–Tax Profits, Minority Interest, and Exceptional Items	13,228	5,418
Tax on Profits	4,860	2,103
Profits Before Minority Interest and Exceptional Items	8,368	3,315
Minority Interest	539	237
Profits Before Exceptional Items	7,829	3,078
Exceptional Losses (Note 6)	473	650
Net Profits for the Year	7,356	2,428
Retained Earnings at Year Start	2,977	1,049
	10,333	3,477
Common Share Dividends	1,500	500
Retained Earnings at Year End	8,833	2,977

© John Wiley & Sons Canada Ltd. All rights reserved.

OMEGA GROUP LTD.
CHANGES IN CONSOLIDATED FINANCIAL POSITION
For the Fiscal Year Ending October 31
(in thousands of dollars)

	1985	1984
Net Operating Income		
Profits for the Year	7,356	2,428
Working Capital Unrelated Items		
Amortization	2,921	2,501
Deferred Taxes	1,806	1,215
Associated Firm (Profit) Loss Sharing	(361)	181
Minority Interest	539	237
	12,261	6,562
Working Capital Variance Excluding Liquid Assets, Deferred Revenue, and Long Term Debt Portion Due within a Year		
Decrease in Customer's Accounts and Other Debtors	137	115
Inventory Increase	(1,056)	(523)
Increase of Other Short Term Asset Items	(884)	(24)
Increase in Suppliers' Accounts and Accrued Liabilities	2,136	1,587
Decrease in Other Short Term Liabilities Items	(61)	(57)
	272	1,098
Others		
Deferred Revenue	991	512
	13,524	8,172
Amount Destined for Financing		
Long Term Debt Increase	1,750	1,000
Repayment on Long Term Debts	(3,000)	(3,000)
Preferred Shares Issue	2,000	
Dividend Payment	(1,500)	(500)
	(750)	(2,500)
Amount Destined for Investment		
Corporate Fixed Asset Acquisition	(12,075)	(3,271)
Accounting Period Liquid Asset Increase	699	2,401
Liquid Assets at Year Start	(3,036)	(5,437)
Liquid Assets at Year End	(2,337)	(3,036)
Consisting of the Following:		
Cash in Hand and Deposit Certificates	3,957	
Loan and Bank Overdraft	(6,294)	(3,036)
	(2,337)	(3,036)

© John Wiley & Sons Canada Ltd. All rights reserved.

OMEGA GROUP LTD.
CONSOLIDATED BALANCE SHEET
(in thousands of dollars)

	1985	1984
SHORT TERM ASSETS		
Cash in Hand and Deposit Certificates	3,957	
Customers and Other Debtors	21,375	21,512
Inventory	6,633	5,577
Services Receivable	1,224	340
	33,189	27,429
LONG TERM ASSETS		
Investment in Associated Firm (Note 9)	4,861	4,500
Fixed Assets, at Cost	29,118	19,842
Non-Corporate Assets	957	1,079
	34,936	25,421
Total Assets	68,125	52,850
SHORT TERM LIABILITIES		
Loan and Bank Overdraft	6,294	3,036
Suppliers and Accrued Liabilities	16,691	14,555
Deferred Income by Way of Subscriptions	2,349	1,289
Taxes to be Paid	264	325
Long Term Debt Fraction Within the Year'	6,800	3,000
	32,398	22,205
LONG TERM LIABILITIES		
Deferred Income by Way of Subscriptions	684	753
Long Term Debts (Note 4)	11,850	16,900
Deferred Taxes and Credits	5,150	3,344
Minority Interest	1,248	709
	18,932	21,706
NET ASSETS		
Capital Stock (Note 5)	7,962	5,962
Retained Earnings	8,833	2,977
	16,795	8,939
Total Liabilities, Capital & Retained Earnings	68,125	52,850

© John Wiley & Sons Canada Ltd. All rights reserved.

Here is an excerpt of the main notes in Omega Group Ltd.'s 1985 financial statements.

1. **STATUS**

   The company was incorporated under the Quebec Companies Act on May 5, 1978.

2. **CONSOLIDATION PRINCIPLES**

   The consolidated financial statements include the corporation's and all its subsidiaries' books. The consolidated companies are:

	Percentage of Participation
Imprimerie Fero Inc. and its Subsidiary	100
Editions Canouk Inc. and its Subsidiary	66 2/3
Messageries Dynamo Ltd.	80

3. **FOREIGN CURRENCY**

   Long term debts in foreign currencies have been converted into $CDN at the year end rate of exchange.

4. **LONG TERM DEBTS (in thousands)**

	1985	1984
Imprimerie Fero Inc.		
—$2,500,000 Loans at 13% Payable Annually	10,000	12,500
Editions Canouk Inc.		
—$200,000 Notes in Belgian Francs at 10.5% – 14.5%, Payable Semi-Annually	1,600	1,300
—$50,000 notes in Deutsche Marks, at 9%, Payable Semi-Annually	750	800
Messageries Dynamo Ltd.		
—Outstanding balance of Subsidiary's Purchase Price, at No Interest, Entirely Payable by 1986	3,800	3,800
Omega Group Ltd.		
—Owed the Administrators, 6%, Payable by the Year 2000	2,500	1,500
	18,650	19,900
Fraction Within a Year	6,800	3,000
	11,850	16,900

5. **CAPITAL STOCK**

   Authorized, Unlimited
   Common shares
   Preferred shares,
   non participating, $2/share cumulative annual dividend redeemable at $12 until October 31, 1987, and at $15 thereafter

	1985	1984
Issued and Paid		
130,000 Common Shares	5,962	5,962
200,000 preferred shares, Issued Sept. 30, 1985	2,000	
	7,962	5,962

6. **EXCEPTIONAL ITEMS**

	1985	1984
St. Jerome Factory Shut Down Charges Incurring $327,000 Exceptional Charges, $185,000 Tax Free	327	
Hebdopin Ltd. Shut Down of Regional Weekly Papers, $78,000 Tax Free	146	
Topo Ltd. Shut Down of Educational Software Production, $557,000 Tax Deductible	—	650
	473	650

7. **PRINCIPAL CUSTOMER**

For the fiscal year ending December 31, 1985, 43.5% of Imprimerie Fero Inc.'s revenue resulted from a supply contract with a Quebec Government corporation (37.8% in 1984).

8. **SECTOR INFORMATION**

For the fiscal year ended October 31, 1985, 78% of the corporation's consolidated revenue came from the printing sector (67% in 1984), 13% from the publishing sector (21% in 1984), and 9% (12% in 1984) from the distributing sector. In 1985, the printing sector contributed 86% of the operating profits (89% in 1984), the publishing sector 5% (negative return of 3% in 1984), and the distributing sector 9% (14% in 1984).

9. **CONTINGENCY**

During the 1985 fiscal year, the corporation has brought before the Superior Court a nullity action and a request for an injunction against Donex Inc. and Donex-Omega Inc. (associated company), and presented before the same Court two incidental proceedings, namely a request for an interlocutory injunction and a request for a writ of sequestration order, so to nullify the 400,000 common shares issued by Donex-Omega Inc. to Donex Inc. at the time of repaying certain advances made by the latter during these past few years. The cancellation of this issue would result in increasing from 30% to 49% the corporation's interest level in Donex-Omega Inc. The hearings of these two incidental proceedings were held on July 31, 1985, and September 27, 1985, and the Superior Court rendered two judgements accepting these two incidental proceedings without pronouncing itself on the substance of the matter. Donex Inc. and Donex-Omega Inc. have appealed these decisions.

10. **COMMITMENT**

On December 5, 1985, the corporation purchased three rotary printing presses and two spreadsheet presses under a lease-back agreement. The corporation may purchase the equipment on December 5, 1995 for $1,250,000. Annual payments due for this lease-back agreement for the coming fiscal years are as follows:

| From 1986 to 1990 | $3,220,000 annually |
| From 1991 to 1995 | $2,250,000 annually |

The current owner anticipates an interest rate of 12% per annum on the rent contract financing.

APPENDIX II
POLY-LOISIRS INC.
BALANCE SHEET
As at February 28, 1986
(in dollars)

ASSETS

Short Term

Receivable from Dealers	88,000
Receivable Share Subscription	3,750,000
Inventory	309,000
Costs Paid in Advance	9,000
	4,156,000

Long Term

Furniture and Equipment, at Cost	193,000
Starting Charges	86,000
	279,000

Total Assets   4,435,000

LIABILITIES

Short Term

Bank Loan, Bank Overdraft and Outstanding Cheques	270,000
Suppliers' Accounts	246,000
	516,000

Shareholders' Equity

Capital Stock

   Authorized

   an unlimited number of common shares, with no face value, voting and participating

   an unlimited number of preferred shares, with a $100 face value each, redeemable, refundable at bearer's option, with a cumulative dividend of 10 1/4% until December 31, 1990, and 9 1/2% thereafter.

Issued

900 Common Shares	9,000
37,500 Preferred Shares	3,750,000

Contributed Surplus

—Dealers' Memberships	160,000
	3,919,000

Total Liabilities & Shareholders' Equity   4,435,000

POLY-LOISIRS INC.
ADDITIONAL INFORMATION

At the beginning of the 1986 fiscal year, Omega Group Ltd. entered an equal partnership with two other companies for the purpose of launching, in the form of franchises, a new retail store concept consisting of record albums, video tapes, books, newspapers and a restaurant. Omega's other partners are the Imasco Ltd., an international company which operates in several sectors, including catering, and the Canadian record album company Capital Inc., a subsidiary of a London based English company.

Already on February 28, 1986, 8 dealerships had been sold in Quebec and Ontario. Poly-Loisirs Inc.'s new management anticipates selling 8 more dealerships before the end of 1986, and opening about 20 new stores throughout Canada in 1987. Each new dealer must pay a $20,000 membership fee which the corporation has entered into its balance sheet under "Contributed Surplus." Each dealer must take upon himself to finance the purchase of his equipment and inventory. However, Poly-Loisirs may help them with the financing. Each franchise owner must abide by certain rules and a rigid code of conduct, as formulated by Poly-Loisirs. The starting-up charges appearing in the balance sheet include advertising and training charges, legal fees, market study fees, etc. It is anticipated these franchise set up charges will amount to about $100,000.

Each partner has 300 common shares, which were paid cash, and has subscribed 12,500 preferred shares, which must be paid up during the 1986 fiscal year. Moreover, in order to finance the rapid expansion anticipated for Poly-Loisirs, each partner has promised to invest into this company, in the form of loans, additional amounts every year, of the order of $3,000,000 in 1986 and in 1987. This new company's auditor will be the international firm of Twopik, Dazout & Co.

APPENDIX III
COSMOS PUBLICATIONS LIMITD.
BALANCE SHEET
as at December 31 (in thousands of dollars)

	1985	1984
ASSETS		
Short Term		
Cash in Hand	2,718	3,146
Customer's Accounts	2,626	2,434
Receivable from Affiliated Companies	164	116
Inventory and Pre–Publication Charges	6,315	5,713
Expenses Paid in Advance	238	198
	12,061	11,607
Long Term		
Land and Improvements	215	215
Buildings	2,447	2,315
Furniture and Materials	993	980
	3,655	3,510
Accumulated Depreciation	(2,621)	(2,393)
	1,034	1,117
Contracts, Copyrights, Trade Marks, Agency Rights and Goodwill at Cost	2,740	2,740
Total Assets	15,835	15,464
LIABILITIES		
Short Term		
Bank Debt	87	127
Suppliers' Accounts and Accrued Costs	1,835	2,105
Dividends Payable	400	450
Payable to Affiliated Companies	273	448
	2,595	3,130
Long Term		
Debenture Payable to Parent Company in $US, Bearing 5% Interest Per Annum, Due in 1998. This Debt is Converted to 1980 Issue Date Rate	8,000	8,000
	10,595	11,130
Tax on Deferred Profits	466	318
Shareholders' Equity		
100,000 Preferred Shares, Redeemable at $12US Each and Bearing $1 Annual Dividend. These Shares are Converted to the 1980 Issue Date Rate	1,000	1,000
2,000 Common Shares	986	986
Retained Earnings	2,388	1,630
Contributed Surplus	400	400
	4,774	4,016
Total Liabilities & Shareholders' Equity	15,835	15,464

© John Wiley & Sons Canada Ltd. All rights reserved.

COSMOS PUBLICATIONS LTD.
STATEMENT OF RESULTS
For the fiscal year ending December 31
(in thousand of dollars)

	1985	1984	1983
Operating Profits			
National Sales	8,400	8,000	9,600
Sales to Affiliated Companies	4,100	4,000	2,600
	12,500	12,000	12,200
Translation & Adaptation Government Subsidies for U.S. Book with Publication Rights Held by Parent Company	600	400	-0-
	13,100	12,400	12,200
Cost of Sales (90% variable charges)	7,598	6,820	6,344
Gross Profits	5,502	5,580	5,856
Operating Expenses			
Amortization	268	256	272
Social Benefits	89	76	72
Sales Commissions — National	107	93	103
Bad Debts	61	16	18
Lighting and Heating	125	111	97
Professional Fees (Including $38,000 Charges on 1984 Share Issue)	52	14	11
Gain on Long Term Debt Repurchase			(47)
Interest	64	68	76
Advertising and Marketing	74	111	284
Dues Paid Back to Parent Company	226	224	212
Dues Paid Back to Affiliated Companies	15	16	14
Loss on Obsolete Inventory	210		
Returns and Discounts on National Sales	80	86	108
Wages	952	886	792
Collection from Legal Proceedings			(78)
Others (Including Moving Expenses of $48,000 in 1984, and $23,000 in 1985)	349	376	34
	2,672	2,333	1,968
Before Tax Profits	2,830	3,247	3,888
Tax on Profits			
— Required	1,036	1,300	1,712
— Deferred	148	135	160
— Investment Tax Credit	(12)		
	1,172	1,435	1,872
Net Profits	1,658	1,812	2,016

COSMOS PUBLICATIONS LTD.
ADDITIONAL INFORMATION

1. If it is sold, Cosmos Publications will automatically loose all the sales it has been making to the affiliated companies. From now on, these sales will be made by the U.S. parent company.

2. As most books are produced outside the company, it is only normal that 90% of the firm's costs of sales are made out of variable costs.

3. If Cosmos is sold, the new owners shall have exclusive rights, for Canada and the Bahamas, over the sales of books published by the American Cosmos Corporation, the current owner of the Canadian company "Cosmos Publications Ltd." These assured sales now represent about 40% of the Canadian Cosmos company's national sales. A 6% increase in the invoiced price of books hereafter sold the Canadian company by the American company must be anticipated.

4. The reduced variable and fixed costs now attributable to sales made to affiliated companies are of the order of 7% of sales.

5. Since 1984, the American parent company has transferred two head office employees to the Canadian subsidiary so it can be advised as to the suitability for the parent company to continue its Canadian operation, or simply to sell this subsidiary. These two employees' annual salaries were $120,000 for the 1984 and 1985 fiscal years, and they were paid by the Canadian subsidiary. These two employees were the ones who insisted that in 1985 the company recorded a loss on obsolete inventory items the Canadian subsidiary had to no avail been keeping for more than 10 years. They also were the ones who required that in 1985 the company eliminated the $40,000 balance a customer had been owing since 1982 and which would never be collected in all likelihood. No provision for bad debts was ever taken in this case.

6. The translation and adaptation subsidy program established by the Manitoba Government ended in 1985.

7. Omega Group Ltd. would also like to have exclusive translation and sales right over books published by the American Cosmos company for all the French speaking countries of the world. According to a quick study by Omega's head office, these exclusive rights would generate an annual net profit of the order of $150,000 minus the $70,000 annual charges necessary to set up a branch or a subsidiary in Paris. The American Cosmos company may be receptive to this proposal and asks for an offer.

8. Dividends paid by the Canadian subsidiary to the American parent company have been as follows for the past three fiscal years:
1983	$1,000,000
1984	900,000
1985	800,000

9. Dividends on preferred shares have always been paid regularly each year.

10. When the long term debt was issued in 1980, the $CDN and the $US were at par value. On Dec. 31, 1985 the $CDN was only worth $0.73 in relation to the $US.

11. On December 31, 1985 the tangible long term assets of the Cosmos Publications had a market value of approximately $3,500,000.

APPENDIX IV
ILLICO EDITIONS INC.
BALANCE SHEET
As at January 31 (in thousands of dollars)

	1986	1985
SHORT TERM ASSETS		
Cash in Hand	517	1,023
Accounts Receivable	-0-	450
Inventory	6,392	6,723
	6,909	8,196
SHORT TERM LIABILITIES		
Accounts Payable	376	2,279
SHAREHOLDERS' EQUITY		
Capital Stock — 100 Common Shares	1,000	1,000
Retained Earnings	5,533	4,917
	6,533	5,917
	6,909	8,196

STATEMENT OF RETAINED EARNINGS AND RESULTS
For the Fiscal Year Ended on January 31

	1986	1985
Revenue		
Reproductions	324	1,420
Books	69	899
Catalogues	646	1,219
Miscellaneous	5	8
	1,044	3,546
Expenses		
Reproduction Cost	286	609
Book Printing	45	839
Copyrights	7	78
Exhibits	-0-	1,702
Postage Stamps	-0-	19
Professional Fees	-0-	400
Bank Charges	31	47
Others	59	82
	428	3,776
Fiscal Year Profits (Losses)	616	(230)
Retained Profits at Year Start	4,917	5,147
Retained Profits at Year End	5,533	4,917

CASE 7

OXFORD COMMUNICATIONS

A. Bhimani
Laurentian University
Sudbury, Ontario

John Rowell, President and owner of Oxford Communications, smiled as he replaced the telephone receiver. He had brought the company a long way in the nine years since 1978 when he started it as a hobby, in his hometown of Woodstock, Ontario. The business, whose annual turnover exceeded a million dollars, offered a range of communication services including paging, telephone answering, two-way radio, and radio air time rental. Paging revenue in particular had increased tremendously in the last year and now accounted for 60 percent of total revenue. John, however, was not sure how much his business was really worth, and he had until the next day to put a price on it. The telephone call had been from one of his suppliers — wanting to buy Oxford Communications!

THE PAGING MARKET

The first Canadian paging company had been launched in 1963, and the pager market potential was estimated to be worth $148 million (412,000 pagers rented out) per annum.[1] Actual pager market size (ie. market penetration), however, was estimated at $46.8 million (130,000 pagers rented out) as presently serviced areas were either only partially served or not served at all. (See Exhibit 1 for worldwide growth in pager services.)

Overall, the market had grown at a rate of 16% per annum, with a range from seven percent to 43%. The paging industry is characterized by a slow and prolonged initial growth period during which user awareness is created, followed by a sharp exponential growth in pager sales, succeeded finally, by a decreasing growth rate until new market segments can be identified. A factor that limits growth is the number of frequencies available on the spectrum; when frequencies become

© John Wiley & Sons Canada Ltd. All rights reserved.

saturated, increases in the pager sales slow down as companies curtail their promotional efforts. With the array of technological innovations designed to improve efficiency of infrastructure utilization a continued growth in the paging industry can be expected; but the pattern of this growth should remain cyclical.

The industry has seen rapid technological advances. Pagers are available in all sizes, colours and shapes. Yesterday, there were "tone-only" and "tone and voice" pagers. Today, there are vibrating pagers, numeric pagers and alpha-numeric pagers. Tomorrow, the industry will see cellular and satellite transmission systems. But with the rapid pace of technological advance comes a decreased life span for any given development, pressing the industry to maximize infrastructure utilization in order to pay back capital investment in new technology. More aggressive competition within the industry can be expected in the future.

The customer profile within the paging industry has changed dramatically since its beginning. At one time, pagers were used solely by the medical profession. Now, a broad range of users can be identified, prompting one trade paper to proclaim: "From Hookers to Priests they all carry beepers"! (Telocator, 1980). The majority of users are males, although the female market segment is increasing. User preference is for the "tone and voice" pager, and most subscribers prefer to rent pagers rather than purchase their own (and rent air time). However, with the introduction of cheap disposable pagers and the consumerization of pagers, an increase in their purchase can be expected.

The industry has traditionally consisted of a large number of small companies. Yet a process of rationalization can be expected as competition for limited licences increases. As larger capital resources will be required to keep pace with technological changes, smaller companies will be squeezed out.

TECHNOLOGY

Operation of a Paging System

A paging system is a one-way communication system, whereby radio signals are used to contact a person. In its simplest form, a radio paging system consists of an encoder transmitter, antenna and receivers; the encoder generates and sends codes to the transmitter. Each receiver in the system contains a decoder that is programmed to respond to a particular code. When the code is transmitted the receiver is activated, emitting a beep tone to alert the user, and with some types of pagers this is followed by a vocal message or a visual display.

Types of Pagers

A tone-only pager receives an alerting beep, letting the user know that he or she is to call a predetermined number to obtain a message. Paging companies prefer tone-only pagers as they use channel capacity more efficiently, (the time required for tone transmission being about 1/2 second).

A tone and voice pager sends a tone followed by a vocal message to the user. A key feature of this type of pager is that it provides an efficient, cost-effective means of receiving messages for users who are constantly away from telephones. Messages, however, use a long transmission time, (four seconds of coded signals plus eight to 15 seconds of vocal message). Also, additional expenses are incurred by the pager company to maintain extra staff to receive, record, transmit and retrieve messages. Technological advances have enabled newer systems to reduce the signalling time by 15 to 23%, through storage of vocal messages, removal of long pauses, and transmittal at slightly accelerated pace.

The newest type of pager on the market is the digital display pager, which is expensive. Here, a visual display of a phone number or an alpha numerical message can be obtained. Also, the digital display pager makes more efficient use of transmission channels than either the tone-only or the tone and voice pager.

Transmission System

The analog transmission system, the only system on which tone and voice pagers can operate, is the most popular system in Canada. It transmits messages through the atmosphere using sine waves. But this transmission system requires a wide transmission span on the frequency spectrum. Also, the maximum capacity with the analog transmission system is 2,200 tone and voice pagers, or 100,000 tone-only pagers.

The digital transmission system, which is relatively new to Canada, is computer controlled and utilizes binary codes for transmission. This system is more efficient than the analog transmission system as it requires less real time to transmit information. Consequently, a larger number of pagers can be carried on one frequency. Thus, if the digital transmission system is fully adopted by the industry, a 20 to 25% increase in band capacity could be expected.

COMPANY BACKGROUND

Oxford Communications was headquartered in Woodstock, a small town about an hour's drive from Toronto. The company had 1802 pagers rented out, and its paging operations consisted of four channels stretching over southwestern Ontario.[2] The company has casual and temporary employees, but few long-term employees. Minimal staff is required to operate the paging service on a regular basis as only one operator is required to send and receive messages.

COMPANY PERSONNEL

John Rowell had been key to Oxford Communications' success, building the company from a hobby into the major paging concern in southwestern Ontario. John's acumen lay in sound technical know-how of the paging business. It was not unusual for him to work sixty-hour weeks, participating in all aspects of the company's operations to ensure a reliable and high-quality service. He was assisted at Oxford by two other essential people: Jim Gordon, the Marketing and Sales Manager, and Harold Burns, the Bookkeeper.

Jim had been with the company for a year, and although he did not have any previous experience with the paging industry, he had a lot of good ideas on how to generate sales. Since his arrival at Oxford Communications, Jim had taken increasingly more responsibilities, and he would discuss his plans in great depth with John.

Harold, who at 65 had no plans to retire for at least five years, had been with the company since its early days. His responsibility was to keep the books up-to-date and provide John with information when requested; Harold also handled much of the clerical work at Oxford Communications.

SOUTHWESTERN ONTARIO'S PAGING MARKET

Oxford Communications' main competitor was MacLean Hunter, a highly diversified communication and information company, reputed to have the world's largest paging network. In the 519 coverage area, MacLean Hunter was estimated to have 1500 pagers rented out. In addition, there were a number of small operators who had between 10 and 200 pagers rented out and were also thought to total another 1500 pagers. Table 1 shows the market shares in Oxford Communications' coverage area.

TABLE 1
Pager Market Share in Southwestern Ontario

Company	Pagers	Percentage
Oxford Communication	1802	37.6%
MacLean Hunter	1500	31.2%
Small Operators	1500	31.2%

The total market size was estimated to be $1,685,000 per year (based on the "2.5% of telephones" index), given the weighted average charge[3] of $28 per month per pager for Oxford Communications, and the average monthly rental charge of $30 for Maclean Hunter and other operators whose charges were known to be higher than those of Oxford. The market potential was thought to be 48,000 pagers.

Companies accounted for 84% of Oxford Communications' clients, the remainder being mostly individual professionals; and 80% of the accounts rented two pagers or fewer. Preference for type of pagers is illustrated in Table 2 and channel preferences in Exhibit 2.

TABLE 2
Pager Preference

Type of Pagers	Individual	Company	Overall
Tone only	35%	35.2%	35.1%
Tone & Voice	65%	64.8%	64.9%

PAGER SALES

Sales at Oxford Communications were generated by agents, by dealers and by Oxford Communications' salesperson. (See Exhibit 3 for market potential in southwestern Ontario.) Agents were paid a commission for each pager service sold. Dealers would sell paging services, assume billing responsibilities and would share in each month's revenue with Oxford Communications. Agents and dealers contributed 6.5% to Oxford Communications' paging revenue. John maintained close contact with his agents and dealers, and revenue from these sources were expected to increase to 10% of total paging revenue. The bulk of Oxford Communications' sales, however, were generated by its own salesmen, who were compensated with a base salary of $150 per week plus a commission (ranging from $35 to $45 depending on the type of paging service sold). (Competitors offered their salesmen compensation packages ranging from $23,000 to

$35,000 per annum.) In general, pager sales growth since the founding of the company had been quite remarkable, as summarized in Table 3.

TABLE 3
Oxford Pager Sales Performance (in dollars)

Year	Sales
1978	18,926
1979	94,630
1980	84,115
1981	103,042
1982	121,968
1983	217,056
1984	605,472

TAX CONSIDERATIONS

The sale of the company will have some significant tax consequences for John Rowell. A cash sale would draw capital gains taxes immediately while an equity exchange would not. Over a period of five years deferred payments can also be considered a possibility to spread the tax burden. Consideration is needed of the most appropriate means to achieve the largest after-tax price for the company.

PRICING OXFORD COMMUNICATIONS

John knew that revenue from non-paging sources had grown by an average of 15% per year, and that his pager sales growth was most encouraging. But as he pulled his company's financial statements (Exhibit 4, 5 and 6) out of the filing cabinet, he wondered how he was going to value his paging business. What was a fair value for Oxford Communications, given all of the information in hand, John wondered, and what terms for the sale would be most suitable?

EXHIBIT 1
OXFORD COMMUNICATIONS
Worldwide Growth in Pager Service

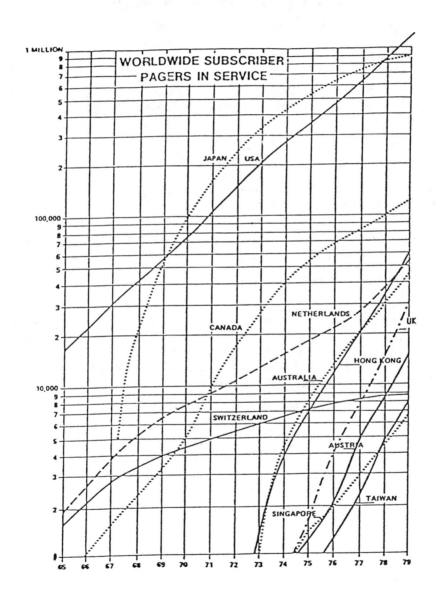

Source

Thomas Waltz, **"Subscriber Radio Paging Companies in Industrialized Nations"** Motorola Incorporated, Communications International Division, January, 1981.

EXHIBIT 2
OXFORD COMMUNICATIONS
Paging System Operation

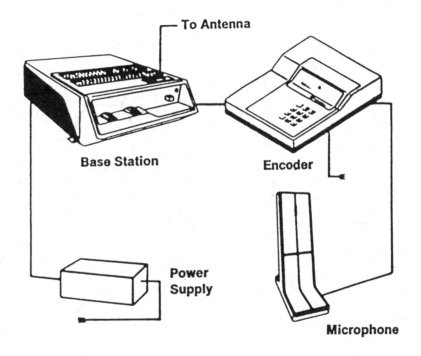

A simple operator assisted paging system.

© John Wiley & Sons Canada Ltd. All rights reserved.

EXHIBIT 3
OXFORD COMMUNICATIONS
Cellular Configuration Models

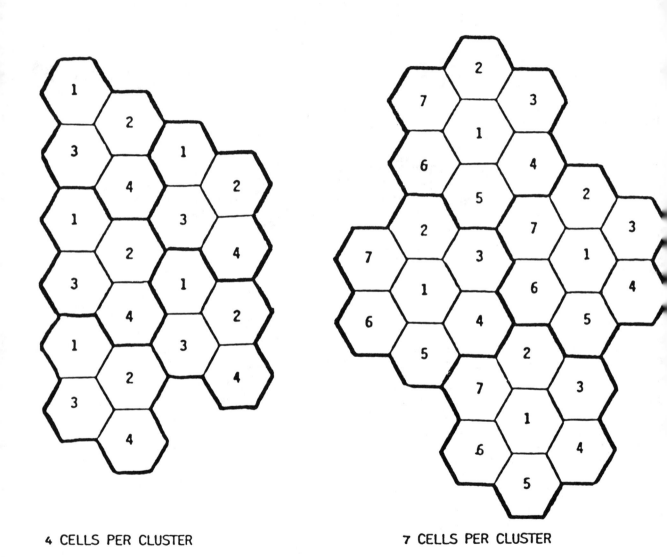

EXHIBIT 4
OXFORD COMMUNICATIONS
Channel Coverage

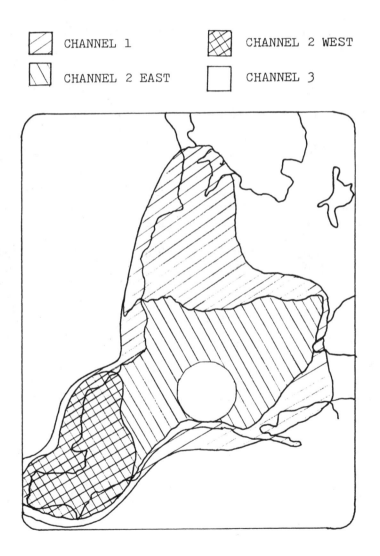

EXHIBIT 5
OXFORD COMMUNICATIONS
Distribution of Pagers Among Channels by Counties

Counties	Percentage of pagers in each county	Channel 1	Channel 2 East	Channel 2 West	Channel 3
Hamilton–Wentworth	0.04	100.0	0.0	0.0	0.0
Niagara	0.04	100.0	0.0	0.0	0.0
Middlesex	4.6	68.0	24.0	0.8	6.7
Essex	5.8	46.7	20.0	33.0	0.0
Waterloo	10.8	60.7	39.3	0.0	0.0
Halton	0.0	0.0	0.0	0.0	0.0
Wellington	0.4	0.0	100.0	0.0	0.0
Lambton	0.0	0.0	0.0	0.0	0.0
Kent	0.4	0.0	0.0	100.0	0.0
Brant	3.0	0.0	100.0	0.0	0.0
Haldimand–Norfolk	0.08	100.0	0.0	0.0	0.0
Oxford	13.9	39.0	61.0	0.0	0.0
Gray	0.0	0.0	0.0	0.0	0.0
Elgin	2.3	66.7	33.3	0.0	0.0
Perth	10.8	47.1	42.9	0.0	0.0
Bruce	0.0	0.0	0.0	0.0	0.0
Huron	5.0	77.0	23.0	0.0	0.0
Overall Channel Distribution	100%	59%	35%	2.7%	3.3%
		[– – – – – – – –100%– – – – – – – –]			

EXHIBIT 6
OXFORD COMMUNICATIONS
Market Potential in Southwestern Ontario

Counties	Population
Hamilton–Wentworth	411,445
Niagara	368,288
Middlesex	318,184
Essex	312,476
Waterloo	305,496
Halton	253,883
Wellington	129,432
Lambton	123,445
Kent	107,022
Brant	104,427
Haldimand-Norfolk	89,456
Oxford	85,920
Grey	73,824
Elgin	69,707
Perth	66,096
Bruce	60,020
Huron	56,127
(This equals 12% of the Canadian population.)	2,935,248

Most populated Towns	Population	Potential Market	Percentage	Present Service*
Hamilton	305,434	6,788	14.0	0.04
St. Catherines	124,018	6,076	12.5	0.04
London	254,280	5,250	10.8	46.0
Windsor	192,083	5,156	10.6	5.8
Kitchener	139,734	5,040	10.4	10.8
Burlington	114,853	4,189	8.6	0.0
Guelph	71,207	2,136	4.4	0.04
Sarnia	50,892	2,037	4.2	0.0
Chatham	40,952	1,766	3.6	0.04
Brantford	74,315	1,723	3.5	3.0
Nanticoke	19,816	1,476	3.0	0.08
Woodstock	26,603	1,418	2.9	13.9
Owen Sound	19,883	1,218	2.5	0.0
St. Thomas	28,165	1,150	2.4	2.3
Stratford	26,262	1,091	2.2	10.8
Port Elgin	6,131	990	2.0	0.0
Stephen	4,177	926	1.9	5.0
		48,430	100%**	100%

* Number of pagers in each area as a % of total number of pagers.
** Percentages may not add to 100 because of rounding.

There are dealers in London, Sarnia, Chatham and Port Elgin and agents in Chatham.

EXHIBIT 7
OXFORD COMMUNICATIONS
Pager Rental Revenue
(in dollars)

Revenue	Voice Pager			Tone Pager	
	Channel 1	Channel 2	Channel 3	Channel 1	Channel 3
Monthly Rental	39.00	34.00	28.00	26.00	20.00
Total Annual Revenue	468.00	408.00	336.00	312.00	240.00
Variable Costs					
Annual Depreciation	81.25	81.25	81.25	34.80	34.80
Watts Line $4.00/mo	48.00	48.00	48.00	48.00	48.00
Accounting $2.00/mo	24.00	24.00	24.00	24.00	24.00
Maintenance $2.00/mo	24.00	24.00	24.00	24.00	24.00
Opening account	15.00	15.00	15.00	15.00	15.00
Interest	39.00	39.00	39.00	17.00	17.00
Commission	45.00	45.00	45.00	35.00	35.00
Total Variable Cost	276.25	276.25	276.25	197.80	197.80

Variable costs of non-paging business averaged 65% of revenue.

EXHIBIT 8
OXFORD COMMUNICATIONS
Balance Sheet as at December 31, 1987 (in dollars)

Current Assets		Current Liabilities	
Cash	15,788	Bank Credit	68,000
Accounts Receivable	227,579	Trade Credits	212,034
Prepaid Expenses	3,890	Accruals	11,457
		Taxes	17,643
Total Current Assets	247,257	Total Current Liabilities	309,134
		Long Term Debt	
		F B D B @ 12 1/2%	100,000
		Bank Loan @ Prime + 2 1/2%	243,575
Rental Equipment (Net)	638,288	**Owner's Equity**	
Transmitting Equipment (Net)	262,500	Common Stock (400 Shares Issued)	400
Other Assets	75,800	Retained Earnings	570,736
Total Assets	1,223,845	**Total Liabilities and Equities**	1,223,845

EXHIBIT 9
OXFORD COMMUNICATIONS
Income Statement for Year Ended December 31 (in dollars)

	1987	1986
Revenue	1,073,530	885,504
Expenses		
Wages	274,986	251,405
Employee Benefits	12,757	11,623
Depreciation	225,705	218,283
Interest	78,000	88,830
Commissions	72,051	27,386
Telephone	70,065	61,707
Maintenance	53,934	47,882
General Administrative	29,662	27,762
Advertising	24,465	12,593
Rent	20,956	20,956
Vehicle	17,440	16,076
Fees, Dues and Licences	10,655	10,104
Bad Debts	7,788	15,834
Insurance	6,526	5,407
Municipal Fees	4,460	3,809
Travel & Convention	1,727	1,694
Miscellaneous Expenses	1,631	1,512
Total expenses	912,808	822,863
Income before tax	160,722	62,645
Income tax	(28,609)	(11,150)
Net Income	132,113	51,495

ENDNOTES

1. *The single most useful indicator of pager market potential is given by taking 2.5 percent of the number of telephones in use in the coverage area. This datum has been tested on historical figures and has proved to be an excellent basis for pager market potential projections*
2. *The "519 telephone code" coverage area.*
3. *The weighted average was a function of the type of pager and the channel rented..*

CASE 8

MURPHY OIL COMPANY LIMITED

B. Boze
Centenary College
of Louisiana
Shreveport,
Louisiana

OVERVIEW

On June 19, 1987, Murphy Oil Corporation announced its intention to purchase the outstanding shares of Murphy Oil Company, Ltd. (Murphy Ltd.), its Canadian subsidiary. The offer was $32 Canadian per share, or the U.S. dollar equivalent, or equity in Murphy Oil Corporation (U.S.). (All dollar amounts are expressed in Canadian dollars unless otherwise specified.)

Mr. C., a former president of Murphy Ltd. and holder of 41,400 shares of its common stock, has retired to the Bahamas and must make a decision about the disposition of the stock. As his accountant, you have been asked to give advice and recommendations on the alternatives.

MURPHY OIL CORPORATION

Murphy Oil Corporation, A Delaware Corporation, is a natural resources company. Started by Charles H. Murphy, Jr., as a partnership with his sisters, 35% of Murphy Corporation remains family owned.[1] It was originally incorporated in Louisiana in 1950 as Murphy Corporation and reincorporated in Delaware in 1964, at which time it adopted the name Murphy Oil Corporation. It was reorganized in 1983 to operate solely as a holding company of the various businesses of the enterprise.

Murphy Oil Corporation is headquartered in El Dorado, Arkansas. Murphy operates through subsidiaries as an:

. . . integrated oil enterprise with major diversifications in offshore contract drilling and diving, and farming, timber and lumber operations. Its exploration activities cover areas in North America, South America, Europe, Africa and Asia, and it produces petroleum substances in North America, the United Kingdom, North Sea, Spain and Africa.[2]

During 1986, principal exploration activities were conducted in the United States, Canada, the U.K. and Danish sections of the North Sea, Spain, Tunisia, Egypt and Gabon. Murphy owns and operates two refineries in the United States and markets refined products at wholesale and retail in the southeastern and upper midwestern United States under the Spur name. Refined products sold in the U.K. wholesale and retail markets and the European cargo market are obtained from a partially owned refinery in the U.K.[3]

Through ODECO (Ocean Drilling & Exploration Company) Murphy is engaged in offshore contract drilling. A wholly owned subsidiary of ODECO provides underwater services to the petroleum industry worldwide.

Deltic Farm & Timber Co. Inc., a wholly owned subsidiary, is engaged in farming, timber and land management, lumber manufacturing and marketing, and real estate development in the United States.

MURPHY OIL COMPANY, LIMITED: THE EARLY YEARS

Murphy Ltd., the Canadian subsidiary, is headquartered in Calgary, Alberta. What began as AMUREX, a joint venture of Ashland Oil Company and Murphy Corporation for purposes of exploration, achieved only modest success and was generally considered a "sick child". Murphy Corporation eventually asked Ashland to either buy them out or to sell to them. Ashland consented to sell.

Murphy Ltd. is engaged in the exploration for the development and production of conventional and heavy crude oil and natural gas primarily in the Western Canada sedimentary basin. The company is also involved in the transportation and marketing of crude oil through pipeline and trucking facilities.[4]

Mr. C., a petroleum engineer and one of the original Murphy Oil employees, was appointed as President of Murphy Ltd., in which capacity he served for ten years.

In an effort to be a good corporate citizen, Murphy encouraged Canadians to invest in the Canadian operations. It separated the U.S. and Canadian ventures while retaining 77.1% of the Canadian operations. Common stock with no dividend was issued at a price of $10 a share and in the early years fluctuated from under $2 a share up to $20 a share.

As part of a promotion to get Canadians to purchase Murphy Ltd. stock, convertible preferred stock was issued at $25 a share with a $.30 annual stock dividend. The preferred stock was convertible to common stock at $10 a share and was callable.

MR. C. AND MURPHY LIMITED

During the early years of Murphy Ltd., Mr. C. decided to bet on himself and his abilities. He purchased 5,000 shares of common stock at an average price of $3.00 a share[5] in 1964, when the Canadian dollar cost $1.06 U.S.

When the Canadian promotion of Murphy Ltd. was offered, Mr. C. borrowed $50,000 to purchase preferred stock at $25 a share. The stock was later converted to common stock at $10 a share, giving him a total of 10,000 shares (his original 5,000 plus the 5,000 converted to common stock). He subsequently bought an additional 350 shares at $10 each, bringing his total Murphy Ltd. holdings to 10,350. A two-for-one stock split left him with 20,700 shares. A second two-for-one split brought the total to 41,400 shares, 36,400 of which now had a base price of $2.50. Mr. C. also held considerable shares of Murphy Oil Corporation, the parent company.

THE ARRANGEMENT

In the spring of 1987 Murphy Oil Corporation began considering the repurchase of the outstanding shares of Murphy Ltd. What was begun under the Trudeau administration to persuade Canadians to invest in Murphy in their own country was unnecessary since Canadians could now invest in the United States or anywhere else. Murphy Corporation wanted to run the Canadian operation like a division instead of a subsidiary. In this way they felt that they could focus and plan for the long run.

Specifically, Murphy Ltd. owned significant amounts of land with heavy oil reserves. It was Murphy Corporation's desire to invest in exploration of these lands even if it did not result in short-term profits.

Since Murphy Corporation still owned 77.1% of the outstanding shares of Murphy Ltd., the majority of the corporate dividends paid by Murphy Ltd. were actually being paid back to the parent company in the U.S.

Murphy Corporation felt that this Arrangement was beneficial both to them and to the shareholders. The company expected to be more flexible in its financing and business affairs and achieve cost savings through not having to prepare and mail quarterly and annual reports, hold annual shareholders meetings, etc., through this Arrangement.

> Public shareholders will have an opportunity to receive a fair and reasonable cash price for their Common Shares. If they elect to receive Murphy Common Shares, public shareholders will have an opportunity to become equity investors in Murphy free of commissions on the disposition of their Common Shares and the acquisition of Murphy Common Shares and they will receive dividends which historically have been greater than the dividends paid on the Common Shares.[6]

On June 19, 1987, after the close of the market, Murphy Corporation announced it had proposed the Arrangement to the Corporation. The closing price of Murphy common stock was $30 on the Toronto Stock Exchange; trading was suspended on the Montreal Exchange.

Public announcement of the first terms of the Arrangement was made on August 17, 1987. The closing price of the Corporation's common shares on the Toronto Stock

Exchange on August 31, 1987 was $31.625 per share and on the Montreal Exchange was $31.50 per share.

An arrangement such as the one Murphy Corporation suggested for Murphy Ltd., under section 185.1 of the Canada Business Corporations Act, is similar to reprivatization or "going private" under United States and other countries' laws. The Arrangement, therefore, is given the protection of the courts so that it does not require the company to get 90% of the 23% of the stock that they did not already own, as would be required in other forms of amalgamation or repurchase.[7]

THE PROVISIONS OF THE AGREEMENT

A package of information dated August 31, 1987, was prepared for distribution to the stockholders. The package was mailed September 3, 1987, and received by U.S. stockholders during the following two weeks, giving them two to three weeks' notice of the stockholders' meeting. The package included:

(1) Information Circular and Proxy Statement

(2) Notice of Special Meeting of Shareholders to be held on September 30, 1987

(3) Notice of Petition to the Court of Queen's Bench of Alberta

(4) Divisional financial statement breakdown for the fiscal year ended December 31, 1986

(5) Interim financial statements for the six months ended June 30, 1987

(6) Notice of Annual Meeting and Proxy Statement relating to the Annual Meeting of Stockholders held on May 13, 1987.

The Information Circular outlined the options available to the stockholders. Stockholders could elect to exchange their shares of Murphy Ltd. for:

a) $32 a share (Canadian), or

b) Murphy Oil Corporation common stock based upon

    (1) the average closing price of Murphy common shares on the New York Stock Exchange on the ten trading days prior to the date of the special meeting, and

    (2) the United States dollar equivalent of CAN $32, based upon the average of the noon rate of exchange, as reported by the Bank of Canada, on such ten trading days, or

c) The U.S. equivalent of $32 (Canadian) a share based upon the average of the noon rate of exchange, as reported by the Bank of Canada on the ten trading days prior to the date of the special meeting.

Canadian Federal Income Tax consequences and United States Federal Tax consequences of the Arrangement are shown in the Information Circular in the Appendix, as are the applicable prices and exchange rates.

THE DECISION

Mr. C. had retired to the Bahamas. On April 23, 1982, Murphy Ltd. was valued at $15.25 a share and the exchange rate on that day was $.8172 Canadian per U.S. dollar.[8]

Upon receipt of the Information Circular Mr. C. sought the advice of his accountants. The meeting is scheduled for September 30, 1987. At that time the rates of exchange and ratio of stock swaps will be announced.

CASE REQUIREMENTS

1. As Mr. C.'s accountant, in what form would you recommend that he exchange his shares of Murphy Oil Company Ltd.? Why?
2. Given that Mr. C. is a resident of a foreign country (both from a Canadian and an American point of view), what are the implications of this transaction for him?
3. How will this transaction be handled by Murphy Ltd. and Murphy Corporation for accounting purposes?

ENDNOTES

1. Murphy Oil Corporation, **Notice of Annual Meeting and Proxy Statement** (El Dorado, Arkansas, 1987), 2-3.
2. Murphy Oil Company, Ltd., **Information Circular and Proxy Statement** (Calgary, Alberta, 1987), 11.
3. Securities and Exchange Commission, **Form 10-K Annual Report, Murphy Oil Corporation** (Washington, D.C., 1986), 3.
4. Murphy Oil Company, Ltd., **Information Circular and Proxy Statement** (Calgary, Alberta, 1987), 12.
5. Paul McDonald, Interview by author, February 17, 1987, El Dorado, Arkansas, Tape recording.
6. Murphy Oil Company, Ltd., **Information Circular and Proxy Statement** (Calgary, Alberta, 1987), 8.
7. Jerry Watkins, Executive Vice President, Murphy Oil Corporation, Interview by author, February 17, 1987, El Dorado, Arkansas.
8. Wall Street Journal, April 23, 1982.

APPENDIX 1
NEW YORK STOCK EXCHANGE DAILY CLOSE
AND
BANK OF CANADA NOON EXCHANGE RATES
September 16 — 29, 1987 and
October 5, 1987

Date	New York Stock Exchange Daily Close	Exchange Rate	Final Ratio
September 16	35.25	.75901	
September 17	34.75	.76028	
September 18	34.00	.76127	
September 21	33.25	.76057	
September 22	35.375	.75890	
September 23	35.875	.75907	
September 24	36.125	.75988	
September 25	35.75	.76214	
September 28	36.25	.76254	
September 29	36.00	.76348	
October 5	(election deadline)		.7645

CASE 9

THE NABU NETWORK CORPORATION

F. Simyar
Concordia University
Montreal, Quebec

K. Argheyd
Concordia University
Montreal, Quebec

On September 21, 1984, John Kelly, Chairman and Chief Executive Officer of the Nabu Network Corporation (NABU), a Canadian-owned distributor of a wide range of computer software by cable television lines, announced to a meeting of employees that the company might have to cease operations if it did not find outside funding sources. His announcement followed a decision by NABU's majority shareholder, Campeau Corporation, to cease financial support after November 13, 1984. But Kelly said to the assembled employees that:

> NABU did not perceive the decision by Campeau Corporation as pulling the plug . . .
>
> Campeau Corporation's support in the form of a $5 million loan for the next two months should provide NABU with sufficient time to organize additional financing . . .
>
> Campeau's support to date ($20.5 million in the past year alone) represented an endorsement of the ultimate financial viability of the corporation, . . . and that employee morale was absolutely superb, and their response had given senior management even more confidence that the company would survive.

Later Kelly began preparing for his upcoming meeting with Robert Campeau, President of Campeau Corporation, during which he intended to raise the question of financing one more time. He had asked his financial manager for a forecast of financial needs for the next six months. He was at the same time considering other options, such as equity or debenture issues, bank loans, joint venture, licensing, etc., in case Campeau's answer remained negative.

© John Wiley & Sons Canada Ltd. All rights reserved.

NABU MANUFACTURING CORPORATION

Background

The Nabu Manufacturing Corporation was established on July 1, 1981, with the amalgamation of five high-tech companies that were engaged in related aspects of the microcomputer and telecommunications industry:

(a) **Nabu Manufacturing Corporation**, a manufacturer of television converters and a cable-related microcomputer development company;

(b) **Andicom Technical Products Ltd.**, a designer and manufacturer of microcomputers;

(c) **Mobius Software Ltd.**, a software development and consulting firm;

(d) **MFC Microcomputer Corporation**, a distributer and retailer of microcomputers;

(e) **Compushop Canada Ltd.**, a retailer of microcomputers.

The amalgamated companies thus covered both the hardware and software aspects of the computer industry. In its first year of operations, NABU achieved sales of $34.9 million (see Exhibit 2, Note 12).

The published financial statements attributed a large part of the revenue and profit contribution to the sale of commercial computers, terminals and systems, especially in the fourth quarter of its first fiscal year. The remainder of the corporation's revenues stemmed from the lease and service operations, computer retail and wholesale distribution, and cable products.

In the corporate annual report for the year ending July 3, 1982, John Kelly stated:

> Over the next two years, NABU's cable-compatible microcomputer systems are expected to add significantly to the existing base of corporate revenues.
>
> NABU's challenge is to take advantage of the technology and distribution strategy it has created. We recognize the objective and we are learning the "how to."

Kelly concluded his letter by adding:

> This vitality, this innovative spirit, combined with solid resources and capabilities and aided by our commitment to meet the challenges and seize the opportunities available to us, places NABU at the forefront of a new era.

The company's corporate mission was:

> To design, manufacture and sell microcomputers capable of providing a wide variety of programmable services through broadband communications.

The emphasis was on a communications network. This described a link between cable subscribers through the use of microcomputers and a central data base through the use of the cable system.

In its first year of operations, the Nabu Manufacturing Corporation and subsidiary products included the NABU 1600 business computer, CRT terminals, lottery terminals and data entry equipment. One of NABU's early products was the microcomputer termed the 1100. It, however, contributed very little to the overall sales figures of the company. John Kelly commented on the 1100 microcomputer:

> It was a product that was almost obsolete when we introduced it. It was stopgap until we could introduce the 1600. The 1100 wasn't designed for our total strategy, which is to sell micro-based systems, not just products.

The 1600 business computer was a multiuser and multitasking 16-bit microcomputer. It was developed for large corporations requiring its multi-use, multi-task applications. Commenting on the 1600 in the corporation's first annual report, John Kelly claimed:

> To the best of our knowledge, it is the most inexpensive and powerful 3-station system on the market today.

Corporate Strategy

The concept of the 1600 business computer was a part of a larger corporate strategy followed by NABU. The corporate objective at the time of creation included obtaining leadership in manufacturing and exporting microprocessor-based delivery systems, as well as becoming Canada's leading microcomputer retailer.

The corporation set out to market and sell a large number of the 1600 business computers. This stand-alone system, along with other NABU computers, would allow clients the necessary communications compatibility to access and be linked through existing communications area networks. These area networks would give NABU's clients access and linkage to one another through high speed cable networks, a concept yet to become reality.

In addition, the Nabu Manufacturing Corporation expressed specific business interests and commitment in the form of investment and involvement in the following areas:

- The design, manufacture and marketing of commercial computers, terminals and systems
- The sale of data entry systems
- The provision of hardware maintenance
- The provision of software consulting services
- The sale of microcomputers manufactured by other companies through a retail store network and direct sales force
- The development of market opportunities outside North America.

Acquisitions

In an effort consistent with NABU's strategic direction, the corporation completed a series of acquisitions. This increased its business base, and accounted for approximately two-thirds of NABU's $35 million in revenue for the fiscal year ending in 1982.

The acquisitions included the following:

(a) Volker-Craig Ltd.   (January, 1982)
(b) Consolidated Computer Inc. (March, 1982)
(c) Financeco Ltd.   (March, 1982)

(a) **Volker-Craig Ltd.**

NABU acquired a 100% interest in Volker-Craig Ltd., a manufacturer of video display terminals, for a total amount of $250,000 cash and 450,000 common shares issued at a deemed consideration of $15 each. As a result of this transaction, NABU had recognized goodwill on acquisition in the amount of $7,314,000. Since the date of acquisition, adverse market conditions had forced NABU to write off the entire amount of the goodwill in its corporate financial statements ending July 3, 1982, because it could not be recovered (extraordinary loss).

(b) **Consolidated Computer Inc.**

NABU acquired from the Government of Canada a 65% interest in the outstanding shares of Consolidated Computer Inc. (CCI) for $1.[1] CCI's business included the design, manufacture, sales and service of data entry systems and advanced on-line lottery terminals. Its markets included Canada, the United States and worldwide locations. In addition, NABU acquired for $100,000 title to $47.4 million of debt owed by CCI to the Government of Canada. The carrying value of the assets of CCI at the date of acquisition exceeded the purchase price that NABU paid by approximately $2 million.

(c) **Financeco Ltd.**

NABU also acquired from the Government of Canada 100% interest in Financeco Ltd. for $1. The business of Financeco involved the purchasing of equipment from CCI, which they in turn leased to customers. As part of this transaction $12.7 million (U.S.) of the total debt owed to the Government of Canada by Financeco and its wholly owned subsidiary, Finecomp, Inc., was forgiven. The balance of the debt, estimated to be $8,001,000, was restructured so as to require Financeco to pay the Government a percentage of the Financeco and Finecomp cash flows at a pre-defined amount over a period of five years, after which any balance owed would be cancelled. The carrying value of the net assets acquired by the company, after adjustment for the debt of $8,001,000, exceeded the purchase price by approximately $7.9 million.

Kelly's peers in Ottawa's high technology community criticized NABU's ambitious acquisition strategy. But replying to some of his critics, Kelly said:

> Acquiring those companies gave us immediate access to established research and development teams, which allowed us to proceed very quickly with the development of the cable micro.

Organization Structure and Strategy

Following these corporate "subsidiary" acquisitions, NABU's management next focused on its internal structure. They felt that there was a need to reorganize structurally. This would enable efficient utilization of capital and ensure that management's capabilities were compatible. Two distinct business areas were identified, based on what were considered to be NABU's strengths, and it was hoped that reorganization would provide the company a competitive advantage. The two areas were:

1. The domestic retail distribution of personal computers and software, and
2. The manufacture and distribution of "cable compatible" computer software.

During the 1982-83 fiscal year, NABU established the Computer Innovations Retail Division as a separate corporation under the name Computer Innovations Corporation. In November, 1983 (16 months after its inception), the company that used to be known as The Nabu Manufacturing Corporation was split into two new companies: The Nabu Network Corporation (NABU) and The Computer Innovations Corporation. Confirming their distinctive entities, these corporations were subsequently listed separately on the Toronto Stock Exchange. The only remaining link was the fact that John Kelly was the chairman of both corporations.

The Computer Innovations business was set up to handle the distribution and servicing of commercial microcomputers, the leasing and servicing of data entry products in Canada, and custom manufacturing of such products as lottery terminals.

The Nabu Network business was set up to develop and market all products related to the Nabu Network home computer system, which used cable television to deliver information, entertainment, and educational computer programs to subscribers.

During this fiscal year and into the next, activities that did not meet the company's strategic objectives were eliminated or wound down. Included in this category were:

- The elimination of production at Nabu's Consolidated Computer Inc. operations
- The phasing out of the company's computer terminal division
- The cancellation of its 16-bit business microcomputer

Commenting on the cancellation of its 16-bit business microcomputer, Kelly said:

> We continued developing the 16-bit business microcomputer until we could determine its economic viability, which seemed a good move until IBM entered the market and made our business plan non-viable.

The phasing out of the company's computer terminal division resulted from the availability of cheaper imports from countries such as Korea and Taiwan. Kelly noted:

> Terminals that cost $800 two years ago are *now* (in 1983) available for under $400.

As for the elimination of employees in production, Kelly justified this move with the corporation's efforts to expand its Computer Innovations chain, thus increasing employment in its retail sector.

Given the new focus of the company and the amount of resources and investment that would have been required to be fully successful in such a business operation, management decided that no further resources would be put at risk and instead began implementing a planned program of divestiture. As a result of these decisions, significant staff reductions were expected during the 1982-83 fiscal year and into the next fiscal year, particularly in the manufacturing sector of NABU's operations. The company expected that 200 employees would be put out of work as a result of the changes.

In further streamlining its manufacturing operations, NABU placed two U.S. subsidiaries of the former Consolidated Computer Inc. for sale for $7 million. Recognition Equipment Inc. of Dallas, Texas, bought the assets of Finecomp Inc. and the stock of Consolidated Computer International Inc. (the U.S. subsidiary), both of Silver Spring, Maryland. These transactions were not expected to have any effect on the Canadian operations.

THE NABU NETWORK

The Nabu Network was described as a new concept in home entertainment, self-education and personal computing available through North America's cable companies. On

October 25, 1983, The Nabu Manufacturing Corporation launched the Nabu Network, a home computing system that transmitted video games, educational software and household information over cable television into the home. Subscribers to the Nabu Network received the NABU personal computer, which provided access to a wide selection of programs transmitted over the special NABU television channel. NABU itself provided the software and loaded it into the system for delivery.

Product and Markets

The Nabu Network offered an integrated communications system consisting of:

- The 80 K NABU personal computer
- The NABU Data Broadcast Computer, a high performance minicomputer
- An addressable communications adaptor
- Software applications including:
- Video games featuring characters from the *B.C.* and *Wizard of Id* comic strips for which NABU had exclusive North American Cable Rights.
- Educational software including programs to teach typing skills, basic computer literacy, and vocabulary skills.
- Information services including metric conversion tables, stock market summaries, news, and dining out guides.
- Computational programs.

The personal computer was an 80 K machine with a three channel sound generator and a separate graphics processor. The network was also developing a full set of peripherals (e.g., disk drives, printers, etc.). The data broadcast system was the most advanced in the world, designed to transmit programs over the coaxial T.V. cable. This was, at the time, a one-way system whereby subscribers received software transmitted on a continuous basis from the main computer located at the cable company's head office. A similar system existed for transmitting data via phone lines, but the network technology was capable of transmitting data 21,000 times faster.

The cable computing system was initially launched in Ottawa, Canada, on October 25, 1983, after an agreement with Ottawa Cablevision Ltd. Ottawa was thus characterized as being the first city in the world to get the cable-computer system. Subscribers to Ottawa Cablevision were able to buy the NABU home computer keyboard and games controller for $695 and rent the software for $9.95 a month, or rent the hardware and software for $29.90 a month. The price list later reflected several options which the consumer would have been able to take advantage of and which NABU had tailored to suit a wide range of needs.

In launching the computer network, a target subscription rate of 5% of Ottawa Cablevision's 90,000 customers was set. The target of about 4,500 network subscribers was anticipated within the first six months of operation. Market studies conducted by NABU indicated that about half the subscribers who would take the service would buy a computer terminal, while the rest would rent. Based upon projections for the Ottawa market, this would mean sales of about $1.6 million for terminals and monthly rental income of about $90,000 within the first six months of operations.

In the first month of operations, NABU received 1200 subscription requests. This greater than anticipated demand created problems in the early stages of the Nabu Network launch, including unannounced price changes and supply problems that left customers waiting six weeks or more for their computer hardware. This backlog was soon straightened out, and customers were able to expect their equipment within 24 hours of ordering.

In a letter to shareholders in the corporation's annual report for fiscal year 1982-83, John Kelly reviewed the year's accomplishments:

> During the past year, we have:
> - Successfully proven the viability of the Nabu Network by the installation of over 200 systems in Ottawa.
> - Negotiated the launch of the Nabu Network in Ottawa with Ottawa Cablevision and in Vancouver with Rogers Cablesystems.
> - Introduced the product into high-volume manufacturing plants in Hong Kong and South Korea.
> - Developed a significant library of software for an initial service offering during the first year of operation.

As of May, 1984, close to 1700 people in the Ottawa region had subscribed to the Nabu Network, which offered more than 70 software titles. Market research indicated that the number of people who would buy the service should increase to about 3400 by the end of 1984.

Date	(Ottawa Region) Subscription Actual	Statistics Anticipated
Oct '83	1200	4500
Mar '84	1500	4500
May '84	1700	3400

Source: Various news clippings.

In addition to the Ottawa region, negotiations were underway at the same time with other major cable companies. NABU expanded into the United States in April, 1984, with the introduction of its cable network in Alexandria, Virginia, a suburb of Washington, D.C. NABU completed an agreement with Rogers Cable to launch the Cable Network in Vancouver in late spring of 1984. In Ottawa, the company negotiated with Skyline Cablevision Ltd. (the second cable company in Ottawa), enabling its potential market to grow to 175,000 cable subscribers with the inclusion of the Ottawa-Carleton district. Market research had indicated that NABU would be able to convince 17% of the 175,000 cable subscribers in the Ottawa-Carleton district to subscribe. By September, 1984, NABU had about 2000 customers of Ottawa Cablevision and Skyline Cablevision subscribing to the Nabu Network. Another 700 customers had subscribed to the network in Alexandria, Virginia. Most subscribers rented the computers at about $20 per month and had the availability of more than 100 software programs.

With respect to the launching of the Nabu Network, one industry analyst commented:

If enough cable T.V. subscribers decide to order the service, and that's a big if, the repercussions could be immense. Besides offering cable firms tremendous potential in expanding their revenues, it would also signal the emergence of an important new channel for distributing software to a mass audience. In short, the era of prime time software could send a jolt through the computer industry and force companies to adapt to consumer-oriented software highways. On the other hand, if cable subscribers stay away from these computer services, then NABU will get a spectacular jolt and this latest venture will go down as an interesting footnote in Canadian corporate history.

Gordon Gow, NABU's senior vice-president of corporate development, commented on existing home computer systems and on the future of the company during the Nabu Computer Network launch:

One of the main drawbacks of existing home computer systems is that the user has to buy software cartridges or diskettes at a cost of about $45, every time he wants new games or functions. NABU will constantly update its software programs so the subscriber can get a variety of entertainment information and educational packages for one monthly rental fee.

Gow considered market research to be the key to success for NABU:

The company intends to spend on market research this year (1984) up to 10 times the amount it will spend on producing its product, computer software distributed by cable to individual homes. Any computer firm providing hardware or software must identify its potential market in order to increase sales.

In an effort to promote itself, its products and services, NABU hired magician Doug Henning for its North American advertising campaign in 1983-84 to promote the "lifetime of software magic" promised by the Nabu Network home computer system. NABU allocated $1.5 million dollars towards this promotional effort and advertising concept.

Research and Development

Given the trend in the industry, NABU had committed itself to an intensive research and development program. In its first year of operations, the company allocated over $8.8 million to engineering research and development. Much of this went towards the development of new products with particular emphasis on the home cable computer and its related hardware and software, that is, the Nabu Network.

On June 28, 1982, the Enterprise Development Board of the Federal Government approved a grant of $8.9 million to NABU for the purpose of research and development expenditures already incurred, and to be incurred during the 15-month period ending March 31, 1983 (see Note 14 in Exhibit 2). In 1982, research and development expenditures were approximately 25% of gross revenue and were expected to be approximately 23% of gross revenue in the following fiscal year.

At the end of the corporation's first fiscal year, NABU emphasized its commitment to the development of the Nabu Network, demonstrated by a planned investment of $16 million in research and development into its 1983 fiscal year. The objective was to complete the development of software and produce an integrated cable communications system. In its year end July 2, 1983, fiscal report, NABU indicated it had spent over $19.1 million during the year in the development of new products, with particular emphasis on the home cable computer and its related hardware and software (Nabu Network). This expenditure in fact represented 32.4% of total sales for that year.

In April, 1983, the Federal Government introduced new income tax legislation whereby investors were able to get tax credits of up to 50% for investments involving research and development, if the companies did not claim the credits themselves; this was a tax incentive program allowing investors to use research and development tax credits that the companies in which they invested did not use. It ended up being a tax scam.

Nabu took advantage of these new income tax provisions for research and development. In February, 1984, the company announced that it would transfer research and development tax credits worth $10 million to outside private investors in return for cash payments totalling $5 million to the company. This sum was to be used for research and development for the NABU home computer system. By March, 1984, NABU was spending at least $300,000 a month developing the Nabu Network and its related software. This was expected to increase in proportion to the network's customer base. By this time the company had already spent at least $25 million in developing the Nabu Network.

Human Resources

In September, 1983, the company began scheduled layoffs involving some 130 of its 225 manufacturing employees, a result of NABU's newly focused structure and strategic direction. John Kelly noted:

> The company has adopted the strategy of "building on strengths and making weaknesses irrelevant." Although layoffs resulted from the company's recognition that it was no longer competitive in certain areas of manufacturing, NABU has shored up its successful microcomputer distribution business by hiring 125 new employees during August and September, 1983.

The decision by Kelly to manufacture the cable microcomputer in Korea and Hong Kong, intended to reduce the price of the microcomputer by a third, led to a deterioration in employee relations. NABU production workers voted to unionize, with the Communications Workers of Canada. However, the union lost its bid at Computer Innovations Corporation, where workers voted two to one against unionization.

John Kelly stated on several occasions that his company was very proud of the fact that so many of its employees had accepted the challenges inherent in the company's business plan with such enthusiasm, dedication and hard work. In his view, NABU's continued ability to attract competent people was one of the company's most significant strengths. He also believed that the continued development of this strength would be the single most important factor in the company's ultimate success.

In a continuing effort to attract competent people, several hirings from the United States were made at a significant price. Thomas Wheeler, former president of the U.S. National Cable Television Network, was hired in 1984 to become president of the Nabu Network's U.S. subsidiary; Wheeler was reported to be earning $150,000 a year in 1983. Other prominent hiring included Vivian Goodier, who was hired away from her post as vice-president of operations of the Disney Cable Channel in the eastern U.S. to become vice-president of cable affiliate relations for NABU in the U.S. Barbara Ruger, former vice-president of Westinghouse, was named vice-president of customer sales for NABU. Kelly claimed that this recruitment effort indicated a "strong team" approach towards the U.S. start up of the Nabu Network. The hiring thus coincided with NABU's efforts at testing the U.S. with its home computer software products on cable television. NABU hoped to go continent-wide within two years of its pilot project (in April, 1984) in Alexandria, VA.

COMPUTER INNOVATIONS CORPORATION (DISTRIBUTION)

In the 1982-83 fiscal year, Nabu had established the Computer Innovations retail division as a separate organization under the name Computer Innovations Corporation. In November, 1983, the company transferred the net assets of its computer innovations retail division to this newly formed wholly-owned subsidiary corporation. This was part of a major corporate restructuring, which saw the Nabu Manufacturing Corporation split into two companies: The Nabu Network Corporation and The Computer Innovations Corporation. Each corporation acted as a separately functioning entity.

In NABU's first year of operations, its computer retail and wholesale distribution activities accounted for $8.6 million out of a total revenue of $34.9 million. The computer innovations retail division operated nine retail outlets that serviced Vancouver, Edmonton, Calgary, Toronto, Kingston and Ottawa. The computer innovations store carried microcomputer hardware supplied by IBM, Apple and Osborne. By 1983, this expanded to include microcomputers, peripherals and software produced by IBM, Digital, Apple, Osborne and Texas Instruments.

In NABU's first year of operations it had established a "working relationship" with the Hudson's Bay Company, joining forces with the Bay to market and sell microcomputers and software throughout Canada. NABU opened computer retail departments at selected Hudson's Bay and Simpson's stores in Toronto and Winnipeg. On July 28, 1983, the Nabu Manufacturing Corporation announced a major expansion of its Computer Innovations retail microcomputer business, following an agreement that was reached between NABU and Hudson's Bay. The Hudson's Bay Company upgraded its working relationship with NABU to that of becoming a major investor in the Computer Innovations Corporation.

Hudson's Bay invested $4 million in cash in the Computer Innovations Corporation for a 41.7% interest in that company. This investment was to result in the addition of 24 stores to the chain by the fall of 1983, and the creation of 125 jobs across the country by the end of 1983. It was further estimated that by 1984 more locations would bring the chain total to 40 outlets, and by 1987 the company expected to have 100 stores in Canada. As part of the agreement, NABU had an option to increase its ownership of Computer Innovations Corporation to 63.75%, up from its current 58.3%.

According to Gordon Gow, NABU vice-president:

> This agreement establishes Computer Innovations as the premier national distributor of microcomputers. With the Bay's vast retail experience and our market position and service capability, Computer Innovations will be even more dominant than it is right now.

While revenues were $8.6 million from computer retail and wholesale distribution activities in 1981-82, by 1982-83 such revenues totalled $25 million. Retail microcomputer sales increased by 300%. According to Evans Research Reports, Computer Innovations had close to a 20% share of the commercial microcomputer market. Thus, it was well positioned for growth opportunities over the next five years. It was expected that the total microcomputer market in Canada would exceed $2 billion annually within a two year period.

FINANCING OUTLOOK

In the corporation's fiscal 1981-82 annual report, management indicated that from a financial perspective, NABU's first year of operations was a success:

- Revenue exceeded management's expectations.
- Three important acquisitions were completed.
- A private placement of common shares yielded $16.8 million.
- A tangible asset base in excess of $38 million was created.

(See Exhibits 1 and 2 for NABU's Financial Statements and some of the accompanying notes to these statements.)

Given that the economic climate at the time was considered poor by most analysts and that these conditions deteriorated steadily throughout 1981-82, NABU's management were encouraged by the company's financial performance. In the corporation's fiscal 1982-83 annual report, management noted both achievements and disappointments over the year's operations:

- In December, 1982, the company raised $26 million in a public stock offering that was believed by management to be the largest initial public stock issue ever placed by a Canadian high-technology company.
- Revenue exceeded that of the previous year by 65%.
- Retail microcomputer sales increased by 300%.
- There were unforeseen delays in the introduction of new products.
- Acceptable levels of profitability were not achieved in some divisions.

According to management, overall performance was adversely affected in its second year of operations.

The reporting procedure in the 1982-83 fiscal report exhibited a change with respect to engineering and market development costs. Previously, such costs had been capitalized on the balance sheet; they would then be amortized over a three-year period. In the 1982-83 financial report, all engineering and market development costs were written off in the year; such costs would thus be charged to earnings when incurred.

This procedural change was attributed to a general trend that was occurring among high-technology companies whereby such costs were being absorbed as incurred. Due to the volatility of the high-technology environment, the life of new technology was uncertain and therefore the determination of an appropriate amortization period was often difficult to assess. The decision by management to write off the full amount as an expense rather than to defer such costs would facilitate comparison of the company's financial statements with others in the industry. Management attributed most of its reported 1982-83 losses to engineering research and development and marketing costs for the Nabu Network.

According to John Kelly:

> NABU will lose up to $50 million on the network over the next two years, . . . but it's all according to plan. We need hundreds of thousands of customers to be profitable on a continuing development mode. We could freeze our operations at any time and be profitable relatively quickly, but we don't want to do that. Yes, we will lose a million dollars a month, but we see it as investing a million a month to create this scenario. What we're doing is building a network and as long as we continue to expand that network we're investing in the future. Developing a new technology and opening new markets is an expensive proposition, and the company will have to raise more money "very privately" within nine months.

In the corporation's 1982-83 fiscal report, Kelly stated, in his letter to the shareholders, that the company's clearer strategic focus provided a strong basis for the future. Other future prospects included:

- Significant improvements in the operating results of the company
- Strong performance from Computer Innovations Corporation and Service Division within Consolidated Computer Inc.
- Contribution to the Company's profitability from its leasing business within Canada
- Ability to implement its key business strategies with a recently announced private placement of a $23 million convertible debenture.

By September, 1984, losses totalling $10 million had added up for the Nabu Network Corporation since November 1983. Most of the losses were attributed to engineering, research and development, and marketing costs for the Network.

In a September 1984, letter to shareholders, John Kelly wrote:

> NABU's development and marketing programs are going according to the company's business plan, but the company is looking for significant additional financing "to maintain the ongoing viability of the company." The company is exploring different equity and joint venture arrangements to obtain this new financing.

On September 18, 1984, the Nabu Network Corporation announced that it would run out of money in mid-November unless it could arrange new financing.

John McArthur, President of NABU and John Kelly, Chairman of the Board, commented in a subsequent press interview:

> We plan to continue serving existing customers while the company looks for new financing, but it would take a minimum investment of about $10 million to support a "bare-bones" operation for the next year. The ideal scenario would be to get an investment of $10 million to $12 million to continue development and expansion of the system over the next year.

NABU gave termination notices to 203 of its 238 employees; investors were pessimistic about the future of the company. This mood was reflected in the rapidly declining price of NABU shares on the Toronto Stock Exchange. Shares that had once traded above $13 in December 1982, had dropped to $2.75 in the first week of September 1984, and financial analysts were of the opinion that the decline had not bottomed out yet.

The Campeau Corporation

The Campeau Corporation, a major real estate development company situated in Toronto, was a major shareholder in the Nabu Network Corporation. In September, 1983, the Campeau Corporation and other investors purchased $23 million worth of debentures from the Computer Innovations Distribution Corporation, subject to approval by the Ontario Securities Commission. Campeau Corporation, which had already invested about $10.2 million in NABU, bought $20.5 million of the debentures. The Computer Innovations Distribution Corporation subsequently loaned $18 million to the Nabu Network Corporation.

The $23 million investment was part of a total $32 million that the corporation announced it had raised in October 1983. The remainder of the investment was attributed to:

- $5 million coming from NABU selling its 20% share of Logo Computer Systems Inc., a Montreal-based software company.
- $4 million coming from Hudson's Bay Co., which acquired 35% interest in Computer Innovations.

As of October 1983, total financing amounted to $74 million, including the $42 million from two previous share offerings.

In a September 1984 announcement, the Campeau Corporation stated that it would not finance the (NABU) Company beyond November 13, 1984. In addition to the $20.5 million of financing, the Campeau Corporation had provided a loan of $5 million to NABU in the two months prior to the announcement. Kelly's immediate response in a letter to shareholders was:

> Although NABU's major shareholder (Campeau) has arranged interim financing in the form of temporary loans, "there is no assurance this interim financing support will continue to be available for any fixed period or in any specified amounts."
>
> Campeau Corporation was under no commitment to totally fund NABU's operations at any time, and its support for the next two months should provide the corporation with sufficient time to organize additional financing. NABU believes that Campeau's support to date, $20.5 million in the past year alone "represents an endorsement of the ultimate financial viability of the corporation" rather than a loss of confidence as to the corporation's opportunities.

On September 27, 1984, more than 60 Nabu Network employees signed an open letter to federal politicians seeking help from the government for NABU. David Daubney, a conservative Member of Parliament for Ottawa West, responded:

> I am concerned about the history of corporate bailouts in Canada, including a notorious one to a NABU predecessor company, Consolidated Computer Inc.

We have to be very selective. However, if that were the only way to save NABU, then I would be prepared to support it.

Industry analysts were not surprised about the financial situation at NABU. Some believed that although NABU was running out of time, a chance still existed for the company; it might be possible for the company to either license its unique technology or find a joint venture or equity partner.

CASE REQUIREMENT

Campeau Corporation did not change its mind and no financing was found. Evaluate the financial strategies and accounting records and establish what went wrong.

ENDNOTES

1. Consolidated Computer Inc., one of the largest Canadian controlled manufacturers of computer data entry equipment, had received federal funds totalling $125 million to keep it afloat during the 1970's.

EXHIBIT 1
FINANCIAL STATEMENTS
NABU MANUFACTURING CORPORATION
CONSOLIDATED BALANCE SHEETS
For the Year Ended July 2, 1983
(in thousands of dollars)

ASSETS	1983	1982
Current Assets (Note 12)		
Cash	862	1,443
Accounts Receivable	10,683	10,237
Investment (Note 15(a))	4,237	-0-
Inventories (Note 2)	12,788	12,443
Prepaid Expenses	485	432
	29,055	24,555
Fixed Assets (Note 3)	14,972	14,548
Engineering and Market Development Costs (Note 14)	-0-	9,771
Other Assets	104	516
Total Assets	44,131	49,390
LIABILITIES		
Current Liabilities		
Bank Indebtedness (Note 4)	6,601	8,900
Accounts Payable and Accrued Charges	14,244	13,916
Provision for Business Rationalization Costs (Note 12)	7,377	-0-
Taxes Payable	331	918
Current Portion of Long-Term Debt	3,089	1,040
	31,642	24,774
Long-Term Debt (Note 5)	9,602	11,014
SHAREHOLDERS' EQUITY		
Share Capital (Note 6)	54,590	24,576
Deficit (Note 7)	(51,703)	(10,974)
	2,887	13,602
Total Liabilities and Shareholders' Equity	44,131	49,390

© John Wiley & Sons Canada Ltd. All rights reserved.

EXHIBIT 1
FINANCIAL STATEMENTS
NABU MANUFACTURING CORPORATION
CONSOLIDATED STATEMENTS OF DEFICIT
For the year ended July 2, 1983
(in thousands of dollars)

	1983	1982
Balance, Beginning of Year as Previously Reported (Note 7)	9,859	1,884
Expenses of Share Issue Transferred from Share Capital (Note 7)	1,115	-0-
Balance, Beginning of Year as Restated	10,974	1,884
Expenses of Share Issue	1,134	1,115
Net Loss for the Year	39,595	7,975
Balance, End of Year	51,703	10,974

CONSOLIDATED STATEMENT OF LOSS

Continuing Operations

	1983	1982
Revenue	49,158	26,592
Operating Expenses Including Interest Expense (Net of Interest Income) of $548 (1982 — $400)	(44,592)	(23,989)
Profit from Continuing Operations Before Engineering and Market Developemnt Expenditures	4,566	2,603
Engineering and Market Development Expenditures, Net of Government Assistance of $4,849 (Note 14)	12,795	44
(Loss) Profit for the Year From Continuing Operations	(8,229)	2,559

Discontinued Operations

	1983	1982
Operating Losses	4,299	2,620
Engineering and Market Development Expenditures, Net of Government Assistance of $2,165 (Note 14)	9,094	-0-
Loss for the Year From Discontinued Operations	13,393	2,620
Loss Before Extraordinary Items	21,622	61
Extraordinary Items (Note 12)	17,973	7,914
Net Loss for the Year	39,595	7,975

(Profit (Loss) per Share — See Note 13)

EXHIBIT 1
FINANCIAL STATEMENTS
NABU MANUFACTURING CORPORATION
CONSOLIDATED STATENENTS OF CHANGES IN FINANCIAL POSITION
For the Year Ended July 2, 1983
(in thousands of dollars)

	1983	1982
WORKING CAPITAL PROVIDED		
Operations – Loss for the Year Before Extraordinary Items	(21,622)	(61)
Items not Requiring an Outlay of Working Capital:		
Depreciation and Amortization	4,176	1,982
Writeoff of Engineering and Market Development Expenditures	21,889	44
Gain on Disposal of Fixed Assets	(310)	-0-
Total Provided From Operations	4,133	1,965
Net Proceeds From Sale of Shares	30,014	22,387
Increase in Long-Term Debt	2,005	2,119
Decrease in Other Assets	69	-0-
Proceeds on Disposal of Fixed Assets	688	-0-
Total Working Capital Provided	36,909	26,471
WORKNG CAPITAL APPLIED		
Provision for Business Rationalization (Net of Items not Requiring an Outlay of Working Capital of $3,074; 1982 – $7,314)	14,899	600
Increase in Investments	-0-	108
Additions to Fixed Assets	6,289	4,397
Engineering and Market Development Expenditures (Net of Government Assistance in 1983 of $7,014) (Note 14)	12,118	8,856
Increase in Other Assets	1,420	169
Non-Current Assets Less Long-Term Liabilities of Acquired Businesses	-0-	10,100
Decrease in Long-Term Debt	3,417	-0-
Expenses of Share Issue	1,134	1,115
Total Working Capital Applied	39,277	25,345
Decrease (Increase) in Working Capital	2,368	(1,126)

EXHIBIT 2
NABU MANUFACTURING CORPORATION
NOTES (12-16) TO FINANCIAL STATEMENTS
For the Year Ended July 2, 1983

12. Business Rationalization

During the year, the Company undertook a review of its business operations to determine the continuing value of operations where the return on invested capital has been inadequate or where the operations are inconsistent with future strategic plans.

Following the completion of that review, a decision was made to discontinue or divest certain of the Company's operations. The assets of the divisions which are to be sold or discontinued have been written down at July 2, 1983 to estimated net realizable value and full provision made for the estimated related costs. These write-downs total $10,596,000.

In addition, the Company has provided for further costs to be incurred during the rationalization period estimated at $6,477,000. These costs consist primarily of employee termination and redundancy, provision for operating losses and other closure costs. Certain costs of reduced corporate functions and provision for losses on disposal of corporate assets have also been provided in the year ended July 2, 1983 and approximate $900,000.

The amounts described above, totalling $17,973,000 have been included in extraordinary items in the Consolidated Statement of Loss. The extraordinary items in 1982 totalling $7,914,000 comprise $600,000 for plant closing costs and $7,314,000 for write-off of goodwill arising on the acquisition of a subsidiary.

The following supplemental balance sheet and operating information has been provided to segregate the assets and liabilities and results of operations of discontinued businesses from that of the Company's two continuing businesses referred to as Distribution and NABU NETWORK.

Supplemental Balance Sheet Information
Industry Segments (in dollars)

	Continuing			Discon-	Total
	Distribution	Nabu Network	Sub-total	tinued	1983
Current Assets					
Cash	862	-0-	862	-0-	862
Accounts Receivable	6,415	2,691	9,106	1,577	10,683
Investment	-0-	4,237	4,237	-0-	4,237
Inventories	7,496	1,222	8,718	4,070	12,788
Prepaid Expenses	129	156	285	200	485
Total Current Assets	14,902	8,306	23,208	5,847	29,055
Fixed Assets	10,046	4,063	14,109	863	14,972
Other Assets	37	67	104	-0-	104
Total Assets	24,985	12,436	37,421	6,710	44,131

	Continuing				
	Distribution	Nabu Network	Subtotal	Discontinued	Total 1983
Liabilities					
Bank Indebtedness	-0-	6,601	6,601	-0-	6,601
Accounts Payable	7,511	3,520	11,031	3,213	14,244
Provision for Business Rationalization Costs	900	-0-	900	6,477	7,377
Taxes Payable	243	6	249	82	331
	8,654	10,127	18,781	9,772	28,553
Long-Term Debt					12,691
Share Capital					54,590
Deficit					(51,703)
					44,131

Supplemental statement of operating results
Industry Segments (in dollars)

	Continuing				
	Distribution	Nabu Network	Subtotal	Discontinued	Total 1983
Revenue	49,158	-0-	49,158	9,695	58,853
Less:					
Operating Expenses	44,592	-0-	44,592	13,994	58,586
Engineering and Market Development Expenses — Current Year	225	7,233	7,458	4,660	12,118
	44,817	7,233	52,050	18,654	70,704
	4,341	(7,233)	(2,892)	(8,959)	(11,851)
Less:					
Engineering and Market Development Expenses — Prior Year	-0-	5,337	5,337	4,434	9,771
	4,341	(12,570)	(8,229)	(13,393)	(21,622)
Less:					
Extraordinary Items	-0-	900	900	17,073	17,973
Net Profit (Loss) for the Year	4,341	(13,470)	(9,129)	(30,466)	(39,595)

Supplemental statement of operating results for year ended July 2, 1982
Industry Segments (in dollars)

	Continuing				
	Distribution	Nabu Network	Subtotal	Discontinued	Total 1982
Revenue	<u>26,592</u>	<u>-0-</u>	<u>26,592</u>	<u>8,371</u>	<u>34,963</u>
Less:					
Operating Expenses	23,989	-0-	23,989	10,991	34,980
Engineering and Market Development Expenses — Current Year	<u>-0-</u>	<u>-0-</u>	<u>-0-</u>	<u>-0-</u>	<u>-0-</u>
	23,989	-0-	23,989	10,991	34,980
	2,603	-0-	2,603	(2,620)	(17)
Less: Engineering and Market Development Expenses — Prior Year	<u>44</u>	<u>-0-</u>	<u>44</u>	<u>-0-</u>	<u>44</u>
	2,559	-0-	2,559	(2,620)	(61)
Less: Extraordinary Items	<u>-0-</u>	<u>-0-</u>	<u>-0-</u>	<u>7,914</u>	<u>7,914</u>
Net Profit (Loss) for the Year	2,559	-0-	2,559	(10,534)	(7,975)

Geographic Segments (in dollars)

	Continuing				
	Distribution	Nabu Network	Discontinued	Total 1983	Total 1982
Revenue					
Within Canada	40,383	-0-	3,524	43,907	24,682
Outside Canada	<u>3,898</u>	<u>-0-</u>	<u>-0-</u>	<u>3,898</u>	<u>3,052</u>
	44,281	-0-	3,524	47,805	27,734
United States	4,877	-0-	4,573	9,450	6,324
Other	<u>-0-</u>	<u>-0-</u>	<u>1,598</u>	<u>1,598</u>	<u>905</u>
Consolidated Revenue	49,158	-0-	9,695	58,853	34,963
Profit (Loss) — Canada	3,887	(12,570)	(11,203)	(19,886)	(125)
United States	454	-0-	(1,931)	(1,477)	242
Other	<u>-0-</u>	<u>-0-</u>	<u>(259)</u>	<u>(259)</u>	<u>(178)</u>
Loss Before Extraordinary Items	4,341	(12,570)	(13,393)	(21,622)	(61)
Extraordinary Items				<u>(17,973)</u>	<u>(7,914)</u>
				(39,595)	(7,975)

Geographic Segments (in dollars)

	Continuing		Discon-tinued	Total 1983	Total 1982
	Distribution	Nabu Network			
Identifiable Assets					
Canada	16,195	12,436	5,659	34,290	27,679
United States	7,819	-0-	1,303	9,122	10,792
Other	-0-	-0-	719	719	1,148
	24,014	12,436	7,681	44,131	39,619
Engineering and Market Development Costs				-0-	9,771
				44,131	49,390

Consolidated revenue excludes the value of transfers between geographic areas. These transfers, which entirely related to discontinued operations, totalled $3,706,000 (1982 — $4,180,000).

13. **Profit (Loss) Per Share**

	1983		1982	
	Basic	Fully Diluted	Basic	Fully Diluted
Continuing Operations				
Profit from Continuing Operations Before Engineering and Market Development Expenditures	0.91	0.76	0.90	0.66
(Loss) Profit for the Year	(1.64)	(1.64)	0.89	0.66
Discontinued Operations				
Loss for the Year	(2.67)	(2.67)	(0.91)	(0.91)
Loss Before Extraordinary Items	(4.30)	(4.30)	(0.02)	(0.02)
Net Loss for the Year	(7.88)	(7.88)	(2.77)	(2.77)

Average number of shares outstanding during the year (thousands) was 5,025 (1982— 2,875).

14. **Engineering and Market Development Costs**

The Company's practice in relation to costs incurred in the development of new products has been to defer such costs and amortize them over a three-year period. Increasingly, prevailing practice among corporations operating in the high-technology industry has been to treat such costs as a charge to earnings when incurred. This is principally because of the volatility of the high-technology environment, which leads to uncertainty as to the probable life of new technology and hence the determination of an appropriate amortization period. For this reason, and in order to permit the comparability of the Company's financial statements with others in its industry, management has decided that it is no longer appropriate to defer such costs and accordingly has written off the full amount as an expense in the current period.

Transactions during the year can be summarized as follows:

	1983	1982
Balance Deferred, Beginning of Year	9,771	959
Expended in Current Year (Including Depreciation of $612; 1982 — $172)	19,132	8,856
Government Assistance	(7,014)	-0-
	12,118	8,856
	21,889	9,815
Written off in Current Year		
Continuing Operations	(12,795)	(44)
Discontinued Operations	(9,094)	-0-
Balance Deferred, End of Year	-0-	9,771

Government assistance received includes $1,556,000 in grants applicable to expenditures incurred in the previous fiscal year, prior to definitive approval of the program.

15. Related Party Transactions

a) **Logo Computer Systems Inc.**

In January 1983, the Company purchased 1,177,050 shares held by Campeau Corporation in Logo Computer Systems Inc. (LCSI). The shares were purchased from Campeau Corporation in exchange for 282,492 Common Shares and 282,492 Share Purchase Warrants entitling the holder to purchase one Common Share at $17.00 for each Warrant, exercisable at any time prior to November 30, 1986. For the purpose of the transaction, the shares of LCSI have an attributed value of $3.60 and one Common Share and one Warrant of the Company have an attributed aggregate value of $15.00. The shares held by Campeau Corporation in LCSI were purchased within the last two years at a price of $1.09 per share and have a current market value of approximately $4.25 per share. The Company intends to sell this investment in the current fiscal year. Subsequent to the year end the Board of Directors approved a reduction in the price at which the shares could be purchased through the exercise of these warrants to $3.00 per share.

As at July 2, 1983, Campeau Corporation beneficially owns approximately 10.7% of the Common Shares of the Company.

b) **CAD/CAM Graphic Systems Limited**

During 1982, the Company agreed in principle with Bytec Management Corporation (Bytec) to purchase all of the shares held by Bytec in CAD/CAM Graphic Systems Limited (CAD/CAM). As at July 2, 1983, Bytec owned approximately 89% of the outstanding shares of CAD/CAM and approximately 5% of the Common Shares of the Company. The agreement in principal provides that Bytec's shares in CAD/CAM will be purchased in exchange for 30,000 Common Shares of the Company (valued at $15.00 per share) and for a release of Bytec's loan guarantee to a Canadian chartered bank in the amount of $450,000 in respect of equipment loans obtained by CAD/CAM. The shares held by Bytec in CAD/CAM were purchased within the last three years for an aggregate price of $450,000. Michael C.J. Cowpland and Glen St.John, who are directors of the Company, are directors, senior officers and major shareholders of Bytec. It is the

Company's intention to sell the shares of CAD/CAM or its underlying business immediately after completion of this transaction. Provision for related costs has been made in these financial statements.

c) **Bytec Management Corporation**

Bytec Management Corporation (Bytec) and the Company acted jointly as purchaser in the initial agreements with the Government of Canada relating to the acquisition of the shares and debt of CCI and the share of Financeco. The Company has agreed to pay to Bytec a monthly fee of $15,000 from March 1982 to February 1985 and to indemnify Bytec in respect of its obligations in relation to CCI. In turn, Bytec has released to the Company any interest it might have in the shares and debt of CCI or the share of Financeco acquired by the Company.

16. Subsequent Events

a) Effective July 3, 1983, the Company transferred the net assets of its Computer Innovations Division, aggregating $4.8 million, to a newly formed, wholly-owned subsidiary corporation, Computer Innovations Corporation, in exchange for 506,919 Class A shares of that company issued at a price of $9.41 each. Subsequent thereto, the Hudson's Bay Company invested $4 million in cash for 362,500 Class A shares of Computer Innovations Corporation at a price of $11.03 each. In addition to the initial subscription, the Company has an option to subscribe for an additional 130,581 Class A shares at $9.41 per share which the Company intends to exercise.

b) In September 1983, the Company arranged, subject to shareholder and regulatory approval, additional financing in the form of a $23 million, 12 1/2% 5-year debenture which will be convertible into common shares at $3.00 per share. The debenture will be secured by a fixed and floating charge on all the assets of the Company to the extent that such assets are not subject to prior liens.

Management believes that this financing is necessary to provide the Company with funds for working capital to support anticipated growth of its distribution business and to enable it to market successfully its integrated cable communications system, The Nabu Network.

EXHIBIT 3
NABU NETWORK CORPORATION
PROFORMA CONSOLIDATED BALANCE SHEET
November 1, 1983 (in thousands of dollars)

ASSETS

Current Assets
Cash	15,667
Accounts Receivable	269
Grants Receivable	36
Inventories	898
Prepaid Expenses	7
	16,877
Fixed Assets	4,372
Other Assets	509
	4,881
Total Assets	21,758

LIABILITIES

Current Liabilities
Trade Accounts Payable	2,785
Provision for Business Rationalization Costs	247
Current Portion of Long-Term Debt	149
	3,181
Long-Term Debt	18,477
	21,658

SHAREHOLDER'S EQUITY
Share Capital	100
Total Liabilities and Equity	21,758

Note

This proforma consolidated balance sheet reflects the issue of $18 million 15% secured convertible debentures on January 16, 1984 and partial use of the proceeds to repay the amount due to the parent company.

APPENDIX A
NABU NETWORK CORPORATION
THE SOFTWARE INDUSTRY

Software are computer programs that come in the form of floppy vinyl disks, magnetic tapes or in cartridges. Software instructs the computer to carry out the commands given to it. It tells the computer what to do and how to do it.

Industry analysts have compared the relationship of software to computers to that of what gasoline is to automobiles or what records are to stereo sets. Without software, a computer would be no more than a mass of electronic parts.

David Strutevant of the Association of Data Processing Service Organizations stated in a mid 1983 interview:

> The computer alone is as dumb as a stump. It won't even keep beer cold.

Consumers in 1983 were willing to spend heavily to get the right software. Industry experts estimated that for every $1000 consumers invested in computer hardware, they would pay out another $300 on software during the first year after they bought a machine.

From a starting point of virtually zero in 1976, sales of software for personal computers have been increasing upward. Sales revenues were $260 million in 1980, $600 million in 1981, $1 billion in 1982 and were expected to reach $1.5 billion in 1983 with upwards of $2.1 billion in 1984. Although sales were increasing at a rate of 50% a year in 1983, industry analysts expected the growth rate to continue but at a rate of 28%.

In 1983, industry analysts characterized the software industry as in the midst of a "business explosion". New companies were springing up almost every week. Big corporations were beginning to move into the market. New programs were being launched with heavy promotion and large advertising budgets. Software only specialty stores were multiplying.

Commodore International Limited announced in mid-1983 that it would be introducing 70 new software titles. This represented more than its total catalogue four years ago.

Software companies were discovering the advantages of being big. In June 1981, an Atlanta-based Software company sold out to Management Science America, a company previously concentrated on programs for mainframe computers for $5.5 million. Sales for the software company increased as a result largely due to the ability of the software to run on the IBM PC.

The Lotus Development Corporation exploited the software market with an integrated software product in 1983. The program called 1-2-3 combined several basic functions in one package. 1-2-3 was deemed the best selling business program at the time.

The Visi Corp. announced in mid-1983 that it would be introducing a new integrated product called VISION.

With so many companies pushing so many products so hard, products were piling up in stores. Dealers were running out of shelf space. Increasingly companies had to persuade dealers into believing that a product would sell. The home computer software industry could be subdivided into systems software and applications software. The systems software controlled the parts of the computer and how they interacted. The application software included programs designated for a particular purpose.

In the late 1970's when the personal computer industry was just getting started, a host of small software companies were growing up. The early applications software for personal computers was developed primarily by computer hobbyists based on their particular need or idea. Many firms were started by one or two people with one computer, a good idea and some knowledge of computer programming. Personal computers were being sold to a very small and limited market. Users had to develop the majority of their own software as the market was not strong enough to support a separate software industry.

As the market expanded beyond the electronics hobbyist to the businessman, homeowner and student, software companies were discovering they could not survive on technology alone. They then developed skills in marketing distribution and advertising. The software industry thus became packaging and marketing oriented.

Many firms in the industry were taking a marketing approach in their business activities. Microsoft, of Bellevue Washington, had sales in 1982 of $34 million. By mid-1983 the company emphasized that it was beyond the point of technology with a new focus on marketing. Microsoft was the company that developed the operating system used on the IBM PC. Bill Gates, president, stated:

> We're past the point where technology is all-important. It's the marketing, the reputations that are important now.

Visicorp, with 1982 sales of $35 million, marketed a financial forecasting program (VISICALC) for businesses, that was the most popular program ever written.

Daniel Fylstra, chairman of Visicorp, stated in 1983:

> Before, anyone with a reasonable product could make a go of it. Now you're seeing larger and larger sums directed toward marketing. Brand names are becoming more and more important.

Softsel Computer Products, based in Inglewood, just outside Los Angeles, grossed $70 million in 1983, distributing 3000 products to 1200 outlets. Softsel began business as a software distributor in 1980. Out of the more than 400 new programs written each month, fewer than eight were selected for sale.

President Robert Liff commented:

> The acceptance rate is very low. Advertising is almost critical. A very good product needs advertising out there generating the interest.

As the computer began being recognized as an essential tool in a changing society, people felt the need to develop some degree of computer literacy. Many of these people had never been exposed to computer programming and had no wish to learn. Rather, they wished to be able to use a computer to solve practical problems. In short, they wanted to be able to work with computers, without having to program them, thus emphasizing the need of predesigned software.

The market for computers in industry had also been affected. Users on the whole tended to avoid in-house programming in favour of off-the-shelf products. Of course some custom software would always be required for various aspects of industry and manufacturing. The resultant emphasis had thus changed the approach in selling computers. Rather than simply selling a computer, a firm had to see itself as selling information handling systems, which required software.

The 2 billion dollar a year computer hardware industry by mid-1983 was characterized by industry analysts as approaching a shakeout.

Texas Instruments, one of the world's largest manufacturers of silicon chips, reported a $110.8 million loss in its third quarter by mid-1983. This was largely attributed to poor hardware and software sales. After having lost $222.9 million in the first nine months of 1983, the company began pulling out of the home computer market. Significant personnel reductions were expected.

Mark Shepar, chairman, and J. Fred Bucy, president, stated:

> The first nine months of 1983 have been the most difficult period in the history of TI. We believe that with the painful but correct, decision to withdraw from the consumer home-computer business, that period has now ended.

The company would continue providing service on existing models and would continue manufacturing its more expensive personal computers aimed mainly at businesses and professionals.

Industry analysts regarded Texas Instruments' withdrawal from the home-computer market as a confirmation that a shakeout was well underway in what was termed a severely competitive industry.

> When a big player drops out like that, that's definitely a shakeout.

Atari's recent multimillion dollar loss confirmed this unsteady segment (computer hardware) of the computer industry. The market for the smallest computers, which had always been competitive, emerged into a full scale price war. Manufacturers were implementing price cuts and rebates, and were spending heavily on T.V. ads. The market was approaching saturation. The higher priced micro computers were not affected by the price cutting that occurred in the bottom portion of the market. Apple and IBM continued to sell full priced personal computers as fast as they were able to introduce them. Towards the end of 1983, IBM introduced a new home computer, the PC Jr. ($998).

Given the interdependence of computer hardware and software for consumer utility, events that occurred in one industry did have repercussions in the other.

By mid-1983, there were an estimated 5000 major microcomputer software products on the market supplied by approximately 200 firms. Manufacturers of software became the stars of the industry. Hardware manufacturers recognized that their ability to sell their computers depended on being able to provide programs to run on their machines. It seemed that, more and more, hardware manufacturers were adapting the computer to accommodate the software.

The high technology software industry was highly competitive. The presence of big companies raised the level of competition and thus made life tougher on smaller firms. This intense competition, while advancing the industry as a whole, had limited the chances of any one firm of becoming a giant software producer. While the industry was in fact booming, competitive factors had limited the average return to software firms.

The number of firms and wide array of products offered was attributed to the demand conditions and revenue potential. In addition, there were no significant barriers to entry into this industry, unlike hardware manufacturing that was capital-intensive. The personal computer software industry lured both big and small companies because of its huge profit margins. In 1983, programs that cost only $5 or $10 to make could sell at retail for $700 or more. The huge profit margins, however, did invite price cutting. This, then, could be a potential source of conflict in the event of a price war by competitors.

As the number of software titles proliferated, consumers were becoming more discriminating and demanding in their choice. Consumers were looking for programs that were more sophisticated while at the same time easier to use. Most did not have the time nor patience to try to decipher complicated instructions. To meet the complex consumer demands required intensive effort in putting together marketable programs. Furthermore, as the lifecycle of many programs tended to be very brief, it was to a software producer's advantage to complete and market a program as quickly as possible. This meant that the larger the staff, the quicker a program could be readied for marketing. Any lag that existed between the development and marketing of a program could render it obsolete. As a result, costs of development and marketing had escalated.

Towards the end of 1983, industry analysts characterized the home video games segment of the software industry as approaching a saturation point. Slow selling inventories, price discounts and huge advertising costs had all caused manufacturers' profits to decline. Industry analysts predicted that one-fourth of the video game competitors would go out of business. Although once a thriving industry, the video games market was being affected by overheated competition, an oversupply of games, and relentless price cutting, resulting in a question of survival for some companies.

By October 1984, industry analysts maintained that although the market was saturated with software, manufacturers kept on producing more and more new programs. New innovations in the market included integrated software packages and programs built into the machines themselves. Software games continued to be the best selling programs for inexpensive home computers while professional programs were favoured by owners of expensive models. Fast becoming popular for an entire range of home computers was educational software. As more school boards were buying computers for instruction, more parents were buying educational software for their children to use at home.

A problem facing the industry was that of piracy. It was estimated that for every software program sold, as many as 10 to 20 copies were made. Although it was illegal, it was also very difficult to control. Software, being intangible, could not be patented. Packaged software being sold to customers could not be protected by the law of trade secrets. Software does, however, have protection under the copyright act. Enforcement of existing provisions of the act not only required interpretation by its very wording; applying the law proved to be even more difficult. One solution that was being developed was by the Vault Corporation. They were developing a "fingerprinting" of floppy disks which would prevent their use when copied to blanks without the "print" on them. If this were successful it would decrease the losses due to piracy.

The computer industry in Canada, from a Canadian perspective, considered both hardware and software to be "high technology." The Ottawa area's high technology manufacturing industry consisted of a variety of companies, both home grown and international, that produced a diverse array of products.

Members of the high technology industry of the Ottawa Valley had recognized that if they did not develop financial and management strengths, they would not succeed at marketing their high technology products successfully. In 1984, many companies that had boasted of doubled or tripled annual growth saw flat sales, sharply reduced profits and in some cases, heavy losses.

Although there were many newcomers to the industry, it was getting tougher and tougher to break into the highly competitive markets for microelectronics, telecommunications and computer software products.

Key industry players in the Ottawa Valley high-tech industry by March 1984 included:

- (Kanata's) Mitel Corp.
- (Manotick's) Gandalf Technologies Inc.
- (Ottawa's) Systemhouse Ltd.
- (Ottawa's) Oratech.
- Domus Software.

Mitel Corporation, a telecommunications company, emerged in 1984 from what was the worst two years of its corporate history. Mitel's drive for leadership in the development of its (SX2000) telephone switching equipment was marked with delays, bugs and cost overruns considered typical of product-development projects. These delays caused the company to lose its market initiative. The SX2000 faced stiff competition in the market place and the company had yet to establish the high-powered sales organization needed to sell it.

Company officials conceded that Mitel could see an overall loss for the fiscal year ending February, 1984. This reported loss, the first in the company's history, would be attributed largely to over-expansion and heavy research and development expenditures.

Although sales exceeded $335 million in the year end fiscal 1984, losses of $8 million were attributed to the first half of the year. The corporation's announced layoffs of 346 production workers were an attempt to implement cost cutting measures.

Gandalf, a manufacturer of modems, reported flat sales and earnings in 1984. Its earnings were being penalized by its investments in research and development and sales development expenses. The company's data communications products were competing in a highly competitive segment of the market.

Systemhouse, Canada's largest software producer and consulting firm, reported losses of $29.5 million in fiscal 1982 and losses of $28.7 million in fiscal 1983. Systemhouse's continued failure to meet its profitability projections had been a major disappointment to investors. Attempts to cut expenses could show up in the profitability figures but a return to its previous growth rate would be much more difficult to achieve. Systemhouse would thus remain essentially a very large, very experienced, customer software house.

Oratech, a designer and manufacturer of equipment for computer aided design, manufacturing and engineering, reported, in 1984, the development of a new product termed CAD-CAM (computer assisted design and manufacturing). This new product was to be developed (in marketable form) at a cost of $8 million. The product development would be in response to unprecedented growth in the CAD-CAM market. The years 1984 and 1985 would thus be deemed development years and were expected to entail all the potential risks of cost overruns, delays, bugs and personnel problems. Such obstacles were considered to be strongly associated with companies entering growth markets.

Problems for Oratech did in fact arise in the following months. In July 1984, Oratech laid off at least 36 of its remaining 65 employees as part of a corporate shake-up that saw the resignation of two of the company's founders. By October 1984, a new repayment plan to its suppliers was being arranged in light of the company's announcement of its inability to meet its then current payments.

Domus Software was established in 1983 by former NABU employees. Originally it was an independent consulting firm under the name "Mobius Software," which in 1981 became part of NABU Manufacturing Ltd. Richard Moxley and two other NABU employees bought the consulting business back from NABU and formed Domus on April 1, 1983.

Domus provided data processing consultation and computer system development services and was involved in microcomputer educational services and computer software products. In its first fiscal year, ending Jan. 29, 1984, revenues of $1.25 million were expected. Consulting accounted for about 80 percent of the company's revenues. The remaining effort was directed towards the expansion of software development and educational areas outside the Ottawa market.

While under NABU ownership, the former Mobius business doubled in size to incorporate product development as well as consulting, working on software for the NABU NETWORK cable television software delivery systems and the NABU 1600 personal computer.

When NABU decided to concentrate its efforts on the cable network and the microcomputer distribution business, the consulting side of Mobius was sold. NABU would then become a client of Domus.

Richard Moxley commented on the relationship between NABU and Domus:

> Of all the changes that have been made at NABU, our split was probably the smoothest and most beneficial to both sides.

Figures from the Department of External Affairs and Statistics Canada indicated annual exports from the high-tech sector were in the $1 billion range by October 1983. The leading export of high technology was in telecommunications. Exports were characterized as being the backbone of the high technology business. High technology exports included computers, telecommunications devices and other microelectronic parts.

Imports of high technology were making inroads into the North American market. In mid-1983, Japan announced a technological agreement that would result in interchangeable game cartridges and programs for their home computers. Microsoft developed the standardized hardware and software system for personal computers. The system would permit programs developed for one computer to run on all others using the same standard. If this computer becomes successful, a substantial market for Japanese software could develop. The owners of such computers would have a much larger selection of software to choose from and force greater price competition.

CASE 10

THE UNIVERSITY AND THE FACULTY ASSOCIATION

J. Amernic
University of Toronto
Toronto, Ontario

A BREAKDOWN IN NEGOTIATIONS

By early January 1981, it had become apparent that the annual salary and benefits negotiations between the bargaining teams representing the University's Administration on one hand, and its Faculty Association on the other, were deadlocked, and that a mediator would be required. This was to be the third time in four years that intervention by a third party was necessary, and reflected the frustrations of the entire university community in the face of declining resources. Although most individuals in both the Faculty Association and the Administration sincerely wanted their collective bargaining to be successful and result in negotiated agreements, both the economic environment and some lingering resentments made bargaining very aggressive.

Jill Allen sat in the Faculty Association's offices at the end of the first week of the New Year, reviewing the progress of the negotiations to date and beginning to work on a **Brief** to the mediator. Since the Faculty Association was not a certified union, the annual negotiations between the two sides took place outside of the Labour Relations Act and operated under a **Memorandum** to which they had agreed some years before. The **Memorandum** provided that a mediator was to be appointed if the negotiating parties were unable to reach an agreement by themselves, and provided further that, if the mediator was then unable to assist them in coming to an agreement, he or she would become an arbitrator who would impose an agreement on the two sides. However, a clause in the **Memorandum** also provided that although the arbitrator's award was **binding** upon the Faculty Association, it could be **overturned** by a majority vote of the University's governing body (i.e., this was true arbitration for the Faculty Association, but not for the University).

© John Wiley & Sons Canada Ltd. All rights reserved.

Jill's accounting firm had been asked the day before by the Faculty Association's bargaining team to help prepare sections of the **Brief**. Since she was both an accountant and a part-time member of faculty, she had followed the negotiations carefully in both the University and Faculty Association press, from their inception in November 1980. The information available to Jill is outlined in the remainder of the case.

THE UNIVERSITY AND THE NEGOTIATING FRAMEWORK

The University is a large and complex organization, with an operating budget at the time of this case of about $300 million. The discussion of its financial affairs in the correspondence in Exhibits 1 and 2 gives some idea of the scope of the institution, and the resulting necessity for the central administration to balance the myriad interests of different schools, departments and faculties, students, faculty members, other employees, etc. The major source of operating funds for the University was provincial government "formula grants", which were based upon the number of students. Thus enrolment projection was a crucial activity.

The negotiations described in this case took place between mid-November 1980, and mid-February 1981, and were in respect to the academic year running from July 1, 1981, to June 30, 1982. The framework within which negotiations took place at the University had evolved from being virtually non-existent in 1973-74, to a more formal contractual arrangement by 1977-78, the first year that the **Memorandum of Agreement** was in effect. In the decade preceding the current negotiations, what the Faculty Association had perceived as "arbitrary paternalism" had been replaced by a more or less meaningful collective bargaining relationship. It might justifiably be said that "union-management" negotiations at the university were evolving away from a "paternalistic-collegial" pattern toward a more "industrial-adversarial" pattern. The shifting to a more traditional union-management relationship had not resulted in smooth agreements, since mediator/arbitrator reports were required both in 1978-79 and 1977-78, the first two years in which the **Memorandum** was in effect.

The relationship between the parties over the past decade had been exacerbated by the sustained underfunding of the university. Since the university was a public institution, it depended for virtually its entire financial resources on government grants, and they had been significantly below the inflation rate for several years. This underfunding had manifested itself in an erosion of faculty salaries over the decade both in absolute terms and also in comparison with other reference groups (see Exhibit 3). Thus a pressure for "catch-up" salary adjustments was created, which became more intense within the Faculty Association as the decade wore on, as the index of the "real" value of salaries went from 98.5 to 85.0.[1]

THE 1980-81 NEGOTIATIONS: A CHRONOLOGY

From local press clippings, minutes of bargaining sessions kept by the Faculty Association secretary, and a long meeting with the head of the Association's bargaining team, Jill developed a chronology of the negotiations. Prior to the commencement of actual face-to-face negotiations the Faculty Association had conducted an intensive review of the erosion of the faculty's economic position over the past decade. Out of these meetings came a list of "demands" — both monetary and non-monetary — which the bargaining team intended to present to the university when bargaining commenced.

Meeting No. 1 dealt with preliminary items, such as introductions and requests for information, most of which came from the Association. (See Exhibit 4.) On balance, one could characterize the response as being what one would expect in a negotiating environment characterized by a somewhat adversarial background — some of the information was helpful but some was not, and some was withheld. Furthermore, the turn-around time was fairly lengthy, especially for the request related to more information and clarification with respect to the university's annual report. Meetings 2 and 3 were exchanges of position by the two parties to allow for examination of differences and similarities forming a basis for negotiations.

At the fourth meeting, the Faculty Association was presented with the university administration's costing of the Association's proposal of eleven days previous. The discussion of this costing carried over to Meeting No. 5. (The administration's costing is shown in Exhibit 5.)

The sixth meeting took place in the New Year, and the University Administration's bargaining team presented its initial offer as follows:

a) an agreement to maintain the existing Dental Plan on the 1977 Fee Schedule;

b) an agreement to base pensions on the best 4 years (48 months rather than the best 5 years (60 months);

c) an increase of the Overload Teaching Stipend to $5,000;

d) the inclusion of Contractually Limited Term Appointees in the career salary progression scheme;

e) the offering of an across-the-board increase of 6.6%.

The "improvement" to the Pension Plan was estimated to cost 0.6% of the salary base. Half of that cost would be covered by an increase of 0.3% in contributions by Plan members; the other 0.3% would take the form of a trade-off against salary gains. The total package was estimated by the administration to cost 10.3% of salary base. It is important to note that this figure (10.3%) includes the 2.8% (itself a gross, not net figure) average merit increase. As the administration itself has sometimes recognized, merit incurs, in the long run, no cost to the University and it does not represent an increase in salary floors, but simply reflects the normal progress of faculty members through the ranks. It is worth noting that the administration consistently included the merit component in its assessment of the value of the "package" it proposed.

During the following five meetings debate continued on the appropriate costing of items, and the Faculty Association dropped its demand for full restoration of 1971 purchasing power. The administration began to allude more frequently to its "inability to pay". Unfortunately, the two sides could not reach agreement, and arrangements were made to summon the mediator.

MEDIATION AND THE "ABILITY TO PAY"

Early in the mediation phase, the mediator announced that insofar as faculty salaries had in his opinion indeed been eroded seriously over the previous decade, he was persuaded that the Faculty Association's wage demand was just. The focus of the mediation then shifted dramatically. Because of the specific nature of the mediation (it was true mediation for the university, but arbitration for the Faculty Association), the mediator felt bound to make the university's "ability to pay" a most important criterion, both during mediation and ultimately in writing his report. He adopted this perspective because of his view that had "ability to pay" been disregarded, the governing body of the university would quite probably vote to reject his award, and, consequently, the **Memorandum** which governed the collective bargaining relationship between the parties would have been significantly weakened. With the failure of mediation in late January, the mediator/arbitrator was required to write a **Report** binding upon both parties unless overturned by the University's governing body.

Background material on "ability to pay" had been collected by a member of the Association bargaining team for Jill's use, and his draft of a portion of the **Brief** to the mediator dealing with ability to pay is in Exhibit 7. Selected portions of the University's budget for the year ended April 30, 1981, are provided in Exhibit 8. The final report position of the Faculty Association immediately before arbitration is set out in Exhibit 6.

CASE REQUIREMENT

As Jill Allen, prepare a brief for the mediator in respect to the faculty and the university positions. Specific emphasis should be placed on the financial implications of each position and on interpretation of the financial records of the university.

EXHIBIT 1

CONTENTS OF FACULTY ASSOCIATION LETTER DATED OCTOBER 1980 TO UNIVERSITY ADMINISTRATION REQUESTING CLARIFICATION OF CERTAIN ITEMS IN THE UNIVERSITY ANNUAL REPORT

Thank you for sending copies of the Financial Statements of the University for the year ending April 30, 1980 and also for the Budget for the year 1980-81.

Members of the Association's Negotiating Team have examined these documents together with the 1979-80 Budget with considerable interest, and we are pleased to note that the administration agrees with our position that the "level of staff salaries" has been jeopardized (Fiscal 1980 Financial Statements, p.2).

We would be pleased if under the provisions of Article II of the **Memorandum of Agreement** you could provide answers to the following questions:

1. The actual financial statements for the year ended April 30, 1980 (Statement A-2) indicate that "Operating results before commitments and transfers" is $3,494,000, while the 1979-80 Budget (published July 1979) anticipated operating results of $625,000. May we have a detailed reconciliation between these numbers?

2. In Statement A-2 concerning "Commitments and Transfers," may we have the following information:

(a) An analysis of the opening and closing balances of $4,969 and $6,049 for "Carry forward of divisional appropriations" (Statement A-3), giving details of the individual amounts making up these balances and indicating to what divisions (and major units of these divisions) these carry-forwards apply.

(b) An explanation of why the "Net carry forward of appropriations to be expended in the following year" (which totals $2,130,000 and is the difference between actual expenditures during the year and total funds committed for specific purposes during the year) is debited to the operating statement.

(c) An explanation of the rationale used to derive the other transfers from (to) B-2, C-3, and D-2.

3. May we have a detailed reconciliation between the July 1979 Budget figure for the Ancillary Enterprise Fund's "Net income before operating funds recovery," and the $896,000 actual figure in the 1980 financial statements (Statement B-2)?

4. Reference: Page 30 (Note 1(h)) — May we have the rationale for charging "the acquisition cost of all equipment. . ." to Statement A-22?

5. Reference: Page 30 (Note 1(h)) — May we have the rationale for charging base stock replacements to Statement B-2?

6. Reference: Pages 31/32 (Note 1(h)) — May we know the difference in Statement A-2 charges between the charge under the method currently used to account for some computer mainframes, and the charge had the rentals been expensed as incurred?

What would have been the effect on Statements A-1 and A-2 had the new capitalization policy been applied to all such assets, whether purchased or leased?

What is the rationale for the new policy?

7. Reference: Page 29 (Note (f)) — The note states that, while staff members must make contributions to the pension plan at a fixed rate, "the balance of the cost must be met by the University." Is it not true that the bulk of the balance is generated by earnings on the assets of the fund?

The note states that the University has followed the practice of making payments in excess of the minimum legal funding requirements "when funds are available." What are the criteria which are used to determine "availability?" What was the amount of the excess for fiscal 1980, and what is the amount projected for fiscal 1981?

8. Reference: Page 28 (Note 1(a)) — May we have a detailed listing of the "quasi-endowed funds" (including principal and revenue therefrom, the date of designation and purpose)?

What criteria does the Governing Council employ to designate certain funds as "endowed"? What criteria are employed to decide on the spending of such funds? Under what conditions may these funds be recategorized?

9. Reference: Page 28 (Note 1(c)) — The note states that the "University follows the accrual basis of accounting by recording. . . expenses when materials are used or

services rendered." How is this policy applied in the case of the items on Statement A-3?

10. Reference: Page 27 (Note 1(a)) — What is the basis of allocating indirect costs against the specific enterprises listed in the 1980 fiscal Budget?

11. Reference: Page 29 (Note 1(d)) — What were the gains/losses on disposal of investments for fiscal 1979 and 1980?

    What is the rationale for the accounting policy adopted for investments? Why are not gains/losses on investments recorded in Statement A-2 (with transfers, where applicable)?

12. Reference: Page 8 — May we know how the restoration of the Sandford Fleming Building is being recorded? How are the insurance claims being accounted for?

13. Reference: Page 14 — What are the criteria that must be fulfilled before "Unearned income. . ." ($1,251,000) is recorded in Statement A-2?

14. Reference: Page 17 — Why have "Investments held for capital purposes" ($1,649,000) been reclassified?

15. Reference: Page 33 — Why are outstanding Update pledges not recorded in Statement A-2?

    May we have a detailed schedule indicating which "comparative figures for 1979 have been regrouped?"

16. May we have schedules detailing the flow of funds (as working capital) for both fiscal 1979 and 1980?

17. In the light of the increased interest in financial reporting of non-profit organizations (as evidenced in Canada by the recent publication of the CICA Research Study entitled, **Financial Reporting for Non-profit Organizations** – 1980), and in order to aid us in our understanding of the University, could we have a statement which sets out the objectives of the University's financial reports?

With thanks,

Yours sincerely,

EXHIBIT 2

UNIVERSITY ADMINISTRATION'S RESPONSE DATED JANUARY 1981 TO FACULTY ASSOCIATION REQUEST FOR CLARIFICATION IN EXHIBIT 4

This letter constitutes our response to your October 27, 1980 letter requesting certain information concerning the University's Financial Statements for the year ended April 30, 1980 and the Budget for the year 1980-81. We will use the same references as in your letter.

This response is submitted in the context that the overall responsibility and accountability for the activities of the University rest with the Governing Council, which establishes policies, and with the President, who manages the affairs of the University within these policies.

Following is our response to your specific questions:

1. **Comparison of Actual Results Before Commitments and Transfers vs. Original Budget**

I have enclosed a schedule (Exhibit 1) comparing the original budget vs. actual and identifying the variances in income and expense.

2. **Commitments and Transfers**

The divisional carry-forward balances and other commitments are set out on Statement A-3 of the Financial Statements. These carry-forward balances are in accordance with policy established by the Governing Council applied on a consistent basis from year to year and confirmed by the auditors.

Net Carry-Forward of Appropriations to be Expended in the Following Year

The actual expenses in respect of these appropriations are recorded as such in Statement A-2. As such expenses are incurred, the appropriation in respect thereof is withdrawn from the reserve and transferred back to Statement A-2 as a credit to appropriations. These credits are offset by appropriations in the current year, resulting in a net increase or decrease, in commitment for the year.

Other Transfers

The transfers to other funds set out on Statement A-2 are similarly in accordance with Governing Council policy, or have been approved specifically by Governing Council.

The transfers between the Current Operating Fund and the Ancillary Enterprises Fund represent the return to Current Operating Funds of a return on its investments in UTLAS.

The transfers to Capital Funds represent the authorized use of Current Operating Funds to partially fund approved capital projects and energy projects. The funds used to fund the energy projects came from utility underspending in the 1979-80 fiscal year, which has been approved under administrative authority for expenditures on energy savings capital projects, having a fast payback period.

The transfer from restricted funds represents a combination of the refund received from Canada Life re: favourable experience for the 1978-79 fiscal year, and the amount required to cover the refunds to U of T staff with respect to the rebates received from Canada Life for the 1977-78 and 1978-79 fiscal years.

3. Statement B-2 — Ancillary Enterprises

The $388,000 variance represents mainly deferred spending on items such as major maintenance and equipment replacement, which funds are appropriated at year end as funds committed for the specific purposes for which they were budgeted. You will note on Statement B-2, a net carry-forward of such appropriations of $343,000.

4. The Acquisition Cost of all Equipment

The generally accepted accounting principle of fund accounting is that acquisition costs of equipment are expensed as a direct charge against the operating fund in the period in which expenditures are incurred.

5. Base Stock Replacements — Ancillary Enterprises

The original cost of equipping a new facility and additions to original complement are not expenses at the time of purchase, but are capitalized on the balance sheet. Subsequent replacements are expensed so that the original complement is maintained as a balance sheet asset at all times (see note 1(h) in the 1979 U of T Financial Statements). This is a generally accepted accounting treatment for such purchases.

6. Computer Mainframes

If the University had expensed the rental payments in respect to computer mainframes, the effect on Statement A-2 would have been an additional expense of $220,000.

No estimate has been made of the impact on Statements A-1 and A-2 if this policy had been applied to all "such assets." By all "such assets" it is assumed that this refers to assets acquired by UTCS only. No significant effect would have resulted, since 1978-79 was the only year capital leases were entered into.

The rationale behind this new policy was to avoid big fluctuation in computer hardware costs from one year to another. By capitalizing the computer leases, the cost is amortized evenly over a number of years. The application of this policy applies to capital leases only, not operating leases, and is consistent with a recent CICA ruling re: capital leases.

7. Note 1(f) — Pension Plan, Page 29

The sources of funding for the pension plan are, as you note, staff member contributions, University contributions and earnings of the fund. Exhibit 3 attached, sets out the contributions of staff and the University for the past four years for Plan P3880. At the present time, for the year under review, the earnings of the fund approximate these contributions to the fund although, historically, they represent only about two-thirds of contributions.

"Availability" of excess funds is determined, under Governing Council authority, by Senior Management as the end of the fiscal year approaches, based upon a forecast of year-end results in terms of our budgeted funds available for allocation.

Actual University payments, in respect of both current and past service liability for the past four years for Plan P3880, are set out in Exhibit 3. The combined budgeted amounts for 1980-81 for Plan P3880 plus Plan P2614 and Teachers' Superannuation Plan are $9,830,524 for current service and $530,977 for past service.

8. Note 1(a) — Restricted Funds, Page 28

The "quasi-endowing" of funds by Governing Council decision has taken place over many years, and except for a few large funds such as the Connaught Fund, no accumulated record has been kept of such funds. As the quasi-endowing of funds is considered permanent, there is no practical distinction made from pure endowments.

Specific Governing Council Policies re: Expenditures of "Quasi-Endowed" Funds

By the process of "quasi-endowing" by Governing Council, the principal of such funds must be maintained intact, and only the income from the investment of such funds may be expensed for the specific purposes identified by Governing Council. The decision to quasi-endow is based upon the immediate need for expendable funds in relation to an on-going requirement which can be met by income on quasi-endowments.

9. Note 1(c) — Accrual Accounting, Page 28

Statement A-3 represents commitments only, i.e. in the case of purchase orders, commitments have been made with the supplier, but the material or services have not been received or supplied. Therefore, these commitments are recorded as an allocation of unallocated fund balances, the actual expense is recorded in the accounting period in which the goods or services are received and the related appropriation restored to its unallocated fund balance in the same accounting period.

10. Note 1(a) — Ancillary Enterprises Funds, Page 27

Under the Governing Council policy applicable to ancillary enterprises, such are to be costed on a "total cost" basis, which includes indirect, as well as, direct costs.

Indirect costs are allocated to ancillary enterprises using the most appropriate basis for the particular type of indirect expense, as determined by management.

11. Note 1(d) — Investments, page 29

Gains and losses on disposals on these investments for the fiscal years 1979–80 are not immediately available.

12. Sandford Fleming Building, Page 8

The restoration of the Sandford Fleming Building is being recorded as a capital project in the Capital Funds section of the Financial Statements.

Operating costs and extra expenses recoverable from insurance are set up as an asset, as incurred, and for balance sheet purposes, are offset by interim advances received from the underwriters in respect of such claims.

13. Unearned Income

Unearned income is income received in advance for which services are to be supplied in future accounting periods. Such unearned income is taken into income as services are provided, as set out in note 1(c).

Accounts Payable and Accrued Charges

The increase in accounts payable and accrued charges in 1980 over 1979 is made up of a large number of small items, none of which reflects any new conditions and all of which are confirmed by our auditors.

14. Investments Held for Capital Purposes

The investments held for capital purposes shown on Statement B-1, ancillary enterprises fund balance sheet, were not reclassified, but rather the wording was changed from "investments held for building programme purposes" to "investments held for capital purposes." The reason for this change is to more correctly identify the specific purposes i.e. residences and parking facilities.

15. Update Pledges

The guide to accounting principles, practices and standards of disclosure for colleges and universities of Ontario, recommends that pledges should be disclosed by means of a note to Financial Statements. This treatment is consistent with this guide.

Comparative Figures for 1979

The attached Exhibit 2 gives a breakdown of the changes we have made to the 1979 comparative figures.

16. Flow of Funds

We do not prepare a flow of funds (as working capital) statement as it is not considered too relevant for fund accounting (e.g. all items in the Current Operating Fund are of a working capital nature).

17. Objectives of the University's Financial Reports

Although we have not specifically addressed the Objectives of our Financial Statements in the context you mention, the main objective is as set out in the last paragraph of the Auditors' Report, and the Financial Highlights section has been included with a view to aiding comprehension.

We hope that this helps in your understanding of the 1979-80 Financial Statements.

Yours sincerely,

Enclosures

EXHIBIT 3
THE UNIVERSITY AND THE FACULTY ASSOCIATION
SALARY EROSION

Year July	CPI* July Figure	Economic Increase(%) Salary Only	Including Benefits	Cumulative Economic Increase Salary Only	Including Benefits	Cumulative Value of Increase in "Real" Terms Salary Only	Including Benefits
1971	100.5	0.0	0.0	0.0	0.0	0.0	0.0
1972	105.1	3.0	3.0	103.0	103.0	98.5	98.5
1973	113.2	3.5	3.5	106.6	106.6	94.6	94.6
1974	125.9	7.0	8.08	114.1	115.2	91.1	92.0
1975	139.8	11.9	11.9	127.6	128.9	91.7	92.7
1976	149.3	7.75	8.8	137.5	140.3	92.6	94.4
1977	161.8	6.2	6.2	146.1	148.9	90.7	92.5
1978	177.7	3.75	4.58	151.5	155.8	85.7	88.1
1979	192.1	5.4	5.7	159.7	164.7	83.5	86.2
1980	211.5	8.0	8.65	172.5	178.9	82.0	85.0

*Statistics Canada

EXHIBIT 4
THE UNIVERSITY AND THE FACULTY ASSOCIATION
REQUESTS FOR INFORMATION OUTSTANDING
WHEN NEGOTIATIONS COMMENCED

Date	Request
Oct. 24, 1980	1. Extension of certain benefits to pensioners; request for clarification of university's position that the Faculty Association did not represent pensioners.
Oct. 24, 1980	2. Request for report on performance of pension fund.
Oct. 27, 1980	3. Request for clarification of several items (17 in ll) in the university's budget and the 1979-80 inancial statements.
	University Response
Nov. 20, 1980	1. Faculty Association has no right to represent pensioners; list of improvements to pensioners' benefits.
Jan. 8, 1981	2. Letter denying request ("While the University is prepared to make available the findings of the Report, it feels it is not appropriate to provide you with a copy of the Report itself. The Report is a sophisticated analytical device. . .")
Jan. 6, 1981	3. Point-by-point response, but some information quite vague or "unavailable". Also, some hard to understand, such as the university's assertion that it did not include a statement of changes in financial position in its annual report because it is "not considered too relevant".

UNIVERSITY BUDGET
For the Year Ending April 30, 1980
WITH ACTUAL COMPARATIVE FIGURES FOR 1980
(in thousands of dollars)

	Actual	Budget	Variance Favourable/ Unfavourable
Income			
Provincial Grants—Formula	170,594	169,575	1,019
Non-Formula	899	725	174
Interest on Capital Debentures	11,027	11,027	-0-
Municipal Taxes	1,592	1,592	-0-
Student Fees	33,393	32,651	742
Endowed Income, Gifts and Non-Government Grants	1,033	960	73
Interest Income	4,817	3,532	1,285
Revenue From Services	8,428	6,449	1,979
Restricted Funds—Assisted Research and Other	54,878	53,000	1,878
Total Income	286,661	279,511	7,150
Expenses			
Academic	149,237	148,085	(1,152)
Academic Services	16,051	16,018	(33)
Student Services	5,081	4,835	(246)
Operation and Maintenance of Physical Plant	27,478	28,232	754
Payment Against Unfunded Pension Liability	1,991	2,058	67
Administration	14,887	14,666	(221)
General University	945	622	(323)
Interest on Capital Debentures	11,027	11,027	-0-
Municipal Taxes	1,592	1,592	-0-
Assisted Research and Other	54,878	53,000	(1,878)
Total Expenses	283,167	280,135	(3,032)
Operating Results Before Commitments and Transfers	3,494	(624)	4,118
Estimated Underspending and Income Variance	-0-	500	(500)
Transfer From Ancillary Enterprises Fund	153	261	(108)
Net Carry Forward of Appropriations to be Expended in the Following Year	(2,129)	-0-	(2,129)
Transfer to Capital Fund	(754)	-0-	(754)
Transfer From Restricted Funds	170	-0-	170
Net Income	934	137	797

© John Wiley & Sons Canada Ltd. All rights reserved.

THE UNIVERSITY AND THE FACULTY ASSOCIATION
CONTRIBUTIONS TO UNIVERSITY PENSION PLAN

Year	Staff Current Service Amount	%	University Current Service Amount	%	University Past Service Amount	%	Total Amount	%
1976-77	4,089,432	28.4	8,522,365	59.4	1,747,074	12.2	14,358,871	100
1977-78	4,530,455	28.1	9,705,137	60.2	1,895,294	11.7	16,130,886	100
1978-79	4,803,955	29.7	9,608,815	59.4	1,763,000	10.9	16,175,770	100
1979-80	5,077,133	29.2	10,367,089	59.6	1,951,181	11.2	17,395,403	100
	18,500,975	28.9	38,203,406	59.6	7,356,549	11.5	64,060,930	100

THE UNIVERSITY AND THE FACULTY ASSOCIATION
UNIVERSITY COMPARATIVE FIGURES FOR 1979 AS RESTATED
(In Thousands of Dollars)

	1979	1979 Restated	Increase/ (Decrease)
Expense (A-2)			
Academic	141,616	141,667	51
Operation & Maintenance of Physical Plant	25,608	26,112	504
Administration	13,245	13,249	4
General University	1,738	1,179	(559)
	182,207	182,207	-0-

i) Salary anomalies adjustment transferred from General University to Academic Expense.

ii) Fire and boiler insurance transferred from General University to Physical Plant expense.

iii) Room rentals transferred from General University to Administration expense.

(A-2) Balance sheet figures are not restated. The 1979 figure for "due from capital funds" (an asset) has been transferred to the liability side for comparative purposes (as a reduction of liabilities) in order to be grouped with the 1980 figures "due to capital funds."

EXHIBIT 5
THE UNIVERSITY AND THE FACULTY ASSOCIATION
ADMINISTRATION'S COSTING OF FACULTY ASSOCIATION DEMANDS

Demand	Administration's Costing at Existing Salary ($000)	%
1. (i) Restore 1971 Purchasing Power as of May 1, 1981.	32,730	32.13
(ii) Salary Increases Effective May 1 Rather than July 1, in Line with University's Fiscal Year.	5,555	5.47
2. (i) Pensions Payable Based Upon Best 3 yrs. Salary, Rather than Best 5 yrs.	1,264	1.24
(ii) Inflation–Proof Pensions.	13,612	13.39
(iii) Elimination of Pension Age Breakpoint.	759	0.75
(iv) Increase Interest Rate on Pension Amounts Due to Terminating Members.	328	0.32
(v) Other Minor Pension Items.	490	0.48

Administration's Assumptions: Details of calculations not disclosed. Each figure consisted of two parts unfunded liability plus additional current service cost. The amounts were provided to the Administration by its actuary.

3. Employer to pay entire cost of Hospital Insurance Plan.	582	0.78

Administration's Assumptions: 100% of faculty would now elect this coverage.

4. Survivor Income Benefits made Inflation-Proof.	97	0.08
5. Improvements in Long-Term Disability Insurance and Employer Pays Entire Premium.	347	0.35
6. Dental Plan Continuation and Improvements	374	0.43
7. Extended Health Care Plan Improvements	21	0.02
8. Family of Faculty to be Admitted to University Athletic Facilities	640	0.46
9. Improvement in Faculty Educational Assistance Plan	41	0.04
10. Research Leave at 100% of Salary, Less 50% of any Outside Support	6,031	5.93

Administration's Assumptions: 100% of faculty will take research leave every 7th year.

11. Minimum Overload Teaching Stipend Increased to $6,000 Per Course	828	0.80
12. Other Minor Items	61	0.05
Total Estimated Cost	**66,102**	**65.23**

This Exhibit is based upon some details provided by the Administration in written form plus interchange during negotiations.

EXHIBIT 6
THE UNIVERSITY AND FACULTY ASSOCIATION
FACULTY ASSOCIATION FINAL POSITION
February 2, 1981

1. That salary scales be adjusted upward by 11.4%.
2. (viii) That pensions payable be based upon the best 60 months' service rather than the best 5 years of service.
   That a committee be established to develop an agreed multi-year program of change in the Pension Plan.
3. Withdrawn.
4. Survivor Income Benefit be indexed to a maximum of 7% (.08).
5. The Long Term Disability Benefit be indexed to a maximum of 7% (.07). The Benefit payable be raised from 70% to 75% (.03).
6. The Dental Plan be continued on the 1980 fee guide (.2).
7. That Extended Health Care, Semi-Private and Dental Plans be modified to allow for the inclusion of:
   i) dependent, unmarried children from age 21 to age 25 provided that such a child attends an accredited school, college or university full-time;
   ii) dependent, unmarried children above age 21 who are physically or mentally incapable of self-support and who became incapable before reaching the age of 21 (.02).
8. That the joint membership plan be modified to permit family access to the University Athletic Facility.
9. Withdrawn.
10. Withdrawn.
11. Withdrawn.
12. Withdrawn.
13. That the career advancement scheme for librarians be modified so that the merit component for librarians above the breakpoint be increased from $315 to $423 (1980 $'s) (.01).
14. That the rank ceilings for Lecturer, Assistant and Associate Professor for Librarians II, III and IV and for Tutors and Senior Tutors, be abolished (.01).
15. That all members of the academic staff on contractually-limited term appointments be included in the PTR scheme (.05).
16. Resolved.
17. Withdrawn.
18. Withdrawn.
19. Resolved.
20. That the Association's right to represent retired faculty members and librarians be recognized by the University's administration.

© John Wiley & Sons Canada Ltd. All rights reserved.

EXHIBIT 7
THE UNIVERSITY AND THE FACULTY ASSOCIATION
DRAFT — THE UNIVERSITY'S ABILITY TO PAY

Introduction

While as a matter of principle the Association rejects the notion that "ability to pay" is the sole criterion for determining salary increases, it recognizes that it must address the issue in its submission. In so doing, the Association stresses the information disadvantages it faces in attempting to get a clear picture of the University's financial position. Details of this information disadvantage will be provided throughout this section of the Association's submission. Briefly, however, this disadvantage is caused by two major factors:

(i) the inappropriateness of the University's financial statements and budgets for gaining insight into the University's ability to pay, and

(ii) the Administration's unwillingness and/or inability to provide certain specific information to the Association for the purpose of negotiation.

This section is organized into three main parts: Part I comments on the inappropriateness of the University's financial statements and budget for providing insight into the University's ability to pay. Part II provides evidence concerning the University's ability to pay and Part III summarizes certain requests for information by the Association. It should be kept in mind that our attempt to assess ability to pay was hampered considerably by the deficiencies discussed in Part I (below) and by the University's unwillingness to provide certain key information (Part III).

Part I — Deficiencies in University Accounting

The University's financial statements are intended to report on the stewardship of the Administration and consequently the accounting principles used to prepare them result in statements which do not provide a fair presentation of the resources available to the University. Since the Administration apparently bases its "ability to pay" decision to a great degree upon its budgets which are prepared using the same procedures of accounting as the financial statements, the Association had serious reservations about the Administration's assessment of "ability to pay".

Accounting as a means of portraying the essential characteristics of an organization has come under increasing criticism in recent years — although the bulk of this criticism has been directed toward the financial statements of profit-seeking enterprises (for example, the lack of success in dealing with inflation in financial statements), as much could be said about the lack of adequacy of statements in non-profit organizations, including universities. Indeed, so deficient is the adequacy of financial reporting by non-profit organizations that the Canadian Institute of Chartered Accountants' Accounting Research Committee initiated a major research project in this area "because the absence of appropriate reporting principles and standards for non-profit organizations is resulting in increasing confusion and misunderstanding among the users of financial information provided by these organizations."[2] Of course, our particular concern is not with the University's financial reporting in general, but with the use of its financial statements and budgets to help us assess its "ability to pay".

Some Shortcomings of the University's Financial Statements and Budget for Estimating "Ability to Pay" (List is not inclusive)

1. The financial statements are based upon historical data. While this may be appropriate for stewardship reporting, we are interested in information on resources for the **future** period under negotiation (i.e. 1981-82). The budget for the year ended April 30, 1981 can be criticized on this score, also, since the period for which negotiations are being held runs from July 1, 1981. Of course, some information from these past records could conceivably be used to help forecast the future.

2. The statements do not contain a Statement of Changes in Financial Position (SCFP). The purpose of this statement, which is a required statement under companies' legislation, is to show changes in the working capital position of the organization and the major financing and investing activities of the organization.

3. The Current Operating Fund in 1980 has been charged with unspent divisional appropriations of $1,368,000 and purchase order commitments for goods and services not yet received of $732,000. This practice of charging the current year's operations with next year's expenditures significantly reduces 1980 operating results of $3,494,000 and is mainly responsible for the continuation of the Current Operating Fund "deficit" which stood at $1,414,000 at April 30, 1980. While this method of accounting might be appropriate for purposes of controlling and monitoring operations, it is inappropriate for reporting the result of operations.

4. Consolidated financial statements are not presented.

Other shortcomings could be cited (e.g. recording depreciation on capital equipment, not recording pledges outstanding at least as assets, etc.), but the above are sufficient to show that the financial statements, while possibly appropriate from a stewardship/control perspective, are not appropriate from a reporting perspective, especially with respect to assessing "ability to pay".

In addition to fund-basis deficiencies, the budgets appear to contain additional shortcomings, that of consistent underestimation of operating results. The Administration's budgeted Current Operating Fund results for fiscal 1980 was a "loss"[3] of $124,972 (after allowing for "estimated underspending and income variance of $500,000), whereas the actual result (from statement A-2 of the fiscal 1980 financial statements) was an "excess" of $3,494,000. The Administration has provided a reconciliation of these two numbers. (See Exhibit 4 of case.)

The "conservative" budget of 1980 appears to be a continuation of past practice, since the 1979 budget called for a loss of $121,740 (again after a variance of $500,000), when in fact the actual reported result was an excess of $1,134,000.

Part of the reason for the consistent underestimation may be in the Administration's poor record of forecasting enrolments. For example, the target for 1980-81 was 37,384.5 full-time equivalents (FTE), whereas the actual enrolment was 38,884.1 FTE, an underestimation of 2.8%.[4] This low forecasting, when combined with the year-to-year increase in actual enrolments (37,972.1 FTE in 1979-80 and 38,848.1 FTE in 1980-81[5]) and the slip-year method of formula funding, strongly suggests that the University will enjoy additional unexpected formula income in 1981-82.

Part II — An Estimation of the University's Ability to Pay

The concept of ability to pay is closely tied to the working capital availability of the organization. Despite the absence of a Statement of Changes in Financial Position in the University's Financial Statements, we are able to estimate that the combined operating fund and ancillary enterprise fund working capital position increased by about $5.1 million over the fiscal year ended April 30, 1980, to approximately $8.2 million by fiscal year end. We recognize that this is an approximation but it suffices to indicate that the need for the Statement of Changes in Financial Position is crucial to reasonable evaluation as to the ability to pay.

We attach as Annex I a document prepared by the Administration and dated January 6, 1981. We should note that this document indicates new income of $22.8 million arising from an assumed government grant increase of 9%, for fiscal year 1981-82. The University's budget for the fiscal year 1980-81 shows a modest anticipated net income of $328,566 in the operating fund (Exhibit 8) and a further modest net income on the ancillary enterprises fund of $455,018 for a sum of $784,000. Although, (as we have pointed out above) we have grave misgivings as to the validity of these numbers, we will use these income numbers to estimate the (lower bound of the) change in the University's working capital position during 1980-81. It is altogether likely that the University's working capital position would be considerably enhanced beyond the approximately $784,000 of projected net income in these two funds. Nevertheless, using these questionable figures, one still arrives at a total of a potential available pool of $31.8 million of working capital as a rough projection of the University's working capital position at the end of the 1981-82 fiscal period prior to the payment of salaries and other increases, which is well in excess of projected increases in equipment, supplies, utilities, and the Association's request (Exhibit 9).

It should be kept in mind that the income numbers we used in the above estimation were total (not operating) income, after deducting commitments and transfers and such other non-uses of working capital as depreciation; thus, this represents a downward bias to our estimate. We recognize that this is an unsatisfactory analysis but submit that the proof that the working capital position of the University will not be impaired by the request of the Association rests entirely on the Administration, since we are not privy to their much more complete information. What insight that we can glean, however, suggests a considerable improvement in the working capital position of the University — apparently more than enough to cover the Association's request.

Part III — The University's Unwillingness to Provide Certain Information

In Part I of this section, the Association provided evidence concerning the inappropriateness of the University's financial statements and budget for assessing "ability to pay". In view of this inappropriateness, the Association requested information from the Administration concerning various policies and accounting principles followed by the University, so that at least some insight could be obtained from the financial reports. It should be noted that, although in some cases the responses were indeed helpful (for example, the response to question 1), in many cases they were so vague as to be misleading (the answer to question 11, concerning investments).

An interesting aspect of this correspondence relates to the degree that the Council of Ontario Universities' guidelines (referred to previously) are adhered to. In point 15 of the Administration's response to our request, the guide is cited as support for not recording pledges, but in point 16 the Administration says that an SCFP (which is recommended for inclusion by the guide) is "not considered too relevant". It appears that the net effect of this selective application of the Council of Ontario Universities' guidelines is to minimize disclosure of the resource flows of the University and also to minimize the University's operating revenue.

Summary

In this section of our submission, we have attempted to address the issue of "ability to pay," while at the same time asserting our position that ability to pay is not the sole criterion for determining salary increases. We have pointed out that the major sources of financial information available to us — the University's financial statements and budget — are not suited to assessing ability to pay.

We have also attempted to indicate that what information we do have bearing on this issue suggests that resources available to the University (as working capital) appear to be more than sufficient to cover the Association's request. Indeed, the data we employed is probably downward biased, as we pointed out in Part II above.

Finally, in Part III of this section we provided copies of correspondence suggesting the Administration has been somewhat less than completely helpful in aiding the Association in its attempt to understand the economic resources of the University [Exhibits 1 and 2 of case].

ANNEX I

Example of the effect of particular changes in Major Variables on the University Budget between 1980-81 and 1981-82.

Assumptions

Increase in formula funding and fees of 8 percent and of 9 percent and increase in other income of $1.2 million.

Increase in salaries and benefits of continuing staff (including PTR and Merit) of 10.3 per cent.

Increase in price of equipment and supplies of 10.4 percent (Toronto CPI for November 1979/78).

Increase in price of utilities of 16 percent.

Formula and Fee Increase	8%	9%
New Income	$20.6 million	$22.8 million
Inflation on Equipment ($6.9 Million x .104)		(.7)
Inflation on Supplies ($40.5 Million x .104)		(4.2)
Inflation on Utilities ($10.6 Million x .16)		(1.7)
Increase in Salaries and Benefits Net of Recoveries		(18.7)
University's Purchasing Power	(4.7)	(2.5)

EXHIBIT 8
THE UNIVERSITY AND THE FACULTY ASSOCIATION
EXCERPTS FROM UNIVERSITY BUDGET
Year Ended April 30, 1981
(with comparative figures for the year ended April 30, 1980)

	1980-81 Budget				1979-80 Budget				1980-81 Increase	
	Total	%	%	%	Total	%	%	%	Total	%
INCOME										
General University Income										
Government Formula Grants	183,347,065	59.8	77.5	81.4	169,526,803	60.7	76.8	82.9	13,822,262	8.2
Government Special Formula Grants	43,257	-0-	-0-	-0-	49,967	-0-	-0-	-0-	(6,710)	(13.4)
Government Non-Formula Grants	700,000	0.2	0.3	0.3	650,000	0.2	0.3	0.3	50,000	7.7
Municipal Taxes	1,600,000	0.5	0.7	0.7	1,591,650	0.6	0.7	0.8	8,350	0.5
Student fees (B.I.U. related)	32,843,967	10.4	13.5	14.2	26,907,145	9.6	12.5	13.1	5,136,822	19.1
Student fees (non-B.I.U. related and miscellaneous)	1,090,000	0.4	0.5	0.5	744,000	0.3	0.4	0.4	344,000	46.1
Endowment income	228,000	0.1	0.1	0.1	213,000	0.1	0.1	0.1	15,000	7.0
Interest income	4,606,000	1.5	1.9	2.0	3,532,000	1.2	1.6	1.7	1,074,000	30.4
Revenue from services (except divisional)	1,709,000	0.6	0.7	0.8	1,406,000	0.5	0.7	0.7	303,000	21.6
	225,367,289	73.5	95.2	100.0	204,620,565	73.2	95.1	100.0	20,746,724	10.1
Divisional Income										
Government non-formula grants	75,075	-0-	-0-		75,075	-0-	-0-			
Student fees (non-BIU related)	5,295,742	1.7	2.2		4,997,962	1.8	2.3		297,800	6.0
Endowment income, gifts and non-government grants	800,000	0.3	0.3		746,680	0.3	0.3		53,600	7.2
Revenue from services	5,482,389	1.8	2.3		5,042,675	1.8	2.3		439,714	8.7
	237,020,595	77.3	100.0		215,482,957	77.1	100.0		21,537,638	10.0
Interest on capital debentures	10,793,452	3.5			11,027,881	3.9			(234,429)	(2.1)
Restricted funds- assisted research and grants	59,000,000	19.2			53,000,000	19.0			6,000,000	11.3
	306,814,047	100.0			279,510,838	100.0			27,303,209	9.8

© John Wiley & Sons Canada Ltd. All rights reserved.

EXHIBIT 8 (continued)
THE UNIVERSITY AND THE FACULTY ASSOCIATION
EXCERPTS FROM UNIVERSITY BUDGET
Year Ended April 30, 1981
(with comparative figures for the year ended April 30, 1980)

	1980-81 Budget				1979-80 Budget				1980-81 Increase	
	Total	%	%	%	Total	%	%	%	Total	%
EXPENSES										
General and Divisional Expenses										
Academic	164,556,947	53.6	69.3		150,318,779	53.7	69.6		14,238,168	9.5
Academic services	16,444,577	5.3	6.9		15,224,877	5.4	7.0		1,219,700	8.0
Campus and Student Services	5,466,492	1.8	2.3		4,877,063	1.7	2.3		589,429	12.1
Physical Plant maintenance and services	20,751,074	6.7	8.7		18,353,129	6.6	8.5		2,397,945	13.1
Physical Plant utilities and rent	10,380,104	3.4	4.4		9,721,680	3.4	4.5		658,426	6.8
Alterations and renovations	500,000	0.2	0.2		500,000	0.2	0.2			
Administration	16,855,941	5.5	7.1		14,898,657	5.3	6.9		1,957,284	13.1
General University expenses	895,317	0.3	0.4		622,094	0.2	0.3		273,223	43.9
Municipal taxes	1,600,000	0.5	0.7		1,591,650	0.6	0.7		8,350	0.5
	237,450,454	77.3	100.0		216,107,929	77.1	100.0		21,342,525	9.9
Interest on capital debentures	10,793,452	3.5			11,027,881	3.9			(234,429)	(2.1)
Assisted research and other	59,000,000	19.2			53,000,000	19.0			6,000,000	11.3
	307,243,906	100.0			280,135,810	100.0			27,108,096	9.7
Budget Net Income (Expense)	(429,859)				(624,972)				195,113	
Estimated underspending and income variance	500,000				500,000					
Transfer from Ancillary Enterprises Fund	258,425				261,687				(3,262)	
Anticipated actual net income	328,566				136,715				191,851	

EXHIBIT 9
THE UNIVERSITY AND THE FACULTY ASSOCIATION
Estimate of Working Capital — 1980
(in thousands of dollars)

	1980	1979
Statement A-1 (Current Operating Fund)		
Current Assets	23,809	16,119
Less Inter-fund Items		
Ancillary Enterprise Fund	2,166	2,058
Capital Fund	(160)	379
Restricted Fund	339	447
	2,345	2,884
Adjusted Current Assets	21,464	13,235
Less Current Liabilities	15,787	12,336
Working Capital (A)	5,677	899
Statement B-1 (Ancillary Enterprises Fund)		
Current Assets	2,981	2,009
Less Current Liabilities	449	364
Working Capital (B)	2,532	1,645
Combined Funds Working Capital (A + B)	8,209	2,544
Combined Increase in Working Capital (8,209 − 2,544)		5,665

Estimate of Funds Available
(Based Upon Working Capital for 1981−82)
(in Thousands of dollars)

Estimate of Working Capital, April 30, 1980 (Exhibit 11)	8,209
Add Budgeted "Income" 1981 — Operating Fund	328
— Ancillary Enterprises Fund	455
	8,992
Add Administration's Estimate of "New Income" Next Year at a 9% Formula and Fee Increase	22,800
Working Capital (Estimated), Prior to Increases	31,792

ENDNOTES

1. Statistics Canada, Various Statistics, 1971–1980.
2. Study Group on Financial Reporting for Non-Profit Organizations, *Financial Reporting for Non-Profit Organizations*, Toronto, Canadian Institute of Chartered Accountants, 1980, Foreword.
3. The term "loss" will refer to the situation in which expenditures exceed revenue, and the term "excess" to the opposite situation.
4. Source: "The University's Enrolment in 1980–81 Compared to Target Levels," Office of the Vice-President (Research and Planning) and Registrar.
5. Ibid.

CASE 11

MARK GOODEN EXPLORATIONS

E. Gardner
University of Lethbridge
Lethbridge, Alberta

Mark Gooden and Cliff Roberts sat in Mark's office at the headquarters of Mark Gooden Explorations Limited. They had been discussing the possible purchase of facilities for the company a few blocks from its present location in Suntown, Saskatchewan. Although present leases would not expire for several years, Mark Gooden considered the time opportune for a move. Penalties for breaking his lease were minimal, and it was evident that more space was needed immediately if the company was to continue to expand. Cliff Roberts was one of the best commercial real estate representatives in Suntown, and he had just agreed to help Mark Gooden find suitable facilities.

BACKGROUND

Mark Gooden Explorations Limited had been in existence under various names for over 20 years. It began as Bergman Mining Company and then was sold to Porter and Porter Explorations Company. When the company encountered financial difficulties, Mark Gooden became a partner and eventually sole owner, at which point the company assumed its present name.

The company engages in minerals exploration for larger integrated mining companies. First Mr. Bergman and then the Porters worked for various companies with a high degree of success. They seemed to have a knack for finding commercially viable mineral deposits, but they had neither the capital nor the inclination to develop the mineral deposits once found. Consequently they usually sold their finds when they owned them, or they took exploration contracts from the owners of the mineral rights when they wanted explorations done. The usual terms of such contracts involved a fixed fee for each exploratory hole and occasionally a royalty on any commercially viable mineral deposits found. Commercial viability depended on the concentrations of the various minerals and it was always stated explicitly in any exploration contract what concentrations were viable. Royalties were paid for minerals actually obtained from the site explored.

Since the founding of the company, exploration techniques have become more and more scientific. The techniques are, however, the same no matter where they are used. In principle, Mark Gooden Explorations could function in any country of the world; it has chosen to limit itself to North America to keep down travel expenses and work permit problems.

Most of the exploration business is obtained by word-of-mouth. Companies that have successfully found minerals through Mark Gooden Explorations have usually provided more business. Even many clients for whom minerals have not been found have returned because of the expert service that has been provided. New clients are obtained through personal contact and through the references obtained from satisfied clients.

PERSONNEL

Mark Gooden is a 43 year old business man with an unusual background for a minerals explorer. He started out as an accounting student with a national accounting firm in Montreal 20 years ago. Three years later, after completing his CA designation, he left the accounting firm and joined a plumbing supplies firm in Sherbrooke as assistant controller. After 10 years with the firm, he changed jobs and joined a national accounting firm in Calgary as a bankruptcy trustee. Two years later, Mark was appointed receiver for Porter and Porter Exploration Company by one of its major creditors, the Arctic Bank. Rather than liquidate the company, Mark left the accounting firm, became a 50 per cent partner and attempted a turnaround. Mark Gooden, three years later, acquired the remainder of Porter and Porter Explorations Company and renamed it Mark Gooden Explorations Limited. He is the sole owner of the company, holding the positions of chairman and president. His knowledge of minerals exploration has been learned since he joined the company because he had no prior experience in the exploration business. He is not an expert and depends on his staff to make the company successful.

The vice-presidents for operations and marketing both have extensive experience in mining and minerals exploration. Karen Driscoll, the vice-president of operations, is a 40-year-old mining and geological engineer. She was hired by the Porters seven years ago and has demonstrated the same uncanny ability to find minerals that the Porters had. Karen was one of the employees that Mark Gooden made sure that he kept on staff when he took control of the company. She is a member of the Board of Directors and a key manager in all aspects of the exploration function.

Dennis Hunter, the vice-president of marketing, is 53 years old and has 30 years' experience in the mining and minerals businesses. His formal education does not extend beyond secondary school graduation, but he is known to be one of the most knowledgeable individuals in the exploration business. He is considered to be an honest man who will always keep his promises. He was hired shortly after Mark Gooden joined the company and he is now considered invaluable. He is also a director of the firm and a trusted advisor for Mark Gooden.

The chief financial officer of the company is Elizabeth Lapointe, age 35, formerly of Sherbrooke. She came to Suntown right after the takeover of the company to join Mark Gooden. She and Mark are both separated from their spouses, and they are known to be involved with each other. Their exact relationship has never been announced, and their friends and co-workers understand that they should mind their own business and respect the privacy of the relationship. Liz, as she is known, is also a director of the firm. She has a community college diploma and a CMA designation, but these were only obtained during the last five years.

Other employees of the company number about 60, divided among the three functional areas (exploration, marketing and financial). Many of these employees are new to the company, but all are carefully selected and competently trained for their jobs. Mark Gooden has generally supervised the hiring process, and he has made sure that he obtains good value for his efforts. Five years ago there were only 20 employees of whom 15 have stayed with the company. The other 45 have been hired by Mark Gooden.

FINANCIAL STATEMENTS

It is quite evident that Mark Gooden has turned the company around over the last six years. Financial statements for the fiscal years from 1983 to 1988 are found in Exhibit I. Operating profits have improved dramatically, but there is one anomaly. In the years 1984 and 1985, some extraordinary profits were achieved. According to Mark Gooden, these profits were a result of asset sales which improved the balance sheet. They happened over a period of 18 months and resolved a number of serious financial problems by providing necessary cash. A number of changes in the revenues and expenses for the company have occurred over the six year period. During the period, long term debt has increased substantially but not smoothly. It now exceeds $1.2 million.

Accounts receivable, income taxes payable and accounts payable have also been substantially increased. The current ratio has, however, decreased. Another asset that is substantial is goodwill, but it is being amortized.

One other crucial issue is the means by which sales have been increased. Substantial customer discounts have been granted in the last two years. These have achieved sales increases, but they now exceed 10 per cent of sales. It is becoming clear that these discounts cannot continue to grow: the limit on the use of discounts to stimulate sales is rapidly being reached.

PURCHASE OPTION

A plant facility has been found which will provide adequate space for all parts of the operation. It has 1200 square metres and will cost approximately $1 million. Cliff Roberts has assured Mark Gooden that the price is reasonable, and the facilities are entirely suitable for his company. After examining the location, Mark Gooden has agreed that it is satisfactory.

Financing arrangements have not been completed, but Gooden has little cash to put into the purchase. He hopes to borrow $250,000 from the bank and obtain a mortgage for $750,000. This arrangement has not been approved by the lenders, but Mark Gooden is optimistic. Interest rates will probably be about 12 percent on the loans.

© John Wiley & Sons Canada Ltd. All rights reserved.

LEASE OPTION

The present lease has two more years to run at a cost of $125,000 per year (payable monthly). The penalty for early cancellation is two months' payments this year and one month's payment next year. The lease can be renewed upon its termination in two years, but the owner of the building is willing to consider earlier renewal.

A proposal has been made to sign a 10 year lease on the current property at $130,000 per year (payable monthly). A renewal clause would allow a five year additional period at the same rates as long as notice is given at the beginning of year 10. The payments will not escalate during the term of the lease unless the owner can obtain the consent of Mark Gooden Explorations. Thus, it is likely that the payments will not change. There is also a bargain purchase option at the end of 15 years for a price of $10,000, exercisable by Mark Gooden on 6 months' notice.

For tax purposes, the new lease will be treated as a capital lease and will appear on the balance sheet, unlike the present situation where it does not. The main reason for the change is the lessor's belief the Mark Gooden Explorations is now financially able to make long term commitments. Previous leases have been for a maximum of three years.

All of the terms of the present lease will be retained except for the time period. Leasehold improvements, utilities and maintenance are all the responsibility of Mark Gooden Explorations. Only all perils insurance on the building is provided by its owner.

OTHER OPPORTUNITIES

Mark Gooden has indicated that, whether he buys or renews his lease, he is not about to sit still. He is actively seeking expansion opportunities whether by internal growth or external purchase. There is no doubt that he will continue to do so.

One of the interesting possibilities for Mark Gooden is the opening of an office in the United States. He hopes that this will happen in 1989 or 1990, but it depends on government policy (Free Trade Agreement) and available funds. He is enthusiastic about the possibility as is the entire Board of Directors. No specific opportunities exist for purchases of similar companies in Canada, and Mark Gooden is not interested in entering another industry. Thus, this expansion vehicle is not open at the moment. Mark Gooden has indicated that he will consider any opportunities for expansion that present themselves in the future.

CASE REQUIREMENTS

Mark Gooden must make some critical choices in the immediate future. He needs to be advised about the following issues:

(1) What is the difference between the lease and purchase options? Consideration must be given to the financial issues and the accounting impact in each case.
(2) Since cash is in such short supply, what must be done in budgeting and financial planning to correct the shortage? Clearly Mark Gooden needs to improve the balance sheet position of the company, and he needs advice on how to do it.
(3) The lack of expertise of the chief financial officer has caused concern among lenders. Mark Gooden has so far ignored the problem. Discussion is needed with respect to ethics and competence, but discretion is also required.

These questions do not exhaust the problems at Mark Gooden Explorations, but they are indicative of the main issues. Mark Gooden, as an accountant, is respected for his knowledge, but he does need some outside advice to lend credibility to his position. He must make a decision about purchase of the facilities as opposed to renewing his lease. While the choice is his, he definitely appears willing to listen to advice from outside.

MARK GOODEN EXPLORATIONS LIMITED
BALANCE SHEETS (in thousands of dollars)

	1983	1984	1985	1986	1987	1988
ASSETS						
Current Assets						
Cash	-0-	4	19	2	-0-	-0-
Accounts Receivable	292	191	406	518	727	781
Advances & Prepaid Expenses	2	4	20	68	10	42
Income Taxes Recoverable	-0-	-0-	27	56	227	613
	294	199	472	644	964	1,436
Fixed Assets (at cost)	414	583	906	718	979	1,283
Other Assets						
Goodwill	-0-	-0-	402	331	297	259
Deposits	-0-	-0-	11	12	15	16
Investment	-0-	-0-	3	3	3	3
	-0-	-0-	416	346	315	278
Total Assets	708	782	1,794	1,708	2,258	2,997
LIABILITIES AND EQUITY						
Current Liabilities						
Cheques O/D	-0-	-0-	-0-	-0-	8	17
Bank Loans	334	158	-0-	146	30	180
Accounts Payable	316	77	200	156	285	524
Current Portion of Long Term Debt	-0-	30	173	145	166	292
	650	265	373	447	489	1,013
Long Term Liabilities						
Long Term Debt	991	613	1,316	1,055	1,292	1,245
Deferred Income Taxes	-0-	-0-	-0-	-0-	72	123
	991	613	1,316	1,055	1,364	1,368
Equity						
Share Capital	15	15	15	15	15	15
Retained Earnings	(948)	(111)	90	191	390	601
	(933)	(96)	105	206	405	616
Total Liabilities and Equity	708	782	1,794	1,708	2,258	2,997

© John Wiley & Sons Canada Ltd. All rights reserved.

MARK GOODEN EXPLORATIONS
INCOME STATEMENTS
(in thousands of dollars)

	1983	1984	1985	1986	1987	1988
Revenues						
Services & Fees	1,329	1,543	1,461	3,047	4,653	4,980
Less Customer Discounts	-0-	-0-	-0-	-0-	318	544
	1,329	1,543	1,461	3,047	4,335	4,436
Expenses						
Operating	1,076	789	906	1,825	2,379	2,488
General and Administration	596	405	366	923	1,303	1,361
Depreciation and Amortization	109	155	151	229	355	323
	1,781	1,349	1,423	2,977	4,037	4,172
Operating Income	(452)	194	38	70	298	264
Income Taxes						
Current	-0-	45	(27)	(31)	27	2
Deferred	-0-	-0-	-0-	-0-	72	51
	-0-	45	(27)	(31)	99	53
Extraordinary Items	-0-	688	136	-0-	-0-	-0-
Net Earnings	(452)	837	201	101	199	211
Retained Earnings (Beginning of Year)	(496)	(948)	(111)	90	191	390
Retained Earnings (End of Year)	(948)	(111)	90	191	390	601

CASE 12

ROLLS-ROYCE PRIVATIZATION

A. Steele
University of Warwick
Warwick, U.K.

On September 23, 1987, Samuel Montague & Co. Ltd. offered for sale 801,470,588 ordinary shares of 20p each in Rolls-Royce Plc (public limited company) at 170p per share payable on application, on behalf of the Secretary of State for Trade and Industry. This sale returned the ownership of Rolls-Royce to the private sector after 16 years in public ownership. In 1971, the British government had acquired the company from the receiver appointed after Rolls-Royce declared bankruptcy. The company had failed because the development of the RB-211 jet engine had been too expensive and sales had not materialized for the engine. Other lines of business had not been sufficiently profitable to save the company.

The objective of this case is to evaluate the financial information in the offer for sale document, in order to understand the performance of the company in the last five years and decide whether the information is useful for helping investors make a decision about subscribing to the shares. The valuation of the shares is not required. All monetary items in the case are in pounds sterling.

To guide the evaluation, consider the following questions:

1) Without calculating any ratios, examine the consolidated profit and loss accounts. What does management wish subscribers to believe about the financial performance?

2) What are the implications of note 7, page 25 in Exhibit I, about net restructuring costs on financial performance?

3) Calculate research and development (R & D) expenditure as a percentage of turnover each year. What does this indicate?

4) The accounting policy of capitalizing R & D as a device for managing the bottom line was abandoned by Rolls-Royce after the 1969 accounts, and their subsequent receivership. In their prospectus Rolls-Royce disclosed, on pages 34 & 35 in Exhibit I, further details about their research and development expenditure. The British Government and the Ministry of Defence (MOD) make significant contributions to support R & D at Rolls-Royce. The net R & D expenditure is the gross expenditure less launch aid for research and development, less contributions to advanced engineering programs, less development contracts from MOD and other customers. Reconcile the net R & D expenditure with the gross R & D expenditure. What does this indicate?

5) In the balance sheets, what caused the balance on the Profit and Loss account in 1984 to change from a deficit of 330 million pounds to a surplus of 106 million pounds in 1985? What were the cash flows involved, and what effect did this have on how the accounts appear?

6) The measurement (or construction) of operating profit depends on a mixture of hard facts (cash flows) plus adjustments which depend on judgement and the choice accounting conventions (income recognition, receivables, provisions for doubtful debts, stock valuation, overhead absorption methods, depreciation methods, accruals, expense recognition, provisions and prepayments, and so on). In order to strip out the items which are due to arbitrary allocations and subjective judgements, analysts sometimes estimate operating cash flow. Operating cash flow is strictly operating cash receipts less operating cash payments. This number is not described in conventional accounts; however, it can be approximated by Funds from Operations (profit before tax add back depreciation and provisions) plus or minus the change in working capital. Appendix I sets out a started analysis of cash flows, which you should complete. Include the projection for 1986.

7) Calculate the operating cash flow as a percentage of sales turnover. What does this indicate about financial performance?

8) Compare the depreciation charge each year and in total for the five years with the net capital expenditure. What does this imply about the years Rolls-Royce were in public sector care?

9) How would the 1986 dividend of 40 million pounds per the proforma profit and loss account be financed? What does this indicate about the long-run dividend paying ability of Rolls-Royce?

10) How useful do you feel the accountants' report is for helping investors make a decision to subscribe to the shares?

QUESTION 6
ROLLS-ROYCE CASH FLOW ANALYSIS
(in millions of pounds sterling)

	1982	1983	1984	1985	1986	Total	Proforma 1986
Operating Cash Flow (a)	(48)	69					
Share Capital	50						
Extra Borrowing	<u>51</u>	<u>33</u>					
	<u>53</u>	<u>102</u>					
Repayment of Borrowing		50					
Net Capital Expenditure	50	48					
Taxation	3	4					
Dividends	—	—					
	<u>53</u>	<u>102</u>					

FOOTNOTES

(a) Profit (Loss) Before Tax	(131)
Add Back Depreciation	38
Decrease in Provisions	<u>(48)</u>
Funds From Operations	**(141)**
Decrease in Stocks	127
Increase in Debtors	(8)
Decrease in Creditors	(3)
Miscellaneous	(4)
Foreign Currency Adjustments	(4)
Decrease in Creditors > 1 yr.	<u>(5)</u>
Operating Cash Flow	**(48)**

(b) Decrease in Cash Balances	22	(i.e. Overdraft & Cash Balance Combined)
Increase in Amounts Falling Due After One Year	<u>29</u>	(i.e. Extra Borrowing)
	51	

EXHIBIT I
ROLLS-ROYCE PRIVATIZATION
KEY INFORMATION

The following information is derived from, and must be read in conjunction with, the full text of this document.

BUSINESS AND ACTIVITIES

Rolls-Royce is one of only three manufacturers in the Western World with the proven capability to design, develop and produce large gas turbine aero-engines. Its aero-engines are in service with more than 270 airlines, 700 executive and corporate operators and 110 armed services. The Rolls-Royce Group also has over 175 industrial customers operating gas turbines for power generation, gas and oil pumping and other industrial uses. Its gas turbines power naval vessels of 25 nations.

In the civil aero-engine market, Rolls-Royce pursues a strategy whereby it can offer an engine to compete within each principal sector of the market, either alone (as in the case of the RB211 family of engines and the Tay) or in collaboration with other manufacturers (such as for the IAE V2500 now under development).

In the military aero-engine market, the fulfilment of the defence requirements of the UK continues to be of major significance, whether through national projects (such as the Pegasus) or on a collaborative basis (as in the case of the RB199); HM Government is Rolls-Royce's single most important customer. From this base of UK defence business, the Group seeks to exploit military and commercial business throughout the world.

The business of the Rolls-Royce Group is international, with approximately 70 percent of sales in each of the last five years being to airframe manufacturers or other customers outside the UK.

The company devotes substantial resources to investment in advanced technology for both manufacturing and research and development. Since the mid 1970's, it has aimed to reduce the technological risk and high cost of engine design and development, where practicable, by proving technologies in advance of the high expenditure phase of an engine project and by making technologies transferable between engines.

The board considers that, on its return to the private sector, Rolls-Royce will have the resources of management, capital and technology to take advantage of the profitable opportunities which the market should provide in the years ahead.

ORGANIZATION

The principal activities of the Rolls-Royce Group in the UK are organized into five business groups (CEG, MEG, I&M, Repair and Overhaul and Nuclear), two service groups (Supply and Corporate Engineering) and a small number of corporate functions. CEG, MEG and I&M are the principal profit centres, each being responsible for the management of its particular engine projects, from engineering development through to assembly, marketing, sales and in service support. The Supply group is responsible for in-house manufacture and external procurement and the Corporate Engineering group for advanced engineering, technology and design, which encompasses fundamental research and development. There are also manufacturing, marketing, repair and overhaul and product support operations overseas. As at 31st December 1986, the Rolls-Royce Group had 42,045 employees, including 3,053 outside the UK.

FINANCIAL RECORD

The information in the following table has been extracted from the Accountants' Report (information is in millions of pounds sterling):

Year Ended Dec. 31	Turnover	Operating Profit	R & D Net Expenditure	Profit (Loss) *	Profit (Loss) **
1982	1,493	122	131	(93)	(138)
1983	1,331	74	131	(115)	(196)
1984	1,409	162	101	26	19
1985	1,601	211	100	81	77
1986–actual	1,802	273	132	120	120
–proforma	1,802	273	132	143	133

*   Before taxation and net restructuring costs
** Attributable to the Company

The Rolls-Royce Group has made a strong recovery from the recession and depressed levels of profitability in the civil airline market in the early 1980's. In 1981, in response to the fall in the level of orders and with the objective of increasing efficiency and competitiveness, the Group began a major program of restructuring its operations. The number of people employed by the Group was reduced by approximately 21,000 by the end of 1984. Other measures taken included greater automation of manufacturing and the introduction of organizational and management changes.

The recovery in orders, both for complete aero-engines and for spare parts, in particular in the civil aero business, commenced in late 1984. Total sales increased in each of the last three years to reach 1.8 billion pounds in 1986. Both operating profit and profit before tax increased sharply in each of these years and in 1986 were 273 million pounds and 120 million pounds respectively. The earlier reduction in manpower levels and other measures to increase efficiency contributed to an improvement in margins; funds generated from operations also improved significantly.

In the last three years, the civil aero-business generated most of the increase in both sales and operating profit reaching 757 million pounds and 137 million pounds respectively in 1986. Military aero sales in 1986 were 740 million pounds and remained stable over this period, while continuing to earn an important proportion of total operating profit, to which they contributed 118 million pounds in 1986.

The total value of orders outstanding at 20th March 1987 was 3.1 billion pounds.

If net proceeds from the subscription by HM Government of the additional share capital (referred to below) had been available to the Group throughout the whole of 1986, the Board estimates that profit before tax for that year would have been 148 million pounds.

During the period 1982-1986, no significant tax charges were incurred. Unabsorbed tax losses of the Company carried forward at 31st December 1986 are estimated at more than 600 million pounds and, consequently, Rolls-Royce does not expect to pay UK mainstream corporation tax for several years.

CAPITAL STRUCTURE AND SUBSCRIPTION OF ADDITIONAL SHARE CAPITAL

In recent years, Rolls-Royce has operated with the backing of assurances given by the then Under-Secretary of State for Trade and Industry on 22nd February 1973, and confirmed by successive Governments, that HM Government would ensure that the debts of Rolls-Royce would be met in the extremely unlikely event of a liquidation.

As part of the arrangements for and at the time of the Offer, HM Government will subscribe for 166.5 million additional Shares which will yield gross proceeds to the Company equal to the net borrowings of the Company and its subsidiaries (including capital obligations under finance leases) at 31st December 1986 and amounting to 283 million pounds. These additional Shares, which will be subscribed at the Offer price, will form part of the 801.5 million Shares made available under the Offer and will be paid for by HM Government out of the proceeds of the Offer. On completion of the Offer, the Government assurances referred to above will be withdrawn and will cease to have effect in respect of the whole of the Group's then existing and future obligations. At the same time, HM Government will subscribe for the Social Share at the price of 1. The major proportion of the proceeds of subscription of the additional share capital will be used to repay most of the Group's borrowings outstanding on completion.

DETAILS OF THE OFFER

HM Government currently owns all the Company's issued share capital of 635 million Shares. On completion of the Offer, it will subscribe for an additional 166.5 million Shares at the Offer price. HM Government is now offering all its existing Shares and the additional Shares being subscribed, which together total 801.5 million Shares, at a price of 170p per Share of which 85p is payable on application and 85p by 23rd September 1987. 80.1 million Shares are being reserved for applications from eligible employees and pensioners under the special arrangements described below. Any Shares not taken up under these special arrangements will be available to meet applications from the general public.

Under the Offer, up to 473.8 million Shares are being placed with certain institutional investors in the UK, and an offer (the "Public and Employee Offer") of up to a further 327.6 million Shares is being made to the general public and to eligible employees and pensioners. If valid applications under the Public and Employee Offer (other than under the Free, Matching and Discount Offers to eligible employees) are received for more than 655.3 million Shares, the placing with institutional investors in the UK will be reduced by approximately 79.0 million Shares (or approximately 17 per cent) and these shares will be added to the number available under the Public and Employee Offer. Other than 11.8 million Shares reserved under the Free and Matching Offers, all the Shares under the Offer have been underwritten. If any of the Shares reserved under the Free and Matching Offers are not taken up either by the employees or under the Public and Employee Offer, they will be sold by HM Government in due course. Following the Offer and the sale of any such shares, HM Government will own only the Special Share.

No allocation or allocations in excess of 10 per cent of the Shares now being offered will be made to any one person or group of associated persons. Under the Articles of Association, the proportion of Foreign-held shares will be limited to 15 per cent. In addition, all individual shareholders will be limited to 15 per cent until 1st January 1989. These provisions of the Articles are protected by the Special Share held by HM Government. The Articles also require the latter's consent to any disposal of a material part of the assets of either the Group as a whole or its nuclear business.

OFFER FOR SALE STATISTICS (monetary amounts in pounds [pence] sterling)

Offer price payable by instalments	170p
Shares in issue following the Offer	801,470,588
Market capitalization at the Offer price	1.36 billion
Actual 1986 earnings per Share (on the number of Shares in issue immediately prior to the Offer)	18.9p
Price earnings multiple on actual 1986 earnings per Share at the Offer price.	9.0 times
Proforma 1986 earnings per Share (on the basis of the number of Shares in issue following the Offer and the assumptions set out in Proforma 1986 profits in Part III)	16.6p
Price earnings multiple on proforma 1986 earnings per Share at the Offer price	10.2 times
Gross dividend yield at the Offer price based on a notional net dividend of 4.99p per Share, which the Directors would have expected to recommend in respect of the year to 31st December 1986 had the net proceeds of the additional share capital been available to the Group for the whole of that year	4.06%
Notional dividend cover on the basis of the proforma 1986 earnings per Share	3.3 times
Proforma net assets per Share at 31st December 1986 after adjustment for the net proceeds of the additional share capital	97.8p

ARRANGEMENTS FOR EMPLOYEES AND PENSIONERS

Special arrangements have been made to enable eligible UK employees of Rolls-Royce and its UK subsidiaries and eligible UK pensioners of Rolls-Royce to acquire Shares under the Offer. Under the Free Offer, such employees, if employed for 16 hours a week or more and with at least 12 months' continuous service, will each be entitled to apply for free Shares up to an aggregate value of 70 plus 2 for each year of continuous service. Under the Matching Offer, they may also purchase up to 88 Shares at the Offer price and receive a further two free Shares for each Share so purchased. Eligible UK employees, irrespective of hours of work and length of service, will each be entitled, in addition, to apply under the Discount Offer for up to 1,176 Shares at a 10 percent discount on the Offer price; and they, together with pensioners receiving a pension in the UK form the Pension Fund, will be further entitled under the Priority Offer to make priority applications at the Offer price for up to a maximum per employee or pensioner of 5,882 Shares.

Applications from eligible employees under the Free, Matching and Discount Offers will be met in full, subject to the personal limits applying under those arrangements. A maximum of 40,073,529 Shares, representing five percent of the offered Shares, are being reserved under the Priority Offer for priority applications from employees and pensioners. However, this number will be reduced to the extent that more than 40,147,058 Shares are allocated under the Free, Matching and Discount Offers. The maximum number of Shares reserved under the Free, Matching, Discount and Priority Offers is 80,147,058. Any such Shares not applied for under these Offers will be available to meet applications from the general public.

BUSINESS AND ACTIVITIES

HISTORY

The Early Years

The origin of the Company can be traced to 1894, when F.H. Royce & Co. Limited was incorporated. 1904 saw the beginning of the manufacture of motor cars, for sale exclusively by C.S. Rolls & Co. under the name "Rolls-Royce." The two concerns were united in 1906 to form Rolls-Royce Limited, which obtained a stock exchange listing for its shares in that year. In 1914, Rolls-Royce piston aero-engines were produced. After the end of the Great War, the development and production of aero-engines continued as an adjunct to its main and growing business of motor car manufacture.

Two significant aero-engine achievements of Rolls-Royce Limited during the inter-war years were the first direct transatlantic flight, made in 1919 by the Eagle engined Vimy aircraft piloted by Alcock and Brown and, in 1931, the powering of the outright winner of the Schneider Trophy with the "R" engine. The latter was the direct predecessor of the Merlin which powered the Spitfire, Hurricane, Lancaster and other aircraft in World War Two. By the end of the War, over 160,000 Merlin engines had been produced in the UK and the US, of which over 80,000 had been produced by Rolls-Royce Limited at Derby, Crewe and Glasgow.

During the early part of the War, Air Commodore Whittle (now Sir Frank Whittle) proved the feasibility of gas turbine power for aircraft propulsion. Rolls-Royce Limited produced components for Whittle engines from 1940 and, in early 1943, took over the development of a Whittle engine variant from The Rover Company Limited. This engine, the W2B/23, was renamed the Welland and entered service in 1944 in the Gloster Meteor, which was the only Allied jet aircraft to see active service in the War.

Development of the Jet Aero-Engine Market

After the end of the War, Rolls-Royce Limited devoted substantial resources to exploiting its technological lead in jet aero-engine development and production, in addition to returning to the manufacture of motor cars. In the military jet aero-engine market, Rolls-Royce Limited achieved considerable success with the Derwent and Nene engines. Its Nene and (first) Tay were manufactured under license in Europe and the Commonwealth and by Pratt & Whitney, Inc. (Pratt & Whitney, now the Pratt &

Whitney Aircraft Division of United Technologies Corporation [UTC]) in the US. This was the first experience in the US of large scale production of jet aero-engines.

Rolls-Royce Limited also developed a strong presence in the civil aero-engine market through a number of engines, principally the Dart turboprop in the Vickers Viscount, introduced into regular airline service in 1953 as the world's first turboprop airliner; The Avon, which in 1958 powered the first jet airliner services across the Atlantic in the de Havilland Comet; and the Conway, which was an alternative engine to the Pratt & Whitney JT3 for versions of the Boeing 707 and Douglas DC8 aircraft and which, later, powered the Vickers VC10. From the 1960s, the Spey powered the Hawker Siddeley Trident, the BAC 1-11 and the Fokker F28. Substantial sales of engines for UK military applications were also achieved during this period.

From 1958, derivatives of gas turbine aero-engines were introduced for industrial and marine applications.

Development of US Competition in the Western World

Over the period from 1960 to 1967, the civil aviation market came to be dominated by the airframe manufacturers in the US, which increased their proportion of total civil aircraft sales in the world excluding the countries of the Warsaw Pact and the People's Republic of China (the Western World) from about 40 percent in 1960 to over 85 percent in 1967. Although the Dart, Conway and Spey aero-engines achieved some success in the US during the 1960s, this was generally in airframes manufactured in the UK or Europe. Once the improved Pratt & Whitney JT3D version became available, and following the introduction of the Boeing 727 and Douglas DC9 aircraft with the Pratt & Whitney JT8 engine, Rolls-Royce Limited did not make significant sales to US airframe manufacturers, other than to power exclusively the Gulfstream Executive aircraft.

Rationalization of the UK Aero-Engine Industry

In 1966, Rolls-Royce Limited acquired its only major UK competitor, Bristol Siddeley Engines Limited, which had been formed in 1958 by a merger of Bristol Aero Engines Limited and Armstrong Siddeley Motors Limited and which in 1961, had acquired the de Havilland Engine Company Limited and Blackburn Engines Limited.

The RB211-22 Project

Against the background of advancing development of the new large CF6 engine by General Electric Company of the US (GE) and the competing JT9D engine by Pratt & Whitney for the proposed new generation of wide-bodied aircraft and for military applications, projections made by Rolls-Royce Limited in 1967 suggested that sales of its principal civil aero-engines then in production would decline from about 59 million pounds in 1969 to under 4 million pounds in 1975. Rolls-Royce Limited therefore considered that it was crucial to receive orders for a large engine from one or more of the US airframe manufacturers, if GE and Pratt & Whitney were not to develop substantial technological and market advantages and if Rolls-Royce Limited was to maintain its position as a major Western World aero-engine manufacturer. After prolonged negotiations, a contract was signed with Lockheed Aircraft Corporation (Lockheed) in March 1968 for the supply of a new engine, the RB211-22m for 150 Lockheed L1011 TriStars (TriStars) for delivery commencing in 1971. This engine development, for which substantial HM Government funding was agreed, involved radical technological advances and was specified to achieve 40,600 pounds force (lbf) thrust, almost twice the level of the largest Rolls-Royce engine then in service. The engine was subsequently rated at 42,000 lbf thrust, as the RB211-22B.

By the end of the negotiations with Lockheed, the engineering task had become significantly more demanding than had originally been envisaged and the timescale for completing the development had been reduced. Unforeseen technical problems arose during the development phase; these problems led to substantial increases in development costs and, ultimately, to a need to postpone delivery of the engines to Lockheed, giving rise to a potential liability to claims for substantial damages from Lockheed and its airline customers. Although further financial support was arranged from banks and HM Government, it subsequently became clear in early 1971 that the costs of continued development and production of the RB211-22B and the potential liability to claims from Lockheed and the airlines could not be met from the existing financial resources of Rolls-Royce Limited.

A receiver and manager was appointed by the holders of debentures in Rolls-Royce Limited on 4th February 1971. Following the passing of the Rolls-Royce (Purchase) Act 1971, HM Government incorporated the Company as Rolls-Royce (1971) Limited, on 23rd February 1971, to purchase from the receiver the undertaking and assets of the gas turbine engine and nuclear propulsion businesses of the old company, together with all rights to the name "Rolls-Royce" and other relevant trademarks. The proceeds of sale of these business, together with the proceeds of sale to the public in 1973 of the shares and unsecured loan stock in Rolls-Royce Motors Limited (a new company, into which the motor car and diesel engine business had been put by the receiver), enabled the receiver to repay the debenture holders. The remaining proceeds also enabled the liquidators to pay all classes of creditors in full and make distributions to shareholders totalling 64.5p per 1.00 share. The receiver had also made separate arrangements to enable the holders of Rolls-Royce Limited Workers' Shares to be paid the full nominal value of their holdings.

In accordance with terms agreed between the receiver and HM Government in 1971, Rolls-Royce Motors Limited was permitted to use the name "Rolls-Royce" and trademarks for certain products, free of charge. Rolls-Royce Motors Limited (now known as Rolls-Royce Motor Cars Limited, a subsidiary of Vickers Plc) has had no other connection with the Company since 1971, except in the limited capacity of a sub-contractor and supplier.

The 1970s

Rolls-Royce (1971) Limited commenced trading on 23rd May 1971. Within a short period, the technical difficulties with the RB211-22 project were largely overcome, although at substantial cost. Deliveries to Lockheed of the first 555 production engines covered by the original contract, and funded by HM Government, were completed in August 1975, with the sales proceeds being paid to HM Government.

The 1970s as a whole were a period of technological and market progress for the Company. The RB211-524, a derivative of the RB211-22B with increased thrust, was launched in 1974 on the TriStar and was accepted by The Boeing Company (Boeing) in 1975 as one of the engine options for the Boeing 747. The Collaborative Olympus 593, with Rolls-Royce's costs fully funded by HM Government, entered service in 1976 in the Concorde; and a major success in the US market was achieved by reaching an agreement with Boeing in 1978 for the 535 derivative of the RB211-22B to be the launch engine for the new Boeing 757 aircraft. The Company continued to be a major supplier to British Airways through the TriStar and the Boeing 747. It also established and strengthened market links with several of the world's major airlines in addition to British Airways, including Eastern Airlines, Trans World Airlines and Delta Airlines in the US, Cathay Pacific in Hong Kong, All Nippon Airways in Japan, Qantas in Australia, Air New Zealand, Saudi Arabian Airlines and Air Canada.

In parallel with these developments in the civil market, successful activities in the military aero-engine market continued with substantial sales of Spey, Avon and Adour engines being achieved. Development of the RB199 collaborative engine for the Panavia Tornado European Multi-Role Combat Aircraft (Tornado) began in 1970 through a three nation consortium company, Turbo-Union Limited. Sales of the Pegasus engine (which had been in service with the RAF since 1969 in the Harrier vertical/short take off and landing aircraft) to the US Marine Corps for the AV8A variant of the Harrier had also started in 1971.

In March 1977, the Company changed its name to Rolls-Royce Limited from Rolls-Royce (1971) Limited (the name of the former company in liquidation having changed to R-R (Realisations) Limited).

The 1980s: Recession in the Civil Market, Restructuring and Recovery

The Company's successful military aero-engine programs continued during the early 1980s with substantial sales of the RB199, Adour, Viper, Gem and Gnome being achieved. However, this period was one of recession and heavily depressed profitability for the civil airline industry resulting from oil price increases and general economic difficulties. The TriStar, for which the Company was the sole engine supplier, was cancelled and sales of wide-bodied aircraft generally, and therefore, of the large engines on which Rolls-Royce had based much of its civil market strategy, were particularly severely affected. Sales of spare parts for engines in service were also depressed. The Company's principal strategies during this period were to broaden its civil aero-engine product range in order to reduce dependence on one or two sectors of the civil market and to prepare to take advantage of the up-turn in demand in the air transport business when airline profitability returned. Significant improvements in productivity were achieved through a major manpower reduction program, coupled with continued investment in manufacturing facilities and automated equipment; between 1980 and the end of 1984, employee numbers were reduced from about 62,000 to about 41,000 through a program of voluntary severance. This was accomplished without industrial relations disruption. Steps were also taken to improve the control and cost effectiveness of research and development activities.

In 1983, the Board initiated organizational and management changes in the Company. The new structure was designed to avoid duplication of effort, to allow progressive moves towards rationalization of component purchases and production and to give individual executive Directors and other senior management clear accountability for either profit or costs.

From late 1984 onwards, the Company was able to take advantage of the strengthened upward trend in civil airline activity and of the customer relationships which it had established during the 1970s, securing substantial orders in the civil aero business. Significant export orders were also obtained for a number of the Company's military engines. The Group recorded a consolidated profit after interest and tax in 1984, following losses in all but one of the previous five years. Substantial increases in consolidated profit after interest and tax were then recorded in 1985 and again in 1986.

Collaboration with other manufacturers, particularly in the military market, had been a long-standing aspect of the Company's business. From the late 1970s, however, the leading aero-engine manufacturers became increasingly aware of the potential advantages of, and need for, collaboration in respect of major civil aero-engine development projects. In December 1983, IAE International Aero Engines AG (IAE) was incorporated as a five member consortium to design, develop and supply the IAE V2500 engine for smaller aircraft in the medium haul market. The major participants are the Company and Pratt & Whitney, each with a 30 per cent shareholding. Pratt & Whitney remains a major competitor of the Company in respect of other products. In May 1984, the Company and its other major competitor, GE, signed a risk and revenue sharing arrangement in respect of the GE CF6-80C2 engine and the Company's 535E4. The Company and GE agreed, however, in November 1986 to terminate this arrangement because of the increasing overlap between the products covered by the arrangement and other products manufactured by the parties. A termination agreement and alternative contractual arrangements were signed in February 1987, under which Rolls-Royce will act as a sub-contractor to GE for a period in respect of the CF6-80C2, and GE similarly to Rolls-Royce in respect of the 535E4, replacing the original risk and revenue sharing agreement.

Following an earlier policy statement by HM Government in July 1983, on 8th November 1985 the Minister for Industry and Information Technology confirmed that, subject to market conditions, HM Government intended to privatize Rolls-Royce before the end of the present Parliament. On 2nd December 1985, the High Court of Justice approved a reduction of 381 million pounds in the paid-up share capital of the Company which eliminated the deficit of 372 million pounds on the Company's profit and loss account at 31st December 1984. On 1st May 1986, the Company was re-registered as a public limited company under the Companies Act 1985, with the name Rolls-Royce Plc.

INTRODUCTION TO CURRENT BUSINESS AND MARKETS

Business by Market Sector

The principal business of the Rolls-Royce Group is the design, production, sale and support of gas turbine aero-engines for industrial and marine applications and produces rocket motors and components for aerospace industry. The Rolls-Royce Group also supplies and supports nuclear steam raising plant for Royal Navy submarines through Rolls-Royce and Associates Limited, in which the Company has a controlling interest. The business of the Rolls-Royce Group is international, with about 70 percent of total sales over the period 1982–1986 being to airframe manufacturers or other customers outside the UK. The Rolls-Royce Group maintains manufacturing, repair and overhaul facilities in Canada, manufacturing, engineering and design facilities in the US and repair and overhaul facilities in Brazil, in addition to maintaining marketing or product support representatives in 30 other countries.

The following table sets out the last five years' results of the Rolls-Royce Group by principal activity:

ROLLS-ROYCE PRIVATIZATION

TURNOVER (m is millions of pounds sterling)

Year End 31 Dec.	1982		1983		1984		1985		1986	
	m	%	m	%	m	%	m	%	m	%
Civil Aero	520	35	388	29	446	32	577	36	757	42
Military Aero	742	50	706	53	735	52	735	46	740	41
Industrial and Marine	137	9	132	10	122	9	143	9	153	9
Other Activities	94	6	105	8	106	7	146	9	152	8
	1493	100	1331	100	1409	100	1601	100	1802	100

Operating Profit/(Loss) (Before Net Research and Development Expenditure)

Year end 31 Dec.	1982		1983		1984		1985		1986	
	m	%	m	%	m	%	m	%	m	%
Civil Aero	(8)	(7)	(35)	(47)	39	24	73	35	137	50
Military Aero	116	95	96	130	111	68	110	52	118	43
Industrial and Marine	7	6	6	8	6	4	20	9	10	4
Other Activities	7	6	7	9	6	4	8	4	8	3
	122	100	74	100	162	100	211	100	273	100

The civil aero activity has increased in importance over the period, accounting for 42 percent of total turnover and 50 percent of total operating profit in 1986, compared with 35 percent of turnover and an operating loss in 1982. Although civil aero sales and operating profits exceeded those of the military aero business in 1986, the latter continued to provide a strong base of operating profit for the Group.

ACCOUNTANTS' REPORT

The following is a copy of a report by the auditors and reporting accountants, Coopers & Lybrand, Chartered Accountants, Plumtree Court, London EC4A 4HT.

The Secretary of State for Trade and Industry
The Directors, Roll-Royce Plc
The Directors, Samuel Montague & Co. Limited
28th April 1987

Rolls-Royce Plc (the Company) was incorporated as Rolls-Royce (1971) Limited on 23rd February 1971 and changed its name to Rolls-Royce Limited on 21st March 1977. The Company was re-registered as a public limited company under the Companies Act 1985 on 1st May 1986.

The Company and its subsidiaries (the Group) make up their annual financial statements to 31st December in each year. We have audited the Group financial statements for the five years ended 31st December 1986.

The financial information set out in this report is based on the audited financial statements of the Group after making such adjustments as we consider necessary. Our work has been carried out in accordance with the Auditing Guideline: Prospectuses and the Reporting Accountant.

In our opinion, the financial information gives a true and fair view of the results and source and application of funds of the Group for each of the five years covered by this report and of the state of affairs of the Group at the end of each of those years.

Audited Accounts of the Group have not been made up for any period subsequent to 31st December 1986.

In our opinion, the proforma financial information set out in this report has been properly prepared on the basis of the notes thereto.

ACCOUNTING POLICIES

The principal accounting policies adopted in arriving at the financial information set out in this report are as follows:

Basis of Accounting

The financial statements in this report have been prepared under the historical cost convention, modified to include the revaluation of land and buildings at 31st December 1980 and at 31st December 1985.

Basis of Consolidation

The financial information consolidates the financial statements of Rolls-Royce Plc and its subsidiaries and the Group's share of profits or losses of related companies for each of the five years ended 31st December 1986.

Turnover and Trading Profit

Turnover excludes value added tax and comprises:

   i)   amounts invoiced to customers, in respect of deliveries made, work completed, or services rendered during the year;

   ii) estimated sales values, where prices have not been agreed with customers; and

   iii) income from licenses and management fees.

Trading profit is taken at the time of sale. In the case of long-term contracts, profit is arrived at by reference to the estimated overall contract profitability.

Foreign Currencies

   i) Transactions of the Company and UK subsidiaries in currencies other than sterling are translated at the average achieved exchange rate for the year, taking account of maturing forward exchange contracts.

   ii) Foreign currency borrowings by the Company are translated into sterling at the exchange rates ruling at the year end. To the extent that such borrowings by the Company act as a hedge against the net assets of overseas subsidiary companies, the differences on exchange arising from the retranslation of those borrowings are taken to reserves.

iii) Foreign currency assets and other liabilities in the Company accounts are translated to the estimated sterling equivalent, account being taken of forward exchange contracts.

iv) Assets and liabilities of overseas subsidiaries are translated into sterling at the exchange rates ruling at the year end.

v) Turnover and profits or losses of overseas subsidiaries are translated at the average exchange rates for the year.

vi) On consolidation, differences on exchange arising from the retranslation of the opening net investment in subsidiary companies, and from the translation of the profits or losses of those companies at average rates, are taken to reserves.

vii) All exchange differences, other than those referred to in (ii) and (vi) above, are charged or credited in determining profit on ordinary activities before taxation.

Research and Development

The charge to the profit and loss account consists of total research and development expenditure, less costs recoverable on development contracts, contributions by HM Government to shared engineering programs and launch aid received from HM Government under the provisions of the 1982 Civil Aviation Act.

Taxation

Provision is made at the rate for the year for UK corporation tax and for overseas taxation on profits of overseas subsidiaries. Deferred taxation is provided where a liability is expected to arise in the foreseeable future.

Stocks

Stocks are valued at cost of materials, labour and relevant manufacturing overheads, less provisions for obsolete and surplus items and where necessary, provisions to reduce cost to estimated realizable value. Progress payments received are deducted from stocks up to the limit of the relevant work in progress. Other advance payments and deposits are included in creditors.

Accounting for Leases

Assets owned by third parties and finance leased from them have been capitalized at amounts equal to the original cost of the assets to the lessors and depreciation provided on the basis of Group depreciation policy. The future capital obligations under finance leases are included as liabilities in the balance sheet and the current year's interest element is charged to the profit and loss account.

Payments under operating leases are charged to the profit and loss account as incurred.

Depreciation

i) Properties

Depreciation is provided on the cost or valuation of properties and is calculated on the straight-line basis over estimated lives advised by the Group's professional valuers. Depreciation is not provided on freehold land. The estimated lives are:

freehold buildings	10-45 years (average 28 years)
leasehold land and buildings	lower of valuers' estimate of life or period of lease

ii) Plant and machinery, fixtures and fittings

Depreciation is provided on the original cost of plant and machinery, fixtures and fittings and is calculated on the straight-line basis over estimated lives in the range 5–14 years.

Provisions

Provisions are made for estimated future expenditure on warranties relating to sales up to the year end and estimated losses on current contracts.

ROLLS-ROYCE PRIVATIZATION
CONSOLIDATED PROFIT AND LOSS ACCOUNTS
Year Ended 31st December (in millions of pounds sterling)

	1982	1983	1984	1985	1986
Turnover (Note 1)	1,493	1,331	1,409	1,601	1,802
Less Cost of Sales	1,213	1,111	1,104	1,235	1,369
Gross Profit	280	220	305	366	433
Less Commercial, Marketing & Product Support Costs	67	67	71	77	82
Less General and Administrative Costs	91	79	72	78	78
Operating Profit (Note 2)	122	74	162	211	273
Less Net Research and Development	131	131	101	100	132
Less Interest Payable & Similar Charges (Note 3)	84	56	35	29	21
Less Share of Losses in Related Companies	-0-	2	-0-	1	-0-
Profit/(Loss) Before Taxation and Net Restructuring Costs (Note 4)	(93)	(115)	26	81	120
Less Taxation (Note 6)	6	6	6	3	(1)
Profit/(Loss) After Taxation and Before Net Restructuring Costs	(99)	(121)	20	78	121
Less Net Restructuring Costs (Note 7)	38	74	-0-	-0-	-0-
Less Attributable to Minority Interests	1	1	1	1	1
Profit/(Loss) Attributable to the Company	(138)	(196)	19	77	120
Dividends	-0-	-0-	-0-	-0-	-0-
Profit/(Loss) for the Year Transferred to Reserves (Note 8)	(138)	(196)	19	77	120
Earnings/(Loss) Per Share (Note 9)	(17.1)p	(19.2)p	3.0p	12.1p	18.9p

ROLLS-ROYCE PRIVATIZATION
CONSOLIDATED BALANCE SHEETS
As at 31st December (in millions of pounds sterling)

	1982	1983	1984	1985	1986
Fixed Assets					
Tangible Assets (Note 10)	388	393	381	383	405
Investments in Related Companies	2	-0-	1	-0-	-0-
	390	393	382	383	405
Current Assets					
Stocks (Note 11)	642	505	511	578	604
Debtors (Note 12)	260	236	258	227	315
Cash at Bank & In Hand	18	15	31	33	21
	920	756	800	838	940
Less Creditors—Amounts Falling Due Within One Year					
Bank Loans, Overdrafts and Other Borrowings (Note 13)	161	191	101	180	171
Other Creditors (Note 14)	224	239	359	379	367
	385	430	460	559	538
Net Current Assets	535	326	340	279	402
Total Assets Less Current Liabilities	925	719	722	662	807
Less Creditors—Amounts Falling Due After more than One Year					
Bank Loans and Other Borrowings (Note 15)	224	174	186	62	79
Other Creditors (Note 16)	111	115	95	118	103
Less Provisions for Liabilities and Charges					
Deferred Taxation (Note 17)	4	5	6	7	1
Other Provisions (Note 18)	96	131	120	82	112
Total Long Term Liabilities	490	294	315	393	512
Capital and Reserves					
Called up Share Capital (Note 19)	508	508	508	127	127
Revaluation Reserve (Note 20)	138	135	132	147	145
Other Reserves (Note 21)	-0-	-0-	-0-	9	9
Profit & Loss Account	(161)	(354)	(330)	106	226
	485	289	310	389	507
Minority Interests	5	5	5	4	5
Total Capital and Reserves	490	294	315	393	512

© John Wiley & Sons Canada Ltd. All rights reserved.

ROLLS-ROYCE PRIVATIZATION
CONSOLIDATED SOURCE AND APPLICATION OF FUNDS STATEMENTS
Year Ended 31st December (in millions of pounds sterling)

	1982	1983	1984	1985	1986
Source of Funds					
Profit/(Loss) After Net Restructuring Costs but Before Taxation	(131)	(189)	26	81	120
Adjustments for Items not Involving the Movement of Funds: Depreciation	38	46	45	50	56
Increase/(Decrease) in Provisions for Liabilities and Charges Excluding Deferred Taxation	(48)	35	(11)	(38)	30
Funds Generated From Operations	(141)	(108)	60	93	206
Issue of Shares for Cash	50	-0-	-0-	-0-	-0-
Increase/(Decrease) in Creditors Falling Due After More than 1 yr.	(5)	4	(20)	23	(15)
Foreign Currency Translation Adjustments	(4)	(3)	(6)	(7)	(2)
Disposals of Tangible Fixed Assets	3	1	1	12	3
Miscellaneous Items	(4)	(1)	(3)	-0-	-0-
	(101)	(107)	32	121	192
Application of Funds					
Capital Expenditure	(53)	(49)	(26)	(56)	(81)
Tax Paid	(3)	(4)	(3)	(6)	-0-
	(157)	(160)	3	59	111
Changes in Net Current Assets					
Increase/(Decrease) in Current Creditors Excluding Corporate Taxation	(13)	16	119	21	(14)
Increase/(Decrease) in Stocks, Net of Progress Payments	127	137	(6)	(67)	(26)
Increase/(Decrease) in Debtors Excluding Corporate Taxation	(8)	24	(22)	34	(91)
Change in Net Liquid Assets and Loans	(51)	17	94	47	(20)

© John Wiley & Sons Canada Ltd. All rights reserved.

ROLLS-ROYCE PRIVATIZATION
CONSOLIDATED SOURCE AND APPLICATION OF FUNDS STATEMENTS
(continued)
Year Ended 31st December (in millions of pounds sterling)

	1982	1983	1984	1985	1986
Represented by:					
Increase/(Decrease) in Cash Balances	(22)	(3)	16	2	(12)
Increase/(Decrease) in Bank Loans Overdrafts and Other Borrowings:					
Amounts Falling Due Within One Year	-0-	(30)	90	(79)	9
Amounts Falling Due After More than 1 yr.	(29)	50	(12)	124	(17)
	(51)	17	94	47	(20)

ROLLS-ROYCE PRIVATIZATION
NOTES TO THE FINANCIAL INFORMATION
Year Ended 31st December (in millions of pounds sterling)

1. TURNOVER	1982	1983	1984	1985	1986
Analysis by Activity					
Civil Aero: UK	39	75	48	79	130
Overseas	481	313	398	498	627
Total	520	388	446	577	757
Military Aero: UK	245	227	252	217	220
Overseas	497	479	483	518	520
Total	742	706	735	735	740
Industrial & Marine: UK	54	34	48	56	58
Overseas	83	98	74	87	95
Total	137	132	122	143	153
Other Activities: UK	69	76	76	105	119
Overseas	25	29	30	41	33
Total	94	105	106	146	152
	1493	1331	1409	1601	1802

ROLLS-ROYCE PRIVATIZATION
NOTES TO THE FINANCIAL INFORMATION (continued)
Year Ended 31st December (in millions of pounds sterling)

1. TURNOVER	1982	1983	1984	1985	1986
Geographical Analysis					
UK	407	412	424	457	527
North America	357	288	332	435	497
Europe	403	394	400	391	397
Asia	180	145	168	235	291
Australasia	48	12	37	38	44
Africa	71	50	25	22	19
Other Countries	27	30	23	23	27
	1493	1331	1409	1601	1802
Exports From UK:					
Direct	691	537	519	712	918
Indirect	313	300	370	313	271
	1004	837	889	1025	1189
Sales by Overseas Subsidiaries	139	123	138	170	165
Parent Company Sales to Overseas Subsidiaries	(57)	(41)	(42)	(51)	(79)
	1086	919	985	1144	1275
2. OPERATING PROFIT					
Civil Aero	(8)	(35)	39	73	137
Military Aero	116	96	111	110	118
Industrial and Marine	7	6	6	20	10
Other Activities	7	7	6	8	8
	122	74	162	211	273
3. INTEREST PAYABLE AND SIMILAR CHARGES					
Interest Payable On:					
Borrowings Repayable Within 5 yrs. Other than by Instalments	20	17	16	14	12
Other Loans	23	12	16	14	10
Finance Leases	9	6	6	6	5
	52	35	38	34	27
Less Interest Received	(3)	(3)	(4)	(5)	(6)
	49	32	34	29	21
Charges Related to US Dollar Borrowings Arising From Movements in Exchange Rates	35	24	1	-0-	-0-
	84	56	35	29	21

© John Wiley & Sons Canada Ltd. All rights reserved.

4. PROFIT/(LOSS) BEFORE TAXATION AND NET RESTRUCTURING COSTS

After charging

Depreciation of Owned Tangible Fixed Assets	31	35	33	35	39
Depreciation of Tangible Fixed Assets Held Under Finance Leases	7	11	12	15	17
Provision for Termination Charges Associated with the Intended Disposal of an Overseas Facility	-0-	-0-	-0-	-0-	7
Operating Lease Rentals:					
Hire of Plant and Equipment	8	10	9	10	9
Hire of Other Assets	6	7	6	7	7
Auditors' Remuneration	0.5	0.5	0.6	0.6	0.6
Directors' Emoluments	0.6	0.5	0.5	0.7	0.6

After Crediting

Rentals Receivable in Respect of Operating Leases	2	2	4	5	7
Profit on Sale of Tangible Fixed Assets	1	-0-	1	5	2

5. EMPLOYEE INFORMATION

Employment Costs

Wages and Salaries	438	424	418	452	482
Social Security Costs	40	36	33	34	37
Other Pension Costs	33	35	34	36	40
	511	495	485	522	559

Number of Employees

The average weekly number of employees during the year was:

UK	48,906	43,247	38,943	38,360	38,824
Overseas	3,316	3,097	2,921	3,046	3,051
	52,222	46,344	41,864	41,406	41,875

6. TAXATION

The taxation charge, which is based on the results for each year, consists principally of overseas taxation. The Group has not paid any significant amounts of UK corporation tax in the five years to 31st December 1986 because the Company has incurred losses, or had unrelieved tax losses available for set off.

7. NET RESTRUCTURING COSTS

In 1981, the Company commenced a major program for the restructuring of its operations. The net costs of voluntary severance, together with other minor costs of this restructuring program, were charged separately in the profit and loss accounts in 1982 and 1983 (in pounds sterling) as follows:

Year ended 31st December	1982	1983
Net restructuring costs	38m	74m

The costs shown are net of amounts recovered under normal contractual arrangements with HM Government. The charge of 74 million pounds in 1983 included a provision of 30 million pounds for costs incurred in the following two years in completing the program. Ongoing voluntary severance costs not related to major restructuring have been included in cost of sales and not charged separately.

8. MOVEMENTS ON PROFIT AND LOSS ACCOUNT
(in millions of pounds sterling)

Year Ended 31st December	1982	1983	1984	1985	1986
Retained Profits/(Accumulated Deficit) at Start of Each Year	(26)	(161)	(354)	(330)	106
Profit/(Loss) for the Year	(138)	(196)	19	77	120
Foreign Exchange Translation Adjustments	-0-	-0-	2	(17)	(2)
Transfer Depreciation Charge Attributable to Revaluation Surplus to Revaluation Reserve (see Note 20)	3	3	3	4	2
Elimination of Accumulated Deficit as a Result of Share Capital Reduction	-0-	-0-	-0-	372	-0-
Retained Profits/(Accumulated Deficit) at End of Each Year	(161)	(354)	(330)	106	226

9. EARNINGS/(LOSS) PER SHARE

Earnings per Share are based on profits or losses after taxation and minority interests but before net restructuring costs and on the average number of Shares in issue each year, adjusted for the share consolidation and sub-division on 27th April 1987 explained in Note 25 below. Except for 1982, the adjusted number of Shares in issue was 635 million. In 1982, the adjusted average number of Shares in issue was 584 million. Proforma earnings per Share information, reflecting the benefit of the additional share capital subscribed by HM Government as part of the arrangements for the Offer, is given in "Proforma financial information" below.

10. TANGIBLE FIXED ASSETS (in millions of pounds sterling)

As at 31st December 1986	Cost or Valuation	Aggregate Depreciation	Net book Value
Land and buildings — Freehold	184	7	177
Leasehold — Long	12	1	11
Leasehold — Short	2	-0-	2
Plant and Machinery	525	347	178
Fixture and Fittings	8	5	3
In Course of Construction	34	-0-	34
	765	360	405
As at 31st December 1985	694	311	383

Land and buildings were revalued at 31st December 1985. Specialized properties, including certain of the Group's major manufacturing sites, were revalued on a depreciated replacement cost basis and the remainder by reference to their open market value for existing use. In the UK, the valuation was carried out by Gerald Eve & Co., Chartered Surveyors and by Fuller Peiser, Chartered Surveyors. The net book value of tangible fixed assets of 405 million pounds (1985 — 383 million pounds) includes an amount of 58 million pounds in respect of assets held under finance leases (1985 — 66 million pounds).

The original cost of assets fully written off, but still in use and included in the figures above, amounts to 150 million pounds (1985 — 134 million pounds).

11. STOCKS (in millions of pounds sterling)

As at 31st December	1985	1986
Raw Materials	71	79
Work in Progress, Jigs and Tools	416	447
Finished Parts and Engines	378	428
Payments on Account	8	9
	873	963
Progress Payments Against Stocks	(295)	(359)
	578	604

12. DEBTORS (in millions of pounds sterling)

As at 31st December	1985	1986
Amounts Falling Due Within One Year		
Trade Debtors	166	205
Amounts Owed by Related Companies	29	34
Other Debtors	19	16
Prepayments and Accrued Income	6	33
	220	288
Amounts Falling Due After More Than One Year		
Trade Debtors	5	14
Prepayments and Accrued Income	2	13
	7	27
Total Debtors	227	315

13. BANK LOANS, OVERDRAFTS AND OTHER BORROWINGS
— Amounts Falling Due Within One Year (in millions of pound sterling)

As at 31st December	1985	1986
Bank Loans and Overdrafts	151	131
Other Borrowings	29	40
	180	171

14. OTHER CREDITORS
— Amounts Falling Due Within One Year (in millions of pounds sterling)

As at 31st December	1985	1986
Trade Creditors	151	168
Payments Received on Account	118	87
Corporate Taxation	1	3
Other Taxation and Social Security	13	12
Other Creditors	73	70
Accruals and Deferred Income	6	10
Capital Obligations Under Finance Leases	17	17
	379	367

15. BANK LOANS AND OTHER BORROWINGS
— Amounts Falling Due After More Than One Year
(in millions of pounds sterling)

As at 31st December	1985	1986
Unsecured		
Bank Loans Repayable 1988–1991 (Interest Rates 9.8% – 11.2%)	51	71
Other Loans Repayable 1988–1990 (Interest Rate 11.7%)	10	7
Secured		
Loans Repayable 1988–1994, Secured by Charges on Related Buildings (Interest Rates 8.8% – 10.5%)	1	1
	62	79
Repayable by Instalments:		
Between One and Two Years	11	19
Between Two and Five Years	39	40
	50	59
Repayable Otherwise than by Instalments:		
Between Two and Five Years	12	20
	62	79

16. OTHER CREDITORS – Amounts Falling Due After More Than One Year
(in millions of pounds sterling)

As at 31st December	1985	1986
Payments Received on Account	33	37
Accruals and Deferred Income	38	29
Capital Obligations Under Finance Leases:		
Payable in the Second Year	16	13
Payable in the Third to Fifth Years	28	23
Payable After Five Years	3	1
	118	103

17. PROVISIONS FOR LIABILITIES AND CHARGES
— Deferred Taxation (in millions of pounds sterling)

	1985	1986
Movements on the Provision		
At 1st January	6	7
Charge/(Credit) to Profit and Loss Account	1	(6)
At 31st December	7	1
Analysis of Provision		
Accelerated Capital Allowances	-0-	1
Other Timing Differences	10	-0-
Losses	(3)	-0-
	7	1

There exists a potential liability of 24 million pounds at 31st December 1986 (1985 – 28 million pounds) in respect of the surplus arising on the revaluation of land and buildings, but no provision is necessary as there is no present intention to dispose of any land and buildings.

The Company has estimated tax losses of 675 million pounds at 31st December 1986 (1985 – 908 million pounds). These are subject to agreement of computations with the Inland Revenue in respect of the years 1982 – 1985, where tax deductions of 42 million pounds are under dispute, and to submission and agreement of the 1986 computations.

18. PROVISIONS FOR LIABILITIES AND CHARGES
— Other Provisions (in millions of pounds sterling)

	1985	1986
Movements on Other Provisions		
At 1st January	120	82
Charge to Profit and Loss Account	36	66
Utilized	(72)	(29)
Released	(2)	(7)
At 31st December	82	112

Other provisions include principally warranty and performance guarantees and estimated future losses on contracts.

19. SHARE CAPITAL (in pounds sterling)

As at 31st December	1985	1986
Ordinary Shares of 25p		
Authorized: Value	150m	150m
Authorized: Number	600m	600m
Issued: Value	127m	127m
Issued: Number	508m	508m

On 27th April 1987, the Company's authorized ordinary share capital was reorganized into 750 million ordinary shares of 20p each of which 635 million were in issue.

20. REVALUATION RESERVE — Non–Distributable
(in millions of pounds sterling)

	1985	1986
At 1st January	132	147
Surplus Arising on Revaluation of Land and Buildings at 31st December 1985 (see Note 10 above)	19	-0-
Transfer Depreciation Charge Attributable to Revaluation Surplus From Profit and Loss Account (see Note 8 above)	(4)	(2)
Net Unrealized Surplus at 31st December	147	145

21. OTHER RESERVES (Non–Distributable)

As at 31st December	1985	1986
Special Reserve	9	9

22. PENSION SCHEMES

The pension schemes for employees of the Company and its UK subsidiaries are administered by trustees and the assets of the schemes are separate from those of the Group and are independently invested. The schemes are funded by contributions from both the Company and its UK subsidiaries and from scheme members. The joint contributions provide for benefit entitlements in respect of pensionable service with the Company and its UK subsidiaries, based upon actuarial valuations carried out not less than once every three years. The actuaries have confirmed, following valuations at 31st March 1985, that the present contribution rates are adequate to meet the benefits provided under the rules of the schemes.

Pension arrangements for employees of overseas subsidiary companies are managed and funded in accordance with local requirements and professional advice.

23. FUTURE CAPITAL EXPENDITURE (in millions of pounds sterling)

As at 31st December	1985	1986
Future Capital Expenditure for which No Provision has been Made: Contracted	19	34
Authorized but Not Contracted	21	26

Future capital expenditure includes amounts both for assets to be leased and for assets to be purchased.

24. CONTINGENT LIABILITIES

Sales Financing Support

The Group participates in guarantees of aircraft financing arrangements which can extend a number of years into the future, including deficiency guarantees on aircraft resale values or future lease payments. The amounts guaranteed are at present either fully supported or substantially supported by the estimated realizable value of any underlying security (generally the related aircraft and spare engines). In certain particular cases, the amounts guaranteed exceed the Company's present estimates of the realizable value of the underlying security, and the aggregate of this excess was 3 million pounds at 31st December 1986 (1985 — 6 million pounds).

Delivery, Performance and Reliability Guarantees

Contingent liabilities exist in respect of guarantees provided by the Group in the ordinary course of business for engine delivery, performance and reliability. These include arrangements made with British Airways to secure the delivery to Boeing and British Airways of RB211-524D4D engines.

General

There are contingent liabilities amounting to 6 million pounds (1985 — 6 million pounds) relating to guarantees, customs bonds, recourse on supplier credit arrangements subject to Export Credits Guarantee Department insurance cover and countertrade obligations.

The Directors do not expect any of the arrangements described above, after allowing for provisions already made, to result in material loss to the Group.

25. POST BALANCE SHEET EVENTS

On 27th April 1987, the 600,000,000 shares of 25p each in the Company were consolidated into 150,000,000 shares of 1 each and then each such share was sub-divided into five shares of 20p each.

By further resolutions passed on that date, conditional upon an underwriting agreement in connection with an offer for sale (the "Offer") of the whole of the issued and to be issued ordinary shares of the Company being entered into and such agreement becoming unconditional and not being terminated in accordance with its terms:

i) the authorized share capital of the Company was increased to 210,000,001 by the creation of 300,000,000 additional Shares and the Special Share;

ii) the Directors were generally authorized to allot relevant securities up to an aggregate nominal amount of 83,000,000 pounds, such authority to expire on 26th April 1992;

iii) the Directors were given certain powers to allot equity securities for cash, pursuant to the authority referred to in (ii) above, as if section 89(1) of the Companies Act 1985 did not apply to the allotment; and

iv) 166,470,588 additional Shares were allotted at 170p per Share in cash and the Special Share was allotted at par in cash, in each case to a nominee of the Secretary of State credited as fully paid.

PROFORMA FINANCIAL INFORMATION

As described in note 25 above, HM Government has agreed to subscribe for 166,470,588 additional Shares which will give proceeds to the Company equal to the net borrowings of the Group (including capital obligations under finance leases) at 31st December 1986. After making payment of certain expenses associated with the Offer, the net proceeds to the Group will be approximately 277 million pounds, the major proportion of which will be used to repay most of the Group's borrowings outstanding on completion of the Offer.

We set out below proforma financial information showing the results for the year ended 31st December 1985 and the balance sheet at that date.

Proforma Consolidated Profit and Loss Account For The Year Ended 31st December 1986

The adjustments made to the consolidated profit and loss account reflect the position as if the net proceeds of 277 million pounds had been available to the Group throughout 1986 and a total dividend of 40 million pounds had been declared in respect of the year. Interest savings have been calculated at a rate of 10 percent per annum (the average rate of interest borne by the Group in 1986 on borrowings other than capital obligations under finance leases) on the net proceeds available to the Group. Taxation has been adjusted to take account of the amount of UK advance corporation tax (at an assumed average rate of 27.7 per cent) which would be payable if this notional dividend were to be paid.

	Unadjusted	Adjustments	Proforma
Operating Profit	273	-0-	273
Research and Development (Net)	(132)	-0-	(132)
Interest Receivable Net of Interest Payable and Similar Charges	(21)	28	7
Profit Before Taxation	120	28	148
Taxation Credit/(Charge)	1	(15)	(14)
Profit After Taxation	121	13	134
Attributable to Minority Interests	(1)	-0-	(1)
Profit Attributable to the Company	120	13	133
Dividends	-0-	(40)	(40)
Profit Retained	120	(27)	93
Earnings Per Share	18.9p		16.6p

The proforma earning per Share are based on 801,470,588 Shares, being the number in issue following the Offer.

Proforma Consolidated Balance Sheet at 31st December 1986

The adjustments made to the balance sheet reflect the position as if the net proceeds had been available immediately prior to the year end and had been employed to discharge all borrowings of the Group (other than capital obligations under finance leases).

	Unadjusted	Adjustments	Proforma
Fixed Assets	405	-0-	405
Current Assets	940	27	967
Creditors—Amounts Falling Due Within One Year	(538)	171	(367)
Net Current Assets	402	198	600
Total Assets Less Current Liabilities	807	198	1005
Creditors—Amounts Falling Due After More than One Year	(182)	79	(103)
Provisions for Liabilities and Charges	(113)	-0-	(113)
	512	277	789
Capital and Reserves			
Share Capital	127	33	160
Reserves	380	244	624
	507	277	784
Minority Interests	5	-0-	5
	512	277	789

RESEARCH AND DEVELOPMENT EXPENDITURE

Total Expenditure

Research and development expenditure in each of the five years 1982–1986 is set out below. Net research and development expenditure, which represents the cost to the Company, is gross expenditure less the aggregate of launch aid received from HM Government, HM Government contributions to shared advanced engineering programs and expenditure on development contracts, as described below (in millions of pounds sterling).

Year Ended 31st Dec.	1982	1983	1984	1985	1986
Gross Expenditure	257	262	227	234	255
Percentage of Turnover	17%	20%	16%	15%	14%
Net Expenditure	131	131	101	100	132
Percentage of Turnover	9%	10%	7%	6%	7%

Trends in levels of gross expenditure reflect, in particular, the phasing of individual programs. Thus, the higher levels of gross expenditure in 1982 and 1983 were associated with the peaking of expenditure on the 535E4, and the rise in 1986 over the two previous years was principally due to the IAE V2500 and RB211-524 programs. Levels of gross expenditure are expected to increase in the short and medium term broadly in line with Group turnover although, as in the past, there will be variations from year to year.

Factors such as greater computerization and more effective project management, discussed in "Research and development" above, have made research and development expenditure more effective; the Company expects this trend to continue. The Company has also benefited from arrangements for collaboration and cost-sharing on new aero-engines between companies, or governments, of two or more countries.

Launch Aid

Launch aid has been provided by HM Government to the Company for certain civil aero-engine projects, generally on the basis of an agreed percentage of the forecast launch costs. During the period 1982–1986, launch aid has been received by Rolls-Royce in respect of the RB211-524B4 and D4 programs, the 535 series and the IAE V2500 (in millions of pounds sterling).

Year Ended 31st Dec.	1982	1983	1984	1985	1986
Launch Aid for Research and Development	45	36	30	28	27
Launch Aid for Tooling and Learner Costs	9	4	5	9	6
Repayment Levies Related to Launch Aid in Earlier Years	13	6	11	17	24

Decisions by the Company on whether to apply for launch aid, and by HM Government on whether to provide it, are taken on a project by project basis. Accordingly, the amount of launch aid, if any, received by the Company will fluctuate from year to year depending on the number of projects in receipt of launch aid and their state of development. No launch aid will be receivable in 1987 or 1988 on current contracts.

Launch aid contracts provide for HM Government to receive levies on subsequent sales of products which have been developed with launch aid. Such contracts may also provide for a fixed schedule of repayments independent of sales, although this does not apply to any of the Company's current projects. Since 1979, the rate of recovery in launch aid contracts has been calculated with the objective of securing a real rate of return to HM Government on its launch investment.

Advanced Engineering Programs

The MoD and DTI provide contributions to shared advanced engineering programs undertaken by the Company and for relevant aero-engine research carried out at the Royal Aircraft Establishment, Pyestock, whose engine test facilities are also used by Rolls-Royce. HM Government contributions to advanced engineering programs undertaken by Rolls-Royce have been as follows:

Year Ended 31st Dec.	1982	1983	1984	1985	1986
Contributions	12	29	35	44	42

Development Contracts

The Company also enters into development contracts with the MoD, generally on a 'non-competitive' basis, subject to the profit formula described in "Sales arrangements with customers" above and with other customers under contracts which reimburse the Company for costs reasonably incurred plus an agreed fee. The proceeds derived from these contracts form part of the Company's turnover. The expenditure attributable to these contracts (which is charged as cost of sales in the Company's accounts) has been as follows (in millions of pounds sterling):

Year Ended 31st Dec.	1982	1983	1984	1985	1986
Expenditure: MoD	66	64	58	54	43
Other Customers	3	2	3	8	11
Repayment Levies Related to Development Contracts with the MoD in Earlier Years	13	10	8	6	7

As in the case of launch aid described above, levies are paid in respect of subsequent military commercial sales where the development of the original engine has been paid for in whole or in part by the MoD.

Accounting For Research And Development And Related Expenditure

Net research and development expenditure is written off to the profit and loss account in the year in which it is incurred. Expenditure of a capital nature on research laboratories and plant is written off over the expected useful life of the asset. Special to product tooling, after deduction of applicable launch aid, is written off to the profit and loss account over a five year period (and is not included in total research and development expenditure above.) Levies paid to HM Government in respect of launch aid received in earlier years for civil aero-engine projects, together with levies paid on sales of military engines to military commercial customers, are charged as cost of sales.

CAPITAL INVESTMENT

Capital expenditure in each of the five years 1982 to 1986 is set out below (in millions of pounds sterling):

Year Ended 31st Dec.	1982	1983	1984	1985	1986
Land & Buildings	3	4	4	6	10
Plant & Machinery	49	44	21	49	70
Fixtures & Fittings	1	1	1	1	1
	53	49	26	56	81

The principal areas of capital expenditure over the last five years have been machine tools and production plant, computing systems and test equipment.

The Group continues to undertake investment in support of its objective of achieving continuing improvements in productivity. As at 20th March 1987, the Group had committed or authorized a total of 64 million pounds capital expenditure (mainly for plant and machinery), which it expects to finance from retained profits.

INTEREST TABLES

Table 1 — Future Amount of 1

Table 2 — Present Value of 1

Table 3 — Future Amount of an Ordinary Annuity of 1 per Period

Table 4 — Present Value of an Ordinary Annuity of 1 per Period

Table 5 — Present Value of an Annuity Due of 1 per Period

TABLE 1 FUTURE AMOUNT OF 1 (Future Amount of a Single Sum)

$$a_{\overline{n}|i} = (1 + i)^n$$

(n) Periods	2%	2½%	3%	4%	5%	6%
1	1.02000	1.02500	1.03000	1.04000	1.05000	1.06000
2	1.04040	1.05063	1.06090	1.08160	1.10250	1.12360
3	1.06121	1.07689	1.09273	1.12486	1.15763	1.19102
4	1.08243	1.10381	1.12551	1.16986	1.21551	1.26248
5	1.10408	1.13141	1.15927	1.21665	1.27628	1.33823
6	1.12616	1.15969	1.19405	1.26532	1.34010	1.41852
7	1.14869	1.18869	1.22987	1.31593	1.40710	1.50363
8	1.17166	1.21840	1.26677	1.36857	1.47746	1.59385
9	1.19509	1.24886	1.30477	1.42331	1.55133	1.68948
10	1.21899	1.28008	1.34392	1.48024	1.62889	1.79085
11	1.24337	1.31209	1.38423	1.53945	1.71034	1.89830
12	1.26824	1.34489	1.42576	1.60103	1.79586	2.01220
13	1.29361	1.37851	1.46853	1.66507	1.88565	2.13293
14	1.31948	1.41297	1.51259	1.73168	1.97993	2.26090
15	1.34587	1.44830	1.55797	1.80094	2.07893	2.39656
16	1.37279	1.48451	1.60471	1.87298	2.18287	2.54035
17	1.40024	1.52162	1.65285	1.94790	2.29202	2.69277
18	1.42825	1.55966	1.70243	2.02582	2.40662	2.85434
19	1.45681	1.59865	1.75351	2.10685	2.52695	3.02560
20	1.48595	1.63862	1.80611	2.19112	2.65330	3.20714
21	1.51567	1.67958	1.86029	2.27877	2.78596	3.39956
22	1.54598	1.72157	1.91610	2.36992	2.92526	3.60354
23	1.57690	1.76461	1.97359	2.46472	3.07152	3.81975
24	1.60844	1.80873	2.03279	2.56330	3.22510	4.04893
25	1.64061	1.85394	2.09378	2.66584	3.38635	4.29187
26	1.67342	1.90029	2.15659	2.77247	3.55567	4.54938
27	1.70689	1.94780	2.22129	2.88337	3.73346	4.82235
28	1.74102	1.99650	2.28793	2.99870	3.92013	5.11169
29	1.77584	2.04641	2.35657	3.11865	4.11614	5.41839
30	1.81136	2.09757	2.42726	3.24340	4.32194	5.74349
31	1.84759	2.15001	2.50008	3.37313	4.53804	6.08810
32	1.88454	2.20376	2.57508	3.50806	4.76494	6.45339
33	1.92223	2.25885	2.65234	3.64838	5.00319	6.84059
34	1.96068	2.31532	2.73191	3.79432	5.25335	7.25103
35	1.99989	2.37321	2.81386	3.94609	5.51602	7.68609
36	2.03989	2.43254	2.89828	4.10393	5.79182	8.14725
37	2.08069	2.49335	2.98523	4.26809	6.08141	8.63609
38	2.12230	2.55568	3.07478	4.43881	6.38548	9.15425
39	2.16474	2.61957	3.16703	4.61637	6.70475	9.70351
40	2.20804	2.68506	3.26204	4.80102	7.03999	10.28572

FUTURE AMOUNT OF 1   TABLE 1

8%	9%	10%	11%	12%	15%	(n) Periods
1.08000	1.09000	1.10000	1.11000	1.12000	1.15000	1
1.16640	1.18810	1.21000	1.23210	1.25440	1.32250	2
1.25971	1.29503	1.33100	1.36763	1.40493	1.52088	3
1.36049	1.41158	1.46410	1.51807	1.57352	1.74901	4
1.46933	1.53862	1.61051	1.68506	1.76234	2.01136	5
1.58687	1.67710	1.77156	1.87041	1.97382	2.31306	6
1.71382	1.82804	1.94872	2.07616	2.21068	2.66002	7
1.85093	1.99256	2.14359	2.30454	2.47596	3.05902	8
1.99900	2.17189	2.35795	2.55803	2.77308	3.51788	9
2.15892	2.36736	2.59374	2.83942	3.10585	4.04556	10
2.33164	2.58043	2.85312	3.15176	3.47855	4.65239	11
2.51817	2.81267	3.13843	3.49845	3.89598	5.35025	12
2.71962	3.06581	3.45227	3.88328	4.36349	6.15279	13
2.93719	3.34173	3.79750	4.31044	4.88711	7.07571	14
3.17217	3.64248	4.17725	4.78459	5.47357	8.13706	15
3.42594	3.97031	4.59497	5.31089	6.13039	9.35762	16
3.70002	4.32763	5.05447	5.89509	6.86604	10.76126	17
3.99602	4.71712	5.55992	6.54355	7.68997	12.37545	18
4.31570	5.14166	6.11591	7.26334	8.61276	14.23177	19
4.66096	5.60441	6.72750	8.06231	9.64629	16.36654	20
5.03383	6.10881	7.40025	8.94917	10.80385	18.82152	21
5.43654	6.65860	8.14028	9.93357	12.10031	21.64475	22
5.87146	7.25787	8.95430	11.02627	13.55235	24.89146	23
6.34118	7.91108	9.84973	12.23916	15.17863	28.62518	24
6.84847	8.62308	10.83471	13.58546	17.00000	32.91895	25
7.39635	9.39916	11.91818	15.07986	19.04007	37.85680	26
7.98806	10.24508	13.10999	16.73865	21.32488	43.53532	27
8.62711	11.16714	14.42099	18.57990	23.88387	50.06561	28
9.31727	12.17218	15.86309	20.62369	26.74993	57.57545	29
10.06266	13.26768	17.44940	22.89230	29.95992	66.21177	30
10.86767	14.46177	19.19434	25.41045	33.55511	76.14354	31
11.73708	15.76333	21.11378	28.20560	37.58173	87.56507	32
12.67605	17.18203	23.22515	31.30821	42.09153	100.69983	33
13.69013	18.72841	25.54767	34.75212	47.14252	115.80480	34
14.78534	20.41397	28.10244	38.57485	52.79962	133.17552	35
15.96817	22.25123	30.91268	42.81808	59.13557	153.15185	36
17.24563	24.25384	34.00395	47.52807	66.23184	176.12463	37
18.62528	26.43668	37.40434	52.75616	74.17966	202.54332	38
20.11530	28.81598	41.14479	58.55934	83.08122	232.92482	39
21.72452	31.40942	45.25926	65.00087	93.05097	267.86355	40

TABLE 2 PRESENT VALUE OF 1 (Present Value of a Single Sum)

$$p\overline{n}_i = \frac{1}{(1+i)^n} = (1+i)^{-n}$$

(n) Periods	2%	2½%	3%	4%	5%	6%
1	.98039	.97561	.97087	.96154	.95238	.94340
2	.96117	.95181	.94260	.92456	.90703	.89000
3	.94232	.92860	.91514	.88900	.86384	.83962
4	.92385	.90595	.88849	.85480	.82270	.79209
5	.90573	.88385	.86261	.82193	.78353	.74726
6	.88797	.86230	.83748	.79031	.74622	.70496
7	.87056	.84127	.81309	.75992	.71068	.66506
8	.85349	.82075	.78941	.73069	.67684	.62741
9	.83676	.80073	.76642	.70259	.64461	.59190
10	.82035	.78120	.74409	.67556	.61391	.55839
11	.80426	.76214	.72242	.64958	.58468	.52679
12	.78849	.74356	.70138	.62460	.55684	.49697
13	.77303	.72542	.68095	.60057	.53032	.46884
14	.75788	.70773	.66112	.57748	.50507	.44230
15	.74301	.69047	.64186	.55526	.48102	.41727
16	.72845	.67362	.62317	.53391	.45811	.39365
17	.71416	.65720	.60502	.51337	.43630	.37136
18	.70016	.64117	.58739	.49363	.41552	.35034
19	.68643	.62553	.57029	.47464	.39573	.33051
20	.67297	.61027	.55368	.45639	.37689	.31180
21	.65978	.59539	.53755	.43883	.35894	.29416
22	.64684	.58086	.52189	.42196	.34185	.27751
23	.63416	.56670	.50669	.40573	.32557	.26180
24	.62172	.55288	.49193	.39012	.31007	.24698
25	.60953	.53939	.47761	.37512	.29530	.23300
26	.59758	.52623	.46369	.36069	.28124	.21981
27	.58586	.51340	.45019	.34682	.26785	.20737
28	.57437	.50088	.43708	.33348	.25509	.19563
29	.56311	.48866	.42435	.32065	.24295	.18456
30	.55207	.47674	.41199	.30832	.23138	.17411
31	.54125	.46511	.39999	.29646	.22036	.16425
32	.53063	.45377	.38834	.28506	.20987	.15496
33	.52023	.44270	.37703	.27409	.19987	.14619
34	.51003	.43191	.36604	.26355	.19035	.13791
35	.50003	.42137	.35538	.25342	.18129	.13011
36	.49022	.41109	.34503	.24367	.17266	.12274
37	.48061	.40107	.33498	.23430	.16444	.11579
38	.47119	.39128	.32523	.22529	.15661	.10924
39	.46195	.38174	.31575	.21662	.14915	.10306
40	.45289	.37243	.30656	.20829	.14205	.09722

PRESENT VALUE OF 1 **TABLE 2**

8%	9%	10%	11%	12%	15%	(n) Periods
.92593	.91743	.90909	.90090	.89286	.86957	1
.85734	.84168	.82645	.81162	.79719	.75614	2
.79383	.77218	.75132	.73119	.71178	.65752	3
.73503	.70843	.68301	.65873	.63552	.57175	4
.68058	.64993	.62092	.59345	.56743	.49718	5
.63017	.59627	.56447	.53464	.50663	.43233	6
.58349	.54703	.51316	.48166	.45235	.37594	7
.54027	.50187	.46651	.43393	.40388	.32690	8
.50025	.46043	.42410	.39092	.36061	.28426	9
.46319	.42241	.38554	.35218	.32197	.24719	10
.42888	.38753	.35049	.31728	.28748	.21494	11
.39711	.35554	.31863	.28584	.25668	.18691	12
.36770	.32618	.28966	.25751	.22917	.16253	13
.34046	.29925	.26333	.23199	.20462	.14133	14
.31524	.27454	.23939	.20900	.18270	.12289	15
.29189	.25187	.21763	.18829	.16312	.10687	16
.27027	.23107	.19785	.16963	.14564	.09293	17
.25025	.21199	.17986	.15282	.13004	.08081	18
.23171	.19449	.16351	.13768	.11611	.07027	19
.21455	.17843	.14864	.12403	.10367	.06110	20
.19866	.16370	.13513	.11174	.09256	.05313	21
.18394	.15018	.12285	.10067	.08264	.04620	22
.17032	.13778	.11168	.09069	.07379	.04017	23
.15770	.12641	.10153	.08170	.06588	.03493	24
.14602	.11597	.09230	.07361	.05882	.03038	25
.13520	.10639	.08391	.06631	.05252	.02642	26
.12519	.09761	.07628	.05974	.04689	.02297	27
.11591	.08955	.06934	.05382	.04187	.01997	28
.10733	.08216	.06304	.04849	.03738	.01737	29
.09938	.07537	.05731	.04368	.03338	.01510	30
.09202	.06915	.05210	.03935	.02980	.01313	31
.08520	.06344	.04736	.03545	.02661	.01142	32
.07889	.05820	.04306	.03194	.02376	.00993	33
.07305	.05340	.03914	.02878	.02121	.00864	34
.06763	.04899	.03558	.02592	.01894	.00751	35
.06262	.04494	.03235	.02335	.01691	.00653	36
.05799	.04123	.02941	.02104	.01510	.00568	37
.05369	.03783	.02674	.01896	.01348	.00494	38
.04971	.03470	.02430	.01708	.01204	.00429	39
.04603	.03184	.02210	.01538	.01075	.00373	40

TABLE 3 FUTURE AMOUNT OF AN ORDINARY ANNUITY OF 1

$$A_{\overline{n}|i} = \frac{(1+i)^n - 1}{i}$$

(n) Periods	2%	2½%	3%	4%	5%	6%
1	1.00000	1.00000	1.00000	1.00000	1.00000	1.00000
2	2.02000	2.02500	2.03000	2.04000	2.05000	2.06000
3	3.06040	3.07563	3.09090	3.12160	3.15250	3.18360
4	4.12161	4.15252	4.18363	4.24646	4.31013	4.37462
5	5.20404	5.25633	5.30914	5.41632	5.52563	5.63709
6	6.30812	6.38774	6.46841	6.63298	6.80191	6.97532
7	7.43428	7.54743	7.66246	7.89829	8.14201	8.39384
8	8.58297	8.73612	8.89234	9.21423	9.54911	9.89747
9	9.75463	9.95452	10.15911	10.58280	11.02656	11.49132
10	10.94972	11.20338	11.46338	12.00611	12.57789	13.18079
11	12.16872	12.48347	12.80780	13.48635	14.20679	14.97164
12	13.41209	13.79555	14.19203	15.02581	15.91713	16.86994
13	14.68033	15.14044	15.61779	16.62684	17.71298	18.88214
14	15.97394	16.51895	17.08632	18.29191	19.59863	21.01507
15	17.29342	17.93193	18.59891	20.02359	21.57856	23.27597
16	18.63929	19.38022	20.15688	21.82453	23.65749	25.67253
17	20.01207	20.86473	21.76159	23.69751	25.84037	28.21288
18	21.41231	22.38635	23.41444	25.64541	28.13238	30.90565
19	22.84056	23.94601	25.11687	27.67123	30.53900	33.75999
20	24.29737	25.54466	26.87037	29.77808	33.06595	36.78559
21	25.78332	27.18327	28.67649	31.96920	35.71925	39.99273
22	27.29898	28.86286	30.53678	34.24797	38.50521	43.39229
23	28.84496	30.58443	32.45288	36.61789	41.43048	46.99583
24	30.42186	32.34904	34.42647	39.08260	44.50200	50.81558
25	32.03030	34.15776	36.45926	41.64591	47.72710	54.86451
26	33.67091	36.01171	38.55304	44.31174	51.11345	59.15638
27	35.34432	37.91200	40.70963	47.08421	54.66913	63.70577
28	37.05121	39.85980	42.93092	49.96758	58.40258	68.52811
29	38.79223	41.85630	45.21885	52.96629	62.32271	73.63980
30	40.56808	43.90270	47.57542	56.08494	66.43885	79.05819
31	42.37944	46.00027	50.00268	59.32834	70.76079	84.80168
32	44.22703	48.15028	52.50276	62.70147	75.29883	90.88978
33	46.11157	50.35403	55.07784	66.20953	80.06377	97.34316
34	48.03380	52.61289	57.73018	69.85791	85.06696	104.18376
35	49.99448	54.92821	60.46208	73.65222	90.32031	111.43478
36	51.99437	57.30141	63.27594	77.59831	95.83632	119.12087
37	54.03425	59.73395	66.17422	81.70225	101.62814	127.26812
38	56.11494	62.22730	69.15945	85.97034	107.70955	135.90421
39	58.23724	64.78298	72.23423	90.40915	114.09502	145.05846
40	60.40198	67.40255	75.40126	95.02552	120.79977	154.76197

FUTURE AMOUNT OF AN ORDINARY ANNUITY OF 1 TABLE 3

8%	9%	10%	11%	12%	15%	(n) Periods
1.00000	1.00000	1.00000	1.00000	1.00000	1.00000	1
2.08000	2.09000	2.10000	2.11000	2.12000	2.15000	2
3.24640	3.27810	3.31000	3.34210	3.37440	3.47250	3
4.50611	4.57313	4.64100	4.70973	4.77933	4.99338	4
5.86660	5.98471	6.10510	6.22780	6.35285	6.74238	5
7.33592	7.52334	7.71561	7.91286	8.11519	8.75374	6
8.92280	9.20044	9.48717	9.78327	10.08901	11.06680	7
10.63663	11.02847	11.43589	11.85943	12.29969	13.72682	8
12.48756	13.02104	13.57948	14.16397	14.77566	16.78584	9
14.48656	15.19293	15.93743	16.72201	17.54874	20.30372	10
16.64549	17.56029	18.53117	19.56143	20.65458	24.34928	11
18.97713	20.14072	21.38428	22.71319	24.13313	29.00167	12
21.49530	22.95339	24.52271	26.21164	28.02911	34.35192	13
24.21492	26.01919	27.97498	30.09492	32.39260	40.50471	14
27.15211	29.36092	31.77248	34.40536	37.27972	47.58041	15
30.32428	33.00340	35.94973	39.18995	42.75328	55.71747	16
33.75023	36.97371	40.54470	44.50084	48.88367	65.07509	17
37.45024	41.30134	45.59917	50.39593	55.74972	75.83636	18
41.44626	46.01846	51.15909	56.93949	63.43968	88.21181	19
45.76196	51.16012	57.27500	64.20283	72.05244	102.44358	20
50.42292	56.76453	64.00250	72.26514	81.69874	118.81012	21
55.45676	62.87334	71.40275	81.21431	92.50258	137.63164	22
60.89330	69.53194	79.54302	91.14788	104.60289	159.27638	23
66.76476	76.78981	88.49733	102.17415	118.15524	184.16784	24
73.10594	84.70090	98.34706	114.41331	133.33387	212.79302	25
79.95442	93.32398	109.18177	127.99877	150.33393	245.71197	26
87.35077	102.72314	121.09994	143.07864	169.37401	283.56877	27
95.33883	112.96822	134.20994	159.81729	190.69889	327.10408	28
103.96594	124.13536	148.63093	178.39719	214.58275	377.16969	29
113.28321	136.30754	164.49402	199.02088	241.33268	434.74515	30
123.34587	149.57522	181.94343	221.91317	271.29261	500.95692	31
134.21354	164.03699	201.13777	247.32362	304.84772	577.10046	32
145.95062	179.80032	222.25154	275.52922	342.42945	644.66553	33
158.62667	196.98234	245.47670	306.83744	384.52098	765.36535	34
172.31680	215.71076	271.02437	341.58955	431.66350	881.17016	35
187.10215	236.12472	299.12681	380.16441	484.46312	1014.34568	36
203.07032	258.37595	330.03949	422.98249	543.59869	1167.49753	37
220.31595	282.62978	364.04343	470.51056	609.83053	1343.62216	38
238.94122	309.06646	401.44778	523.26673	684.01020	1546.16549	39
259.05652	337.88245	442.59256	581.82607	767.09142	1779.09031	40

TABLE 4 PRESENT VALUE OF AN ORDINARY ANNUITY OF 1

$$P_{\overline{n}|i} = \frac{1 - \frac{1}{(1+i)^n}}{i} = \frac{1 - p_{\overline{n}|i}}{i}$$

(n) Periods	2%	2½%	3%	4%	5%	6%
1	.98039	.97561	.97087	.96154	.95238	.94340
2	1.94156	1.92742	1.91347	1.88609	1.85941	1.83339
3	2.88388	2.85602	2.82861	2.77509	2.72325	2.67301
4	3.80773	3.76197	3.71710	3.62990	3.54595	3.46511
5	4.71346	4.64583	4.57971	4.45182	4.32948	4.21236
6	5.60143	5.50813	5.41719	5.24214	5.07569	4.91732
7	6.47199	6.34939	6.23028	6.00205	5.78637	5.58238
8	7.32548	7.17014	7.01969	6.73274	6.46321	6.20979
9	8.16224	7.97087	7.78611	7.43533	7.10782	6.80169
10	8.98259	8.75206	8.53020	8.11090	7.72173	7.36009
11	9.78685	9.51421	9.25262	8.76048	8.30641	7.88687
12	10.57534	10.25776	9.95400	9.38507	8.86325	8.38384
13	11.34837	10.98319	10.63496	9.98565	9.39357	8.85268
14	12.10625	11.69091	11.29607	10.56312	9.89864	9.29498
15	12.84926	12.38138	11.93794	11.11839	10.37966	9.71225
16	13.57771	13.05500	12.56110	11.65230	10.83777	10.10590
17	14.29187	13.71220	13.16612	12.16567	11.27407	10.47726
18	14.99203	14.35336	13.75351	12.65930	11.68959	10.82760
19	15.67846	14.97889	14.32380	13.13394	12.08532	11.15812
20	16.35143	15.58916	14.87747	13.59033	12.46221	11.46992
21	17.01121	16.18455	15.41502	14.02916	12.82115	11.76408
22	17.65805	16.76541	15.93692	14.45112	13.16300	12.04158
23	18.29220	17.33211	16.44361	14.85684	13.48857	12.30338
24	18.91393	17.88499	16.93554	15.24696	13.79864	12.55036
25	19.52346	18.42438	17.41315	15.62208	14.09394	12.78336
26	20.12104	18.95061	17.87684	15.98277	14.37519	13.00317
27	20.70690	19.46401	18.32703	16.32959	14.64303	13.21053
28	21.28127	19.96489	18.76411	16.66306	14.89813	13.40616
29	21.84438	20.45355	19.18845	16.98371	15.14107	13.59072
30	22.39646	20.93029	19.60044	17.29203	15.37245	13.76483
31	22.93770	21.39541	20.00043	17.58849	15.59281	13.92909
32	23.46833	21.84918	20.38877	17.87355	15.80268	14.08404
33	23.98856	22.29188	20.76579	18.14765	16.00255	14.23023
34	24.49859	22.72379	21.13184	18.41120	16.19290	14.36814
35	24.99862	23.14516	21.48722	18.66461	16.37419	14.49825
36	25.48884	23.55625	21.83225	18.90828	16.54685	14.62099
37	25.96945	23.95732	22.16724	19.14258	16.71129	14.73678
38	26.44064	24.34860	22.49246	19.36786	16.86789	14.84602
39	26.90259	24.73034	22.80822	19.58448	17.01704	14.94907
40	27.35548	25.10278	23.11477	19.79277	17.15909	15.04630

PRESENT VALUE OF AN ORDINARY ANNUITY OF 1   TABLE 4

8%	9%	10%	11%	12%	15%	(n) Periods
.92593	.91743	.90909	.90090	.89286	.86957	1
1.78326	1.75911	1.73554	1.71252	1.69005	1.62571	2
2.57710	2.53130	2.48685	2.44371	2.40183	2.28323	3
3.31213	3.23972	3.16986	3.10245	3.03735	2.85498	4
3.99271	3.88965	3.79079	3.69590	3.60478	3.35216	5
4.62288	4.48592	4.35526	4.23054	4.11141	3.78448	6
5.20637	5.03295	4.86842	4.71220	4.56376	4.16042	7
5.74664	5.53482	5.33493	5.14612	4.96764	4.48732	8
6.24689	5.99525	5.75902	5.53705	5.32825	4.77158	9
6.71008	6.41766	6.14457	5.88923	5.65022	5.01877	10
7.13896	6.80519	6.49506	6.20652	5.93770	5.23371	11
7.53608	7.16073	6.81369	6.49236	6.19437	5.42062	12
7.90378	7.48690	7.10336	6.74987	6.42355	5.58315	13
8.24424	7.78615	7.36669	6.98187	6.62817	5.72448	14
8.55948	8.06069	7.60608	7.19087	6.81086	5.84737	15
8.85137	8.31256	7.82371	7.37916	6.97399	5.95424	16
9.12164	8.54363	8.02155	7.54879	7.11963	6.04716	17
9.37189	8.75563	8.20141	7.70162	7.24967	6.12797	18
9.60360	8.95012	8.36492	7.83929	7.36578	6.19823	19
9.81815	9.12855	8.51356	7.96333	7.46944	6.25933	20
10.01680	9.29224	8.64869	8.07507	7.56200	6.31246	21
10.20074	9.44243	8.77154	8.17574	7.64465	6.35866	22
10.37106	9.58021	8.88322	8.26643	7.71843	6.39884	23
10.52876	9.70661	8.98474	8.34814	7.78432	6.43377	24
10.67478	9.82258	9.07704	8.42174	7.84314	6.46415	25
10.80998	9.92897	9.16095	8.48806	7.89566	6.49056	26
10.93516	10.02658	9.23722	8.54780	7.94255	6.51353	27
11.05108	10.11613	9.30657	8.60162	7.98442	6.53351	28
11.15841	10.19828	9.36961	8.65011	8.02181	6.55088	29
11.25778	10.27365	9.42691	8.69379	8.05518	6.56598	30
11.34980	10.34280	9.47901	8.73315	8.08499	6.57911	31
11.43500	10.40624	9.52638	8.76860	8.11159	6.59053	32
11.51389	10.46444	9.56943	8.80054	8.13535	6.60046	33
11.58693	10.51784	9.60858	8.82932	8.15656	6.60910	34
11.65457	10.56682	9.64416	8.85524	8.17550	6.61661	35
11.71719	10.61176	9.67651	8.87859	8.19241	6.62314	36
11.77518	10.65299	9.70592	8.89963	8.20751	6.62882	37
11.82887	10.69082	9.73265	8.91859	8.22099	6.63375	38
11.87858	10.72552	9.75697	8.93567	8.23303	6.63805	39
11.92461	10.75736	9.77905	8.95105	8.24378	6.64178	40

TABLE 5 PRESENT VALUE OF AN ANNUITY DUE OF 1

$$Pd_{\overline{n}|i} = 1 + \frac{1 - \frac{1}{(1+i)^{n-1}}}{i} = (1+i)\left(\frac{1 - P_{\overline{n}|i}}{i}\right) = (1+i)\,P_{\overline{n}|i}$$

(n) Periods	2%	2½%	3%	4%	5%	6%
1	1.00000	1.00000	1.00000	1.00000	1.00000	1.00000
2	1.98039	1.97561	1.97087	1.96154	1.95238	1.94340
3	2.94156	2.92742	2.91347	2.88609	2.85941	2.83339
4	3.88388	3.85602	3.82861	3.77509	3.72325	3.67301
5	4.80773	4.76197	4.71710	4.62990	4.54595	4.46511
6	5.71346	5.64583	5.57971	5.45182	5.32948	5.21236
7	6.60143	6.50813	6.41719	6.24214	6.07569	5.91732
8	7.47199	7.34939	7.23028	7.00205	6.78637	6.58238
9	8.32548	8.17014	8.01969	7.73274	7.46321	7.20979
10	9.16224	8.97087	8.78611	8.43533	8.10782	7.80169
11	9.98259	9.75206	9.53020	9.11090	8.72173	8.36009
12	10.78685	10.51421	10.25262	9.76048	9.30641	8.88687
13	11.57534	11.25776	10.95400	10.38507	9.86325	9.38384
14	12.34837	11.98319	11.63496	10.98565	10.39357	9.85268
15	13.10625	12.69091	12.29607	11.56312	10.89864	10.29498
16	13.84926	13.38138	12.93794	12.11839	11.37966	10.71225
17	14.57771	14.05500	13.56110	12.65230	11.83777	11.10590
18	15.29187	14.71220	14.16612	13.16567	12.27407	11.47726
19	15.99203	15.35336	14.75351	13.65930	12.68959	11.82760
20	16.67846	15.97889	15.32380	14.13394	13.08532	12.15812
21	17.35143	16.58916	15.87747	14.59033	13.46221	12.46992
22	18.01121	17.18455	16.41502	15.02916	13.82115	12.76408
23	18.65805	17.76541	16.93692	15.45112	14.16300	13.04158
24	19.29220	18.33211	17.44361	15.85684	14.48857	13.30338
25	19.91393	18.88499	17.93554	16.24696	14.79864	13.55036
26	20.52346	19.42438	18.41315	16.62208	15.09394	13.78336
27	21.12104	19.95061	18.87684	16.98277	15.37519	14.00317
28	21.70690	20.46401	19.32703	17.32959	15.64303	14.21053
29	22.28127	20.96489	19.76411	17.66306	15.89813	14.40616
30	22.84438	21.45355	20.18845	17.98371	16.14107	14.59072
31	23.39646	21.93029	20.60044	18.29203	16.37245	14.76483
32	23.93770	22.39541	21.00043	18.58849	16.59281	14.92909
33	24.46833	22.84918	21.38877	18.87355	16.80268	15.08404
34	24.98856	23.29188	21.76579	19.14765	17.00255	15.23023
35	25.49859	23.72379	22.13184	19.41120	17.19290	15.36814
36	25.99862	24.14516	22.48722	19.66461	17.37419	15.49825
37	26.48884	24.55625	22.83225	19.90828	17.54685	15.62099
38	26.96945	24.95732	23.16724	20.14258	17.71129	15.73678
39	27.44064	25.34860	23.49246	20.36786	17.86789	15.84602
40	27.90259	25.73034	23.80822	20.58448	18.01704	15.94907

PRESENT VALUE OF AN ANNUITY DUE OF 1   TABLE 6-5

8%	9%	10%	11%	12%	15%	(n) Periods
1.00000	1.00000	1.00000	1.00000	1.00000	1.00000	1
1.92593	1.91743	1.90909	1.90090	1.89286	1.86957	2
2.78326	2.75911	2.73554	2.71252	2.69005	2.62571	3
3.57710	3.53130	3.48685	3.44371	3.40183	3.28323	4
4.31213	4.23972	4.16986	4.10245	4.03735	3.85498	5
4.99271	4.88965	4.79079	4.69590	4.60478	4.35216	6
5.62288	5.48592	5.35526	5.23054	5.11141	4.78448	7
6.20637	6.03295	5.86842	5.71220	5.56376	5.16042	8
6.74664	6.53482	6.33493	6.14612	5.96764	5.48732	9
7.24689	6.99525	6.75902	6.53705	6.32825	5.77158	10
7.71008	7.41766	7.14457	6.88923	6.65022	6.01877	11
8.13896	7.80519	7.49506	7.20652	6.93770	6.23371	12
8.53608	8.16073	7.81369	7.49236	7.19437	6.42062	13
8.90378	8.48690	8.10336	7.74987	7.42355	6.58315	14
9.24424	8.78615	8.36669	7.98187	7.62817	6.72448	15
9.55948	9.06069	8.60608	8.19087	7.81086	6.84737	16
9.85137	9.31256	8.82371	8.37916	7.97399	6.95424	17
10.12164	9.54363	9.02155	8.54879	8.11963	7.04716	18
10.37189	9.75563	9.20141	8.70162	8.24967	7.12797	19
10.60360	9.95012	9.36492	8.83929	8.36578	7.19823	20
10.81815	10.12855	9.51356	8.96333	8.46944	7.25933	21
11.01680	10.29224	9.64869	9.07507	8.56200	7.31246	22
11.20074	10.44243	9.77154	9.17574	8.64465	7.35866	23
11.37106	10.58021	9.88322	9.26643	8.71843	7.39884	24
11.52876	10.70661	9.98474	9.34814	8.78432	7.43377	25
11.67478	10.82258	10.07704	9.42174	8.84314	7.46415	26
11.80998	10.92897	10.16095	9.48806	8.89566	7.49056	27
11.93518	11.02658	10.23722	9.54780	8.94255	7.51353	28
12.05108	11.11613	10.30657	9.60162	8.98442	7.53351	29
12.15841	11.19828	10.36961	9.65011	9.02181	7.55088	30
12.25778	11.27365	10.42691	9.69379	9.05518	7.56598	31
12.34980	11.34280	10.47901	9.73315	9.08499	7.57911	32
12.43500	11.40624	10.52638	9.76860	9.11159	7.59053	33
12.51389	11.46444	10.56943	9.80054	9.13535	7.60046	34
12.58693	11.51784	10.60858	9.82932	9.15656	7.60910	35
12.65457	11.56682	10.64416	9.85524	9.17550	7.61661	36
12.71719	11.61176	10.67651	9.87859	9.19241	7.62314	37
12.77518	11.65299	10.70592	9.89963	9.20751	7.62882	38
12.82887	11.69082	10.73265	9.91859	9.22099	7.63375	39
12.87858	11.72552	10.75697	9.93567	9.23303	7.63805	40

GLOSSARY

ABSORPTION COSTING: a method of product costing that assigns fixed manufacturing overhead to the units produced.
ACCRUAL: revenue earned but not received nor past due.
ACID TEST RATIO: see Quick Ratio.
ACTIVITY RATIO: see Turnover Ratio.
ADJUSTING ENTRY: an entry made at the end of an accounting period to recognize all accounting items.
ADMINISTRATIVE EXPENSES: expenses incurred by the managerial and policy-making aspects of a business.
ALLOCATION: assignment of items of cost or revenue to one or more segments of an organization according to benefits received or some other logical measure of use.
AMORTIZATION: liquidation of a future obligation in an orderly process of payments.
ASSET: property or resources of a person or organization.

BALANCE SHEET: an itemized statement of total assets and total liabilities of a business to show its net worth.
BREAK-EVEN POINT: the level of activity (volume) at which a company earns zero profits, occurring when total revenue equals total expenses.

CA: Chartered Accountant (Canada).
CANADIAN INSTITUTE OF CHARTERED ACCOUNTANTS (CICA): the association of provincial institutes (ordre in Quebec) which confers the CA designation and safeguards professional standards and ethics.
CAPITAL BUDGET: a budget that identifies expenditures for buildings and capital goods and which identifies the sources of the funds required to meet the expenditures.
CAPITAL COST ALLOWANCE: sums set aside in financial statements to write off the initial costs of investments or equipment, buildings, and improvements to land, usually treated as a cost of production; synonymous with depreciation.
CAPITAL STOCK: securities representing the ownership interest of the firm.
CASH BUDGET: a schedule of cash receipts and disbursements.
CASH DISCOUNT: a deduction from the selling price to encourage prompt payment.
CASH FLOW: the net income of a corporation plus amounts charged off for depreciation, depletion, amortization, and extraordinary charges, which are not actually paid out in cash.
CHARTER: articles or incorporation granted to an organization.
CONSISTENCY: the application of the same accounting policies and procedures from period to period.
CONSOLIDATION: a combination of two or more organizations into a new entity.
CONSTANT DOLLAR: the adjustment of dollar values to a constant level (removing inflation).
CONTINGENT LIABILITY: liability caused by the responsibility for the actions of some other person or persons.
CONTRIBUTION MARGIN: the excess of revenue over variable cost.
CONTROL: the concept of monitoring activities and taking action to correct undesirable performance.
CORPORATION: a legal entity which has many of the characteristics of a person or proprietor of a business.
COST: the value given up in order to receive goods or services; all expenses are costs, but not all costs are expenses.
COST ACCOUNTING: a branch of accounting that deals with the classification, recording, allocation, and reporting of current and prospective costs.
COST ALLOCATION: the assignment of common costs to cost centres in accordance with the matching principle.
COST-BENEFIT ANALYSIS: a branch of operations research that aids in evaluating alternative courses of action; it is primarily concerned with the selection of equipment, products, etc.
COST OF CAPITAL: the weighted-average cost of a firm's debt and equity capital; also the rate of return that a company must earn to satisfy the demands of owners and creditors.

COST OF GOODS MANUFACTURED: all direct material costs, labour costs, and overhead costs transferred from work in process inventory to finished goods inventory.
COST OF GOODS SOLD: the costs incurred for goods sold during a specified period, including transportation costs.
COST PLUS PRICING: the practice of adding a percentage or amount to the cost of goods to establish the selling price.
COST-VOLUME PROFIT ANALYSIS: a method used for examining the functional relationships among the major aspects of profits and for identifying the profit structure.
CPA: Certified Public Accountant (United States).
CPP: abbreviation for Canada Pension Plan.
CREDITOR: an entity owed money by another.
CURRENT ASSET: an asset which will be liquidated within a year.
CURRENT LIABILITY: a liability which will be required to be paid within a year.
CURRENT RATE METHOD: a method of translating foreign currencies based on their current exchange rates.
CURRENT RATIO: the relationship between current assets and current liabilities.

DATA BASE: a collection of information specific to an organization.
DECENTRALIZATION: the placing of the decision-making point at the lowest managerial level, involving delegation of decision-making authority.
DEFERRAL: an item on which payment is delayed to a future time.
DEMAND CURVE: a graphic representation of the quantity of goods demanded in relation to their price.
DEPLETION: the changing of an expense against income for a wasting asset.
DEPRECIATION: see Capital Cost Allowance.
DIFFERENTIAL COSTS: the difference in costs between two situations.
DIRECT COST: the cost of a good or service that contributes to the production of a commodity or service.
DIRECT LABOUR: the dollar value of wages paid to workers.
DIRECT MATERIAL: raw material that is part of the finished good and can be assigned to specific physical units.
DISCOUNTED CASH FLOW METHODS: capital budgeting techniques that take into account the time value of money.
DISCOUNTED RATE OF RETURN: the rate of return that equates future cash inflows with cash outflows of an investment.
DISCRETIONARY COSTS: fixed costs arising from periodic, decisions that directly reflect top-management policies and can be varied by its actions.
DIVIDENDS: a portion of profits of a firm declared by the Board of Directors to be paid to shareholders.
DIVISIONALIZATION: the existence of autonomous units in an organization; responsibility for performance rests with a divisional or sectional manager who operates the division as if it were separate from the parent organization.

EARNINGS PER SHARE: the portion of profits accruing to each share in the corporation.
EOQ (economic order quantity) MODEL: an inventory decision-making approach used to create a formula for determining what quantity of supplies to order.
EQUITY: stockholder's or owner's funds invested in the firm.
EXPENSE: cost of resources used in revenue creation; all expenses are costs but not all costs are expenses.
EXTRAORDINARY ITEM: non-operating gains or losses that are material in amount, but unusual in nature.

FACTORY OVERHEAD: manufacturing costs that are not direct material and direct labour.
FIFO (first in-first out): a term relating to inventory valuations that means that the cost shown for the first shipment of an item is used for valuation in accounting.
FINANCIAL ACCOUNTING: the area of accounting concerned with measuring and reporting on the financial status and operating results of an organization.
FINANCIAL ANALYSIS: the use of specific techniques to study a firm's financial statements (also Financial Statement Analysis).

FINANCIAL CONTROLS: the vital factors in control processes; namely budgets, financial analysis, and break-even analysis.
FINANCIAL EXPENSE: interest expense on long-term debt.
FINANCIAL LEASE: a lease that is for the life of an asset and is primarily a financing arrangement.
FINANCIAL LEVERAGE: the use of debt by the firm.
FINANCIAL POSITION: the financial status of a company, indicated by the assets and liabilities on a balance sheet.
FINANCIAL REPORTING: periodic reporting of the financial position of an organization in terms of operating results and financial transactions.
FINISHED-GOODS INVENTORY: all completed, manufactured items made for sale to customers.
FISCAL YEAR: the time period over which a business keeps its financial records (normally a 12 month period).
FIXED ASSETS: permanent assets required for the normal conduct of a business which normally are not converted into cash (e.g. fixtures, buildings and land).
FIXED CHARGES: business expenses not related to the level of activity.
FIXED COST (expense): a cost (expense) for a fixed period and range of activity that does not change in total.
FLEXIBLE BUDGET: a budget that is established for a range rather than for a single level of activity.
FOB (free on board): a term identifying the point from which transportation charges are paid by the purchaser.
FULL-COST PRICING: the practice of including all appropriate manufacturing costs in determining inventory values and prices.
FUND (working capital): current assets less current liabilities.

GOING CONCERN: an entity that will have a continuing existence for the foreseeable future.
GROSS MARGIN: amount determined by subtracting cost of goods sold from net sales. (Synonymous with gross profit.)
GROSS REVENUE: revenues received from selling goods or performing services before any deductions have been made for returns, allowances, or discounts.

HISTORICAL COST: the principle requiring that all financial statements be presented in terms of the item's original cost to the entity.

INCOME STATEMENT: the statement of profit and loss for an entity.
INDIRECT COSTS: costs not identifiable with or incurred as the result of the manufacture of specific goods or services but applicable to a productive activity generally.
INTANGIBLE ASSET: an asset with no physical substance.
INVENTORY: an asset that consists of materials or supplies used in a business.
INVENTORY CONTROL: the control of goods on hand by accounting and physical methods.
INVENTORY TURNOVER: the average number of times that inventory is replaced during a period, calculated by dividing cost of goods sold by average inventory.
INVESTMENT: the use of money to gain income or increase capital or both.
INVESTMENT CENTRE: a unit of an organization in which a manager has responsibility for costs, revenues, and investments.

JOINT PRODUCTION COSTS: the costs of two or more produced goods made by a single process not identifiable as individual products up to a certain stage of production known as the split-off point.
JOURNAL: an account book kept for various purposes.

LEAD TIME: the elapsed time between the beginning of a function and its completion.
LEASE: a contract providing use of property or equipment for a payment or set of payments, usually called rent.
LEASEHOLD IMPROVEMENT: any improvement made on leased property.
LESSOR: a landlord (owning the property or equipment).
LIABILITY: an obligation imposed by law, usually financial.
LIFO (last-in--first-out): value of last item is used for valuation or cost of inventory.

LIQUIDITY ANALYSIS: use of liquidity ratios to assess a firm's financial position.
LONG-TERM ASSET: an asset that will not be liquidated within a year.
LONG-TERM LIABILITY: a liability or debt that will not be paid within a year.

MAKE-OR-BUY DECISION: a firm's decision about whether to produce an item or purchase it elsewhere.
MANAGEMENT ACCOUNTING: a resource for management that supplies financial information to be used in planning and administering the business.
MANAGEMENT INFORMATION SYSTEM (MIS): a specific system that is designed to furnish management and supervisory personnel with current information in real time; data are recorded and processed for operational purposes; problems are isolated for referral to upper management for decision making.
MANAGERIAL ACCOUNTING: the area of accounting concerned with assisting managers in decision making for planning, budgeting, and controlling costs and revenues.
MANAGERIAL CONTROL: the monitoring and modification of activity and resource use so that predetermined standards are met and plans are carried out.
MANAGERIAL PERFORMANCE: the extent to which a manager achieves coordinated work and results through the efforts of subordinates.
MANUFACTURING COSTS: costs incurred in the process of bringing a product to completion, including direct-materials, direct-labour, and manufacturing overhead costs.
MANUFACTURING FIRM: a firm that produces goods by some process.
MANUFACTURING INVENTORY: a term covering all items of inventory for a manufacturing entity, including raw materials, work in process, and finished goods.
MANUFACTURING OVERHEAD: all expenses arising from manufacturing activities except labour and materials.
MARGIN: the difference between the cost of items sold and the net sales income.
MARGINAL ANALYSIS: analysis of information by examining the value added in one variable when another variable is increased by a single unit.
MARGINAL COST: the increase in the cost of production that results from manufacturing one more unit.
MARGINAL COST PRICING: the rule in competitive markets that price should equal the cost of producing the final (marginal) unit.
MARGINAL REVENUE: the added revenue received from the sale of one additional unit.
MARGIN OF SAFETY: the amount by which sales exceed the break-even point, providing a cushion against a drop in sales or other unforeseeable forces.
MARKET VALUE: the value that can be obtained for an asset on an open market.
MASTER BUDGET: a budget composed of all the various departmental budgets.
MATCHING: the process of taking revenues and expenses from the same period of time to arrive at a profit.
MATERIAL COST: the cost of an item directly resulting from the cost of raw material.
MATERIALITY: the concept that accounting should disclose only those events important enough to have an influence on the reader.
MBO (management by objectives): a process in which superiors and those who report to them jointly establish objectives over a specified time period, meeting periodically to evaluate progress in meeting these goals.
MERCHANDISING FIRM: a firm that buys and sells goods but does not produce them.
MOVING AVERAGE: a perpetual inventory cost-flow assumption in which the cost of goods sold and the ending inventory are determined as a weighted-average cost of all merchandise on hand after each purchase.

NEGOTIATED PRICE: the result obtained by a purchaser who desires something different from what is usually available or who is powerful enough to obtain prices lower than those usually charged.
NET BOOK VALUE: the value of an asset after depreciation (capital cost allowances) is subtracted from its purchase price.
NET PRESENT VALUE (NPV): the difference between the present values of an investment's expected cash inflows and cash outflows.
NET REALIZABLE VALUE: the selling value of an item less reasonable costs of disposal.
NON-CURRENT ASSET: an asset not to be liquidated for more than a year into the future.

NON-MANUFACTURING EXPENSES: expenditures that are not associated with the manufacture of products, but which include selling and administrative expenses.
NORMAL CAPACITY: the expected activity level (however defined) for the accounting period assuming normal operations.
NOTE PAYABLE: a liability which is a promise to pay, in writing at a fixed future date.
NOT-FOR-PROFIT: describes the activities of an organization established with the goal of providing service for a group in society rather than for the purpose of making a profit.

OBJECTIVITY: the characteristic of accounting data that makes it verifiable by some means.
OPERATING BUDGET: a quantitative expression of a plan of action that shows how a firm will acquire and use its financial resources over a specified period of time.
OPERATING INCOME: income to a business produced by its tangible assets and by fees for services rendered.
OPERATING LEASE: a lease that is not financial, but is purely a means of obtaining temporary use of an asset.
OPPORTUNITY COST: the maximum alternative profit that could have been obtained if the productive good, service, or capacity had been applied to the next best use.
OTHER ASSET: an asset that is not a current asset nor a fixed asset, but is usually intangible or some form of investment.
OWNER'S EQUITY: the portion of the firm that represents the ownership interests.

PARTNERSHIP: a contractual relationship among two or more people (entities) in a joint (but not necessarily equal) relationship.
PAYBACK PERIOD: the period of time that passes before the incoming cash flows equal the outgoing cash flows on a specific project.
PERFORMANCE APPRAISAL: a methodical review of performance on the job to evaluate the effectiveness or adequacy of the work.
PERIODIC INVENTORY: a method of identifying and controlling inventory recorded periodically.
PERPETUAL INVENTORY: a method of identifying and controlling inventory as each transaction happens.
PLANNING: an activity that requires establishment of a predetermined course of action, beginning with a statement of goals and objectives.
PREFERRED STOCK: stock with a preference on earnings and/or assets over common stock.
PRESENT VALUE: the discounted value of a certain sum that is payable for a specified future date.
PRICE: the amount of money received for goods or services at the factory or place of business.
PRODUCT COSTING: the assignment of manufacturing costs to products to determine the cost of finished goods.
PROFITABILITY ANALYSIS: the study of the financial activities of a firm through examination of profit ratios.
PROFIT CENTRE: a segment of a business responsible for both revenues and expenses.
PROFIT MARGIN (per unit): sales less all operating expenses divided by the number of units sold.
PROPRIETORSHIP: a business owned by one person.
PURCHASE PRICE: the dollar amount for which any item can be bought.

QUICK RATIO: the ratio of quick assets to current liabilities, where quick assets are usually cash marketable securities and accounts receivable.

RATIO ANALYSIS: analysis of financial statements through the use of various financial ratios.
RAW MATERIAL: unprocessed resources utilized in manufacturing an item.
REALIZABLE VALUE: See Net Realizable Value.
RELEVANCE: that characteristic of accounting information such that it meets the needs of users.
RELEVANT COST: a cost needed in the decision-making process with two characteristics: it is an expected future cost and it is a differential cost.
RELIABILITY: the accuracy and dependability of financial data.
REORDER POINT: the inventory level at which an order is placed for some specific item.
REPLACEMENT COST: the value of an item if it had to be purchased in the market now.

RESIDUAL INCOME: the net income of a profit centre or investment centre less the imputed interest on its assets used.
RESIDUAL VALUE (also salvage value or scrap value): predicted disposal value of an asset.
RESPONSIBILITY ACCOUNTING: a system under which a manager is held responsible for each activity that occurs in his particular area of the firm.
RETAINED EARNINGS: funds retained by a firm after taxes and dividends paid to shareholders.
ROI (return on investment): the dollar amount earned divided by the capital invested.

SAFETY STOCK: a minimum inventory providing a cushion against reasonably expected maximum demand and variations in lead time.
SALES MIX: the proportionate combination of the various products leading to a firm's total sales.
SEGMENTED REPORTS: reports that identify costs, revenues, profits, contribution margin, and other variables for segments of an organization.
SELLING PRICE: the dollar price that a customer must pay to purchase items.
SENSITIVITY ANALYSIS: a method of assessing the reasonableness of a decision that was based on estimates, testing the impact of differences from an estimate.
SERIAL BOND: a bond issue where a portion is retired at regular intervals.
SERVICE DEPARTMENT: an organizational unit not directly producing goods but serving other departments.
SHIPPING EXPENSE: cost of transporting goods.
SPECIAL ORDER: an order priced differently from the normal price in order to utilize excess capacity, thereby contributing to company profits.
STANDARD COSTS: an estimate of what costs would be under projected operating conditions.
STATEMENT OF CHANGES IN FINANCIAL POSITION: one of the basic financial statements in an annual report describing the financing and investing activities of an enterprise.
STOCK DIVIDEND: the payment of dividends in additional shares rather than cash.
STOCK-OUT: something that occurs when all inventory has been used or sold.
STOCK SPLIT: the division of shares of a corporation into a larger number of shares (generally an increase of more than 25%).
SUBORDINATED BOND: a bond which has a claim on the assets inferior to other bonds.
SUNK COST: a cost already incurred that is now irrelevant to the decision-making process.
SYSTEMS ANALYSIS: the analysis of business activity to establish goals and means to achieve them.

TARGET NET INCOME: a desired profit level predetermined by management.
TARGET PRICING: a means of setting prices to reach a profit objective.
TIMELINESS: a characteristic of financial data that indicates that it is available quickly.
TRANSFER PRICE: the price charged by one part of an organization for a product or service supplied to another part of the same firm.
TREASURY STOCK: stock reacquired by a firm from outstanding shares.
TRIAL BALANCE: a list of all account balances used to test whether debits equal credits.
TURNOVER RATIO: a measure of the activity of a firm with respect to the use of its assets.

UIC: Unemployment Insurance Commission (Canada).
UNIT COST: the cost of producing and distributing one unit of a processed or manufactured item.
USEFUL LIFE: period over which an asset is assumed to have value to a firm.

VARIABLE COST: a cost, uniform per unit, that changes in total in direct proportion to changes in total activity or volume.
VERIFIABILITY: a characteristic of financial data that allows its accuracy to be checked.

WEIGHTED AVERAGE: a means by which an asset is valued as an average of all available items.
WORKING CAPITAL: excess of current assets over current liabilities.
WORK-IN-PROCESS INVENTORY: the cost of all accumulated products that have entered the manufacturing process but have not been completed.
WORKSHEET: a chart of accounts used to prepare financial data for financial statements.